BALANCING ACT
MEMOIR OF A FLORIDA YOUTH

*For Carol Carol
from a friend,
from a friend,
Sept 2015 Sarah
Grand Rapids Chapman*

BY
SARAH CHAPMAN

Typesetting for this book is Bodini for the text, Anastasia for the title and similar headers, and DecoCaps for the drop caps at the beginning of each chapter. All book layout done by BookBurrista.

Library of Congress Control Number: 2014932951

Copyright ©2014 by Sarah Kate Chapman. All rights reserved.

ISBN-10: 0961117230
ISBN-13: 978-0961117238

To the memory of my brother, MIW III

CONTENTS

Acknowledgements   vii
Prologue   1

PART ONE

A Bad Person   3
Playland   11
Practice   21
Showtime   29
Sussie   33
Confusion   41
Truth or Dare   49
Rules   57

PART TWO

First of May   65
Obedience   75
Blue Skies   85
Red Leotard   95
The Big One   107
Second Half   119
Ringling Years   133
Touring   143
Class Act   151
Aerial Ballerina   161
Backyard   171
Tough Season   181
Down the Road   191

PART THREE

Interlude	201
Cursed Trip	209
Running Away	221
Feelings	233
Delicate Wings	239
Serenity	251
After The Show	259
Finding Balance	273

ACKNOWLEDGEMENTS

I've heard, "You've led an interesting life," frequently followed by, "let me know when your memoir is done." I first thought why a person would want to know my facts. I think I had a happy childhood, albeit strange. Then I joined the circus and had to admit my life was different.

Many thanks to all who helped my saga's progress. Starting in 1998 was Priscilla Dugan who told me to enlighten, not shock the reader. Exposing my secrets inflicted pain on both my adult children. I'm sorry for that. Several polite friends also read early versions without wincing.

Winston Chapman gave me a Windows accessible computer. Edward Hoagland told me why he chose me the most beautiful girl on Ringling. Joy Dey's skill designed the cover and chose David A. Harvey's 1973 photograph and the title, a suggestion from Maggie Schacker. Patricia Weaver Francisco recommended my story as a memoir. Circus historian Fred Dahlinger proofed my circus years. Mara Kirk Hart and members of Lake Superior Writers Memoir Group will be friends forever.

All those who insisted I dig deep in my emotional well. Aitkin Writers Group kept me motivated. Vibrant Dona Lee Gould did the final edit and titled chapter 23. Harlan Community Librarians for wisdom beyond books. Book Burrista Michael Burris for turning coarse type into gossamer wings.

I didn't embellish my memoir, I omitted details. I portrayed people through my experience with them and wish no harm to anyone. Each encounter enriched my memory and imagination. Lastly I thank God for the mind's ability to heal physical ailments. I have faith my story will help someone decide a better path.

skc

PROLOGUE

We don't know what will happen to our babies. Some parents wish for good health, happiness, wealth, beauty. I don't think a parent wishes a newborn to meet up with thievery, drunkenness, and rape. If that was my mother's curse to me, it explains why I've dodged danger from birth.

PART ONE

CHAPTER ONE
A BAD PERSON

I was two in 1947, a year that turned sour for Mama. Daddy asked her for a divorce and child custody based on her frustrations with my older brother and sister and me. Since my birth he hired one of his workers to care for me days.

Mama balked at the divorce, and they compromised on a legal separation putting us in her fulltime care with monthly child-support from Daddy. That covered our expenses but she wanted spending money so she took food industry jobs and cooked in local restaurants. One job, making cottage cheese, lasted for several years at the Land of Lakes Dairy. She also waitressed there, wearing a pink uniform with a hankie in her chest pocket held tight with a gold clasp. Her coworkers called her Dottie. I believe she liked those jobs because she made friends.

My mother's mother had multiple kids at home, but treated them well. My grandfather beat Mama and her siblings silly so Mama defiantly left home at age ten with only four years of school. Boxed in by her marital dilemma and the feeling that life wasn't fair, I believe Mama turned her frustration into displaced aggression on us kids. At five, I vividly recall my brother Merritt hitting me, causing downfalls of tears. When I went to Mama looking for justice, I got the worn response, "I'll give you something to cry about." Her huge hand slapped my cheeks leaving stinging welts that hurt far more than my brother's angry punches. Her strikes brought bigger tears with no comfort in sight. If I didn't brighten quickly, she'd glare at me and sneer, "I suppose you want some more."

Another technique she preferred occurred when I violated the fifth commandment, "Honor Thy Mother and Father." Mama relished this punishment—"Stand at arm's length and look at me." WHAP! "Now turn your face," she belittled mechanically. WHAP! Sometimes, her viper slaps came without warning. I grew up not looking at people and especially not in their eyes. As late as high school, teachers told me to look at them when they talked to me. Mama used the phrase, "eye for an eye" right out of the Bible. When she heard me repeat her cuss words, she ground a bar of wet Ivory soap back-and-forth on my tongue. She valued honesty and feared the devil. Afterlife to her was hell or nothing because she didn't talk about heaven. With her negative view, there were no rewards for good deeds on Earth.

We kids never figured out what turmoil brewed inside Mama's head. Whatever her demons were, she needed to rid herself of them before she could praise us. Neither happened. She didn't punish in public places, she saved that for inside the car, or on our property.

Almost daily while on enforced evening strolls to the mailbox and back, Mama would take a paring knife from her pants pocket and cut switches from green shrubs, stripping off the leaves. One-long-thin switch easily controlled us, even my sister Lucy, five-years older than me.

Mama pointed out various plants during these parades. Her bizarre incongruity scared me, "Remember to look for the evening star, the moon is made of cheese, who's first to see a lightning bug?" I peeked through dense shrubs hoping to see the bird that made its cruel WHIP-her-WILL, WHIP-her-WILL call. High above in the live oak canopy, noisy jays screeched in overhanging limbs alerting each other of egg or chick robbing snakes lurking nearby. I didn't know the tiny eggs stood a better chance of maturing than me.

If we went too far forward or lagged behind, Mama sharply struck our legs. We never knew what to expect and sometimes clung together with Lucy leading us in marching songs hoping Mama had other interests. Anytime we got within her reach, our whipping chances increased. We knew she could easily outrun us and helplessly stood still during switching.

Besides twigs and palms, Merritt, older than me by eighteen-months, endured broomstick beatings. Once she assailed both of us with a can of dog food held in each hand. If I whimpered when she parted my hair for braiding, she gripped my jaw tightly and tugged on my tangled mop with her free hand. If my fingers reached up for either my hair or my jaw, she struck them with the brush and, kept her bone-crushing grip. If she happened to stride across the room, she yanked me alongside by my hair like a dog on a leash. Mainly I wanted grooming to end and tried with all my might to hold still and be quiet. Mama's stature outstripped Merritt and me, her two active kids. Often subdued by pain from new bruises, we comforted each other.

* * *

One fall day when it got dark earlier, Mama and I ate supper without Merritt in eerie silence in our small hot kitchen. She figured where he was and when the clock passed fifteen minutes she left. I moved to his side of the table and stared out the window. Why was Mama standing by the house? Merritt rounded the corner in his barefoot lope smack into her stern face.

They had words and his head dropped down to his chest. He started a reluctant march in front of her catching frayed jean cuffs on grass runners. She nudged him forward with her palm directing him to a young oak tree where I saw a dangling cotton rope. She tied the rope to his wrist.

I stole down the back steps and crept alongside the house. She looped a second rope in a branch of a nearby tree and tied the free end to his other wrist stretching his arms away from his ribs with his tanned back facing her. Mama never tied us up before. Is he too big for her? Twelve year-old Merritt was six-feet-tall, lean, but still no match for Mama's strength.

Was she duplicating a story she read in a murder mystery magazine? Mama told us more than once a coward shoots a person in the back, so I knew she wasn't going to shoot him. Was she was going to beat him to death or let him live? Was I next? I slid behind the copper bushes peeking through my fingers, compelled to watch.

Mama stepped away from Merritt allowing striking room. She bent, picked up a one-inch-wide hardened leather belt, and folded it lengthwise. He wiggled side to side after the first lash. I couldn't see his tears yet knew they were there. Mama whipped passionately as though she had done it before. Slaaap. Slaaap. Slaaap.

"Stop! Stop! I'm sorry, I'm sorry...I won't do it again!" Merritt screamed between gasps for breath. Slaaap. Slaaap. "I won't. I promise." Blood trickled from criss-cross lacerations.

His screams turned to profuse sobbing. If her goal was to break his spirit into repentance, she accomplished that when he twisted his body, slumped down to his knees, and hung limp.

Tangled woods muffled the beating. No one ever stopped Mama. Her disciplinary job done, she looked satisfied like when she completed stacking the last of the rinsed dishes. Without emotion, Mama untied Merritt's grimy arms blandly ordering, "Go to the front steps and wait."

As evening light faded, she removed the cap on a tube of Vitamin A cream. He moaned lightly when she rubbed it into the long gashes.

Twenty minutes late, I thought to myself. I left the shrubbery and quietly positioned myself beside the two figures, one bent and wincing, and the other proudly sitting upright on the broad wooden planks. With us together, she calmly said, "It's a bad person who doesn't see to it that the wounds don't get infected."

As fast as I could, I tore strips from a white cotton sheet and rolled them up for Mama. She dutifully wound them around

Merritt's ravaged torso concealing each blow administered earlier. She secured the thick bandage in place with strips of adhesive tape. Then she stood up tall and left.

I helped him crawl through the doorway and onto his cot. He lay on his side and faced the wall.

Mama briskly entered the room setting a slice of buttered white bread on a plate and a glass of cold milk on the floor. I crouched on the opposite wall. *Twenty minutes late. I'm sorry Merritt. You don't deserve whipping. I don't want you to have scars on your back like slaves or outlaws. I wish you came home for supper on time.*

* * *

I knew Mama's family well. Named Dorothy Mae Raines on May Day 1917, she was the first child of a rural pioneer family in Cass County, Minnesota. Her father worked in the woods as a sawyer. Her mother grew babies—sixteen of them. Their homestead nestled near the Boy River, nine miles west of Remer.

Mama longed for knowledge at a clapboarded schoolhouse. She trudged two miles to school on snowy trails shared with bears, deer, and wolves.

She was ten and had five siblings when she left home to do kitchen help and childcare for moneyed families.

Need for domestic skills determined where young Dorothy went. Some families employing her owned businesses, attended Catholic churches, and lived inside city limits. Others lived in northern summer homes and during the school year, returned to either St. Paul or Minneapolis.

At eighteen, Mama tried living in St. Paul with a younger sister who had also escaped Remer. Mama detested her menial job operating a mangle and longed for a finer life, one like she observed working for the well-to-do.

She hired out as the Parson's nanny in 1938 and they took her to Sarasota to winter away from the cold and snow. Come spring Mama abandoned their three young daughters to live at Brown's Apartment House in downtown Sarasota.

I know she preferred warm winds, palm trees, and pristine, snow-white beaches to Minnesota's icebox any day of the year.

She thought her large-boned five-foot seven-inch frame, ample figure, size ten feet, hazel eyes, and fine black hair all detrimental. Simply put, she believed she wasn't attractive as younger sisters, who had married their beaus and birthed babies.

She quickly met Florida girlfriends and they went as a group to places of interest, the Ringling Bros. Circus Winter Quarters, the beaches, and the bars. One bar had a forty-five-year-old single owner who was raising a foster son.

Mama wanted children, her own beautiful, bright children. She aimed for Daddy and succeeded. At the end of 1939, she was Mrs. Merritt Ives Wheeler II and expecting my sister.

* * *

Daddy was born in 1894 in Great Barrington, Massachusetts. He had an older brother, Robert, and they both stood five-foot seven-inches tall on medium frames with dark brown eyes, wavy black hair, and spoke in thick New England dialects.

Daddy's family history was in reference books under Nathan Hale; James Merritt Ives; Robert Hale Kellogg, and Captain Truman Wheeler.

Grandfather Wheeler died from tuberculosis in 1898 and Grandmother Wheeler, a former schoolteacher, went to work at Wheeler and Taylor Insurance. When Daddy graduated high school Grandmother Wheeler gave her share of the insurance business to Uncle Robert.

Free to roam, Daddy ventured away from the cozy Berkshire Hills. He rode a cavalry horse in the Great War as a 2nd Lieutenant in Company A 9th Engineer, in El Paso, Texas. After an honorable discharge, he wandered about the US, taking a variety of jobs; first in Texas, then Florida, and back to Massachusetts.

Along the way he married Violet Soul, a widow with a young son, Roy. After my grandmother died in 1933, Daddy moved with Violet and Roy to Sarasota. He toyed with potential patent ideas from instant coffee to a Florida Professional Football League. Daddy eagerly wanted his contributions added to the 20th century.

Warm Florida with its simple, casual lifestyle suited Daddy. He owned and operated the Off Shore Bar, a wooden-barracks-style saloon built during WWI. He invested the saloon profits into several real estate tracts. His community involvement included the Episcopal Church of the Redeemer, the American Legion, the Boy Scouts, sports refereeing, and notary public.

Violet left twelve-year-old epileptic Roy with Daddy when she divorced him to remarry. Daddy liked kids but ran a business twelve hours a day. Mama, newly hired in the Off Shore kitchen seemed interested in both Roy and Daddy. He wooed and won her in marriage.

Mama only wanted Daddy so my foster brother finished growing up in a Gainesville institution as a ward of the State of Florida.

With Roy tucked away, Daddy built a house and improved Off Shore for WWII crowds. Mama helped where she could and her first pregnancy didn't interfere with attending parades, beach parties, and the county fair. At the homestead, Daddy raised fighting cocks. That pleased Mama with fresh brown eggs for custard or breakfast.

Together they saw his horse, Yo Yo, boarded at Captain Hyer's stable next to the Ringling Winter Quarters. On the way home, they dropped by Texas Jim and Mae Mitchell's wild animal compound at the corner of Tuttle Avenue and Fruitville Road. Mama and Daddy seemed to have things in common mostly, when they went out in public.

CHAPTER TWO
PLAYLAND

My family life was different for many reasons. It contributed to my reclusive behavior. Pivotal facts were an older dad, an abusive mom, siblings with exceptional identities, and a homestead unlike any other in Sarasota, with so few people who visited or even wanted to come on our property. We didn't live in the boonies, we were in town with respectable folks on four sides, i.e., Oyster Bay's luscious home sites. Some places you just don't go in or question who lives there. Sometimes it's best to walk on by.

My home, every square foot of it, was five exotic acres including 500 feet bordering US Highway 41 (also called the Tamiami Trail or the Trail). The northern boundary met a crushed shell sidewalk and a few scattered houses on the unpaved Worrington Street. Daddy and I loved Oakairs' trees—massive live and laurel oaks, towering pines, and miniature scrub oaks. Dense, spiraling palmetto plants, resembling jumbled up caterpillars with pointed fan-shaped leaves for antennae clustered in thickets below the pines.

In 1939, six years before I was born, Daddy put a mailbox on the two-lane Trail with Oakairs, Sarasota, Florida painted on the side. Fifteen years later Daddy proclaimed in closing a letter to his childhood friend in Great Barrington, "I have been instructed to change our address to 1840 Worrington Street." Daddy preferred the novelty of our rural address.

A large white gate warning, "Positively No Trespassing" graced the entrance driveway to Oakairs. A second sugar-sand road forged in from Worrington Street.

A short third road joined the first two forming a densely wooded triangle in front of the house. Occasionally, at night, speeding cars raced through Oakairs from the Trail to Worrington Street hoping to lose someone in a chase. From junior high on, cars that went silent mid-way kept me suspenseful and breathing shallow until I heard rumbling from a muffler leaving our sanctuary. I don't know what my siblings or parents heard or what they would have done had I reported the cars.

Besides encountering sugar-sand roads to the hub of our arboreal maze, there was Mitzy, my little brown dog with four white feet and a white tip on her tail, who loved to dig in gopher holes. She also bit people in the heel. "Mitzy's barking at someone. Go get her," Lucy or Mama called out. I'd grab Mitzy by the collar and stare at the newcomer deciding if I wanted to let them make friends with her or hang on to her until they left and then say, "Sic'em." Most people stayed out with the exception of the Green's Fuel man, the milkman, and the insurance man. Despite my training, Mitzy bit all three.

I learned about the 1940 smallish vacation-style house Daddy built by looking at pictures in a photo album. My attachment to the odd structure grew from childhood. I knew the covered cream can and nearby paintbrush was for swabbing oil on knee-high concrete pyramids to keep termites away from the knotty pine lumber floors, framework, and interior woodwork. Fragrant red cedar boards lined the clothes closets and wide overlapped cypress boards wrapped the exterior in brown ribbons. I begged Daddy to let me brush the lower rough sawn unstained cypress boards with number two fuel oil while he did the higher ones.

Rain slid off the metal, pitched roof after it made a cacophony from deafeningly loud bass drum thudding to tiny droplets plinking treble notes. Windows were shut and clothes taken down from the line leaving little to do but take a nap. "Where's Sarah? Where are you?" Merritt called out opening cupboards and doors until he found me in my favorite cubbyhole with my panda bear. The three of us went to the kitchen where food was waiting. I outgrew the cubbyhole but not the feeling of peace coming from falling water.

The original bedroom was also a sunroom with sliding windows along the south side. Daddy built a great room for Lucy when she turned seven. As mentioned, my parents split up when I was two. Mama reassigned bedrooms. Lucy moved into the sunroom until she was fifteen. Mama, Merritt, and I shared the great room with me in a crib and he on a cot. Later on, Merritt's cot shifted to the front door corridor. Living was sparse: a bed, a lamp, a place to hang clothes, a small table and chair for schoolwork. We rose up with the sun, went inside after dark. It was a simple life.

Daddy slept six blocks away at the Off Shore in a lean-to attached to a one-stall-garage. When I did overnights at friends' houses or stayed with relatives, I learned that parents had the same room and sometimes with just one bed. I thought their parents odd, not mine.

* * *

The large dining room's twelve-foot cathedral ceiling covered a built-in closet, drawers, and a desk. It was perfect for holiday meals and a towering cedar Christmas tree. Like most families of the era, we listened to nightly and weekend radio programs.

The small kitchen paired a gas range and oven next to a cast iron sink. A wooden stick pushed open a trap door that turned on an exhaust fan sucking heat and kitchen odors up and out through the cupola. Daddy's innovations gave the place a unique charm.

We ate at an oak picnic table between two built-in benches. Much of the time, my knees peeked out at the table's edge. As I grew Mama lessened her catchword, "Put your knees down," before she struck at them with the either end of the fly swatter.

Once, when barely four, my highchair fell backward and I hit my head on the stove making a big bump and noisy tears. I cried from the hurt and I cried because my parents argued whose fault it was that the chair tipped.

"If you had built the chair as I asked this wouldn't have happened," Mama squawked at him, pressing ice on my bump.

"I can saw the bottom flat, Dorothy," Daddy muttered with downcast eyes.

By age six I realized Mama blamed Daddy for her many annoyances; the food we ate, the inadequate kitchen, and the lone Green's Fuel heater we huddled in front of when dressing for school and after baths at bedtime. A sixth sense told me Daddy wasn't the one at fault then or later. Some things just happen. Mama dominated our irrational family life with her harsh words and unpredictable actions.

* * *

The rest of the house consisted of a breezeway where the pantry and refrigerator faced each other and a small bathroom with a tub.

Wherever one looked outside, native bromeliads made their home in tree crotches, and populous succulents served as ground cover. Spanish moss resembling limp Afros, liberally hung below pine and oak limbs. Black and yellow swallowtail butterflies danced around Meyer lemon tree blossoms, the sole citrus at Oakairs.

Several outbuildings surrounded the house, the cypress shower house closest and most notable. Night or day, we showered in sulfated water. I often dashed to the house butt naked because I forgot a towel and no one heard my yells to bring one.

Through a grove of laurel oaks a brown, wooden dayroom rested on concrete pyramids. Merritt claimed this building for his tool shed and tolerated my presence. He never told me to leave. I felt close to him amid lawn mower fumes, greasy rags, and half-eaten candy bars.

One day I hopped on playground equipment Daddy built near the back door. I pretended I was a gymnast and jammed my pubic bone on the chinning bar. Warm blood stained my underwear and shorts. I didn't run to Mama because I wasn't sure what she would do. That night I put my clothes in the burn pit.

There were many chicken coops scattered about under oak trees. One large fenced pen contained many free-range laying hens. I admired Daddy's comforting morning ritual of standing in the middle of the hens and tossing scratch on the ground.

The chickens roosted in an elevated house and laid eggs in another. I swirled dried pine needles into thick nests for the hens. We gathered eggs daily, keeping rampant egg sucking snakes at bay. "Eat mice and rats," I told full-bellied snakes lifting them, still asleep, off nests.

Merritt grew and explored the territory bringing home all types of wild and tame animals and housing them in wire pens. Opossums and raccoons, often young enough to play with, non-poisonous snakes, rabbits, fancy tumbler pigeons, pigs, and horses all called Oakairs home.

The early morning air resounded with a symphony of song; roosters crowing, dogs barking, pigs squealing, blue jays screaming, and eagle and hawk cries harmonized in Earth's orchestra.

* * *

Merritt and I scouted the entire property, even blindfolded we knew our land. Heat and mosquitoes didn't bother us when we camped on blankets under the stars or slept in the tree house Daddy built for Merritt.

"Why didn't you help build the tree house?" I questioned my sibling one dark night.

"Because I didn't ask for it, that's why," my handsome brother said gazing into the night sky. "You can use it. Look! Did you see the falling star?"

My brother and I were of the land and the land thrived within us. Lucy couldn't stand being in our woods. She never joined us in our pursuit of adventure, climbing any tree in the chicken coop area, or going by treetops to the northwest corner of the property to an algae covered pothole filled with oily, stagnant water.

"First one there without touching the ground wins!" Merritt crowed.

I usually won.

* * *

A source of Oakairs' income derived from three full-sized billboards facing traffic on the Trail. Mature oaks and dense native shrubs framed each billboard. Merritt and I knew vagrants slept off drunken stupors behind the signs. When they sobered, they hitchhiked further south. Daddy drilled explicit instructions into our heads, "I want you children to leave the tramps alone in the woods. It's our job to keep our family happenings to ourselves. Can you do that?"

"Yes, Daddy," we both answered, anxious to bound off yet again.

* * *

Oakairs' five acres endured all we Wheeler's put upon it. At first, the house was probably a nice shelter for a young family… with faults, which Mama pointed out to Daddy. In 1954 she made it clear, "The house is inadequate for a family of five. New arrangements have to be made."

"Dorothy, I am putting in a telephone to help you out," he mumbled, then sighed, "I can draw-up a plan for an addition."

"That suits me," she said returning to the steamy kitchen. Not much later I spied them looking at a building plan.

"The addition has four bedrooms just as you wished and one bathroom. It's connected to the cypress house by a breezeway," Daddy proffered to Mama.

Next, Daddy came to me saying, "Miss Sarah, you are getting older and Mummy says you need a room of your own. To do this, there will be some changes in the way things look." He gazed out at trees left to shade the house, then returned his eyes to me.

"What trees are you cutting down?" I asked holding my breath.

"We'll keep as many as possible."

He kept to his word and I handled the stacks of oak firewood okay because he sold them to smoke ribs.

The addition went up as planned. The exterior had board-on-batten cypress on the top half with concrete block below. Mama painted the bottom half bright-aqua that never faded enough to suit me and some days, its loudness embarrassed me. The only new landscaping were ginger plants placed outside my window. After a rain, the eves drip-dropped a melody on their broad flat leaves, soothing me to sleep.

Each of us moved into our modern decorated bedrooms except for Daddy. The sunroom became his bedroom. I appreciated him saying good night to Merritt and me. He played little piggies ending with, "Sleep tight and don't let the bed-bugs bite." The great room where Mama and I slept became our living room with new rugs, lamps, drapes, and Bahama lounge furniture. Aluminum window blinds replaced the two-inch wooden Venetian slats.

On weekends, we ate store-bought frozen dinners on TV trays in the living room and watched the evening news on a used black and white console television. For the Boston Red Sox games, Daddy and I snacked on saltine crackers, butter, and grape jelly. On Saturday night we stayed up for *Gunsmoke* and wandered off to bed after an orchestrated Lord's Prayer ended the eleven o'clock news.

* * *

In early 1964, Daddy announced, "Oakairs has been sold."

"Why?" I whined, not yet nineteen, "Couldn't we just sell off the highway frontage and live on the back half?"

"No, Mummy and I agreed to sell it all. Besides, none of you are prepared to pay the taxes," he honestly answered. Except for Daddy, none of us gave anything to the homestead. We took from it. We lacked work ethics, loyalty, love, and family tradition.

"What will happen to the house? Where will we live?"

"Mummy is buying her own house. The cypress house will be moved to Worrington Street," Daddy said trying to keep his dignity about the downsizing.

Before we moved, I announced, "I'm reclaiming my baby room." Lying in bed next to the same window where my crib sat, I stared out into the night at oaks that had grown much larger. I recalled Mama reading *Uncle Remus* stories to Merritt and me for bedtime. And all of us watching the "Ed Sullivan Show." Meat cooled from butchered hogs on tables with the aid of the window air conditioner. During those few months, slumber came easily when I let Oakairs' woodsy cocoon securely wrap around me in the night.

Once the deconstruction started, Daddy offered friends free used lumber from the new addition. Each pine, cedar and cypress board was removed as carefully as when he nailed them on a mere nine years earlier. Doors, lamp fixtures, and windows went too, leaving an empty shell. Landscape plants were soaked and potted for replanting at Worrington Street. Strangers bought chickens and carted away pens and fencing. Power and gas supply ceased. Daddy removed the water pump and capped the well.

Next, bulldozers dug a long deep coffin into the golden, white, and gray colored sands of Oakairs, ripping through any giant tree roots getting in the way. The crater was large enough to hold the twelve-inch-thick concrete flooring, the same size roof, hundreds of concrete blocks, and the shower and tool outbuildings.

Disorder and confusion affected Oakairs wild animal population. So many ran for their lives that day; scurrying, slithering, and screaming away from lost habitat, to refuge in adjoining land, out of harms way.

When the earth holding their life giving roots rumbled from the immense weight of advancing bulldozers, trees shook worse that from any storm I knew of. One by one, magnificent oaks, stately pines fell before the onslaught, unwillingly laying prone on the very soil that had nourished them. All vines and moss once pristinely draped from extended limbs tangled in a mess amid flowering bromeliads and succulents. Heavy equipment scooted the heap on top of the construction debris. Palmettos decorated the near full hole with a casket blanket of grass-green-fans and brown-leathery-stalks. Finally, a thick dense layer of mottled sugar sand neatly obliterated Oakairs. It was a funeral fit for Eden.

Lazy puffy clouds, with no intention of dropping rain, floated over the barren-raped-property, now development readied. Nighttime stars looking for familiar shadows wept meteors for this jungle, once a brother-sister playground. No animals or people cry out. The land lies mute. Cars and trucks whiz by on the Trail blind to the cut-off to Worrington Street.

Mama redesigned the original cypress house. She had Daddy install the outside shower, now smaller, near the back steps. She added a second great room, remodeled the kitchen, and returned to Lucy's childhood great room where she permanently closed the sliding wooden windows shutting out street noises. I'm sure the air conditioner worked triple time cooling the tempests hidden within those walls.

CHAPTER THREE
PRACTICE

Probably by age five, I learned a knack for creating a façade that others couldn't penetrate, not even those closest to me. The answer to anything that seemed wrong was to hold it inside. I didn't need a rope attached to a concrete block like the one my mother threatened me with to sink me to the bottom of the ocean, my secrets would sufficiently take me deep down and keep me there. Maybe that dread of not surfacing prevented me from making high dives or sharing memories for decades. When I thought about what I hid, I felt like I was inside a robust balloon yet suffocating for lack of air. I wanted the vinyl to pop open, so I could breather in all the air I wanted, float freely through life, and not be burdened by pressure holding me trapped. I wanted to have frivolous secrets to teehee about with girlfriends. Mine were heavy, dark, and ugly ones etched into my soul.

I shared what was important like 4-H awards and making honor roll (Daddy gave me $1 for each A or B), but the usual chitchat of sharing hopes, dreams, and miseries wasn't there. Junior high counselors in the 1950's and 1960's were for kids with bad behavior or poor grades. No one wanted to hear about my life, besides what could one—besides my dog Mitzy—do for me?

I met Charles at a coed square-dance class during gym. His blonde flattop and green eyes caught my eye. I can't say what he saw in me, but he asked me out.

Only thirteen and on my first date I didn't know what was and wasn't acceptable behavior. My sister Lucy bubbled when she heard the news. Turns out Charles' sister was popular at Sarasota High. "You've done well, little sister. I'll help you dress." She picked out a pleated-blue-plaid skirt, white-long-sleeved blouse, and red mohair pullover sweater, warm clothes for a chilly December night. Charles's mother dropped us off downtown at the Florida Theater.

Halfway through the movie, Charles reached under my sweater, unbuttoned my blouse, and rested his hand on my cotton bra feeling my small firm breasts. I did nothing, feeling neither joy, despair, nor embarrassment. I looked at the screen instead of yelling, "Pervert!" and running out to the lobby. Two years earlier I played spin the bottle for kisses with neighborhood kids. The tomboy in me told me kissing wasn't fun, so I left. My desire to fit in in ninth grade made me numb.

Afterward, while his mother waited in an idling car, Charles walked me to the rear of my house, planting my backside in the sticky sap of a mature pine tree. Squeezing my shoulders, he whispered in my ear, "Do you know what I did to you in the movie?"

"No, I don't," I confessed, swishing my ponytail back and forth in the bark. "Does it matter?"

Straightening up he looked into my eyes, "Promise me you won't tell anyone. I love you, Sarah," he said clearly, before kissing me on the lips. It was my first real kiss.

Weakened, I replied, "I promise. I love you too." From that moment on I felt bad and helpless with Charles. I accepted bruises from Mama because there were other black and blue kids at school. Striking your kids wasn't reported in 1960. I thought no one had a mother like mine. The guilt I felt from Charles eroded my soul, I knew I was doing something illicit. I didn't have a girlfriend to blab to or a diary for confession. I'm as quiet now as I was then. I felt annoyance with Charles rather than the joy associated with a new love. It was the little things he did like sticking me by a sappy tree and not participating with my family activities. He liked taking me to dark places. It's hard to imagine I stayed with him for the next five years.

Charles came on hot and heavy, giving me his solitaire ring, a gold charm bracelet, and all the sexual forcefulness of a growing teenage boy. I elected the status of going steady and crossed my heart thinking, *I'll stay with Charles as long as possible. Lucy, my beauty queen runner-up sister, has too many boyfriends.* That is a polite way of saying she had a tawdry reputation in Sarasota. More than once my parents got late night calls from the police to pick her up and she would return screaming at them because they brought her home. Her tastes were for professional men, not students like her. I thought one boy couldn't get me in to trouble with my parents or other ways, but I didn't see what was coming.

Charles sold his small motorcycle and bought a 1954 brown Ford, thus gaining him liberal access to my body. He parked on isolated dead-end roads after dark and told me it was important for him to insert his fist into my vagina to prove, "that you're big enough."

"Will it hurt?"

"No, not if I go slow. Other boys do it to their girls," he calmly assured me. As he penetrated, I screamed for mercy; the same sobbing cries as Merritt's cries to Mama a few years before.

Afterward I somehow became his property. Charles used any portal of my body, often several times a night. I enjoyed some places he took me, especially the prestigious Junior Cotillion dances yet, I found no pleasure in our sexual orgy. He grew into a habit. I concealed my sexual life with Charles inside my head right alongside Mama's abuse.

I know I said, "Please stop," "Take me home," "It hurts," so faintly he couldn't possibly have heard me. I wanted that perfect image of the girl who will do anything for her man. Maybe I was afraid of Charles the same way I was afraid of Mama. An example of this is spending all my savings to replace a necklace he gave me instead of telling him I lost it.

Time away from Charles occurred during summer vacations when Mama drove Merritt and me to Minnesota. Another saving grace was that Charles and I went to different high schools. I felt normal at my 4-H meetings, church, Sailor Circus, and Tri-Hi-Y activities. Separated from him I knew I was an average teenage girl, not someone's steady.

* * *

When I was barely fourteen, a man knocked on the front door. "Hello, I'm Danny Chapman," he grinned at me, "I'd like to see Mr. and Mrs. Wheeler."

"Okay." I replied, "Come into the kitchen and I'll get them." Mama prepared coffee and they talked while I busied myself in the dining room rooting for an ashtray. A visitor at Oakairs was rare and someone for me even more so.

Danny announced, "I think you understand what I'm saying. Can Sarah join us?"

I slid next to Daddy on the bench at our wooden table. He asked, "Sarah, do you know this man?"

"I've seen him around. He coaches clowning at Sailor Circus."

"I know him from picking up his dad at my bar." That established Daddy continued, "Danny has a proposition for you."

Mama pushed the ashtray to Danny.

"You're a natural performer," Danny began, snuffing out his cigarette. "You can earn a living as a performer. I checked with the Hanneford's offer for you to learn bareback riding. You declined them to stay home and finish high school. How about learning an act at home and staying in school?"

"What kind of act?"

"Aerial—the single trapeze, the balancing trapeze, or the contortion trapeze. The single trapeze is the most common and performed at one time or another by almost all females in the business. The contortion trapeze involves daring heel and toe catches and long swings. The finish is usually a dangerous backward somersault to a separate web. The balancing trapeze is harder to learn because it involves balance. This trapeze is not stationary—it moves all the time."

Standing up, Danny talked and gave a mock demonstration. "It's also the most elegant, graceful, and feminine of the solo trap acts."

I was interested and felt challenged to pick one. As he talked, my mind's eye envisioned my tricks on the contortion and single trapezes when I was smaller and weighed less than 110 pounds. Although I'd never heard of the balancing trapeze, it might work for me.

"Tell me about the balancing trapeze."

"There are only three women in the world who do it. It compares to the balance beam in the Olympics, except half as wide. The bar swings and twists and the object is to keep it under you at all times. A person needs strong legs plus upper body endurance. Balance is learned by developing specific foot muscles," Danny concluded.

"Then I choose the balance trapeze," I stated, confidant of my parent's approval.

* * *

Within a week, Daddy brought home a crude metal trapeze forty-inches long, two-inches wide, with two-by-six-inch uprights welded to each end. "This cost me twenty dollars young lady. Let's see how much progress you can make." He wasn't concerned for his investment; he wanted to see if I could stand on it.

In the front yard, Daddy and I clamped hooks on both ends of a set of one-fourth-inch thick, fourteen-foot-long cables. One hook hung in an eye of a crossbeam on a sixteen-foot rigging and the other went to the trapeze. Guyed out, I hopped on the bar—a mere six-inches off the ground.

A month later Danny returned to see how I was doing. I met him by the trap as he destroyed a cigarette butt between his fingers. With both hands free he started talking, "I turned to clowning after I fell fifty-feet in the Cirque Royale in Brussels. My left leg is forty-percent paralyzed. I gave up aerial work, but I know balancing basics."

He had a tanned face below his Panama hat and his hands fluttered in front of an old blue T-shirt until he thrust them straight out from his chest, bent his knees, and said, "This is the position you take to rotate the bar. Try it on the ground first."

He rotated his arms left to right, grinning. "You can also learn sideways, circular, and back and forth swings. Swinging it straight backwards and forwards while facing front is the hardest." I stepped on the bar and took the basic position letting my forearms touch the cables when I felt like falling off. I turned sideways next and starting swaying the bar back and forth.

"Soon you'll be doing figure eights." Danny joked while he studied the set up. "The bar isn't heavy enough. I'll talk to your dad."

"Thanks for checking on me." I waved when he pulled out of the yard driving his shabby Nash Rambler on the pine needle strewn path.

Daddy brought the improved bar home from the machine shop with two iron rods welded to the underside. At forty pounds, it took more power to move and less effort to keep it under me.

Looking in again, Danny advised a location change. "Hang it in the pine tree. I'll get you a crane bar and guy it out with four cables to iron stakes in the ground."

My thirty-minute daily practice waxed and waned like former piano lessons. On the other hand, it was something unique and I wanted to be the fourth woman doing this act. The word balancing sounded magical to me. Each time I placed my feet on the narrow bar, delicate muscles keenly worked, pressuring the bar to my command. When I bent my torso instead of bending my knees, I lost equilibrium, grabbed the cables, and started again.

The trapeze merged with my identity. I wanted to master the final trick—a head balance. Danny Chapman didn't know how to teach me, so he told me to sit on the bar in a wooden kitchen chair the same way I leaned a chair backwards at school.

"Saw the back legs off on an angle," Danny said then quipped, "If you were older, you could light a cigarette. Hah ha!" Changing his tone he said, "I see you are weak in upper body strength. Stick to grace, elegance, and poise and you'll have a first class act. How about picking up a handkerchief?"

"How do I do that?"

"Take a piece of cloth and put it on the bar between your knees. Bend down and pick it up with your mouth. And don't hit your teeth."

I drew a paper napkin from my pocket, shook it out, and laid it across the middle of the bar. I flexed my knees straddling the napkin, put my arms forward, and waited for the trapeze to stop its constant slow-motion swing. Careful and unhurried, I glanced downwards viewing the object I was supposed to pick up. *Sarah, you're only inches off the ground. Not too far too fall. Keep bending. Slow. Slower. Got it! Now what?*

Still frozen in a tucked position, Danny teased me, "Great! You're doing great! See you in a couple of weeks."

I reached for the support cables and stood up similar to a newborn chick on wobbly legs. *Hmm, elegance and poise...I'll work on that.* What I didn't know at the time was Danny telling me I was weak put him in control of my body. Without strength, I was fatigued throughout my circus career.

As time went by, I showed Danny other tricks. "The bar's moving."

"Don't worry. Take your time," he responded, leaving his eyes on me, giving me confidence. "You'll be working under a variety of conditions. Get used to the bar shifting up and down and forward and back. Sometimes it'll do both. Remember, it's a balancing act," he chuckled. I took practice seriously and didn't comprehend his humor.

Balance depends upon excellent inner ears. My portable radio blared pop music during practice. I never realized I blocked it out and unexpected sounds and distractions until Mama came out to get me for supper. Not a rooster crowing or a loud truck on the Trail interrupted my concentration. On weekends I spent extra time swinging, either standing or kneeling, in big lazy circles. Each minute spent on the narrow beam subconsciously developed muscles aligning me on top of the bar during twists and swings.

CHAPTER FOUR
SHOWTIME

Early in 1963, an idea grew to perform my trap in Sailor Circus. I'd already performed aerial acts in this youth circus for four seasons. On a whim during physical education class, I saw Sailor Circus Director, Bill Lee, sitting idly on a chair in the gym. "Coach, can I do my trap in the show? I'm a senior and it means a lot to me."

"You'll have to pass tryouts, like everyone else," Coach Lee answered giving me his "I'm not a pushover" look.

After school I sped in the family car to Daddy's business, the Off Shore Bar, grinning all the way. I quizzed my bartending dad, "Guess what?"

"What?" He suspected nothing more than a request for a few dollars.

"I'm going to try out my act in Circus. What do you think?"

"You'll need to get there," he responded raising his eyebrows.

"I'm so excited!" I practically squirmed, "Yes, you can pick me up at Riverview and please bring something to eat before practice." He nodded and rustled my hair with his hand.

I drove the short distance home dazzled. *No one has done balance trap in Circus. I know I'll do my act because Coach will say, "Yes."*

Circus practice was in the tent located behind Sarasota High School. Daddy helped me rig the heavy bar knee-high off the ground and I began a practice session. When I rested, sophomore Raul Segura, watched, and fussed. "You don't know how to practice do you? My aunt, Pinito Del Oro, did balance trapeze."

"She's your aunt? People say her forward balance was thrilling. I wish my act closed with a swinging headstand like hers. She's really your aunt?"

"She is." He was straight-faced. "She's my father's sister. She retired to have a family and her trap's at my house. You can use it."

"Gosh, thanks, Raul." I digested the news, and then told Daddy.

Raul brought Pinito's trapeze bar to the tent. "I'll help put it up and your dad can watch. You have to work harder, Sarah. Concentrate on each trick until its right. Be serious about practice and you'll be good. No practice, no act." I've often wondered how Raul knew how to coach me and how it made him feel.

Pinito's bar was one-inch wide and hung with rope, not cable. Weight and length were the same. Her bar gave me the added incentive I needed to master a gyrating iron slab. When I stopped overbalancing, the bar did the work, leaving me to hold poses.

During the month of practice, Daddy took me to the tent. Mama waited at home with our evening meal. I'd inform her of the day's events, not sure she listened as she hardly ever commented. I suspect she felt the circus was encroaching on my goal to be an extension agent. To me circus was just a senior activity.

"Guess what Raul did?" He raised my bar up to my shoulders. Coach said I need a net," I shared between bites. "The wardrobe mistress gave me an old Ringling leotard decorated with feathers. It's pretty."

I knew Daddy supported my talent. Each year he took our family to see the Ringling Circus in Sarasota when it was under canvas. At pre-school age, I didn't let go of his hand in the crowd. When we climbed planked seats, he put me on his shoulders. On the way out of the five-ring big top, he stopped in front of the bandstand to say hello to his friend, Merle Evans, a famous bandleader. I felt special when Daddy let me pick a colored balloon. Those early circus visits deluged my senses. Performing in Sailor Circus changed that because I felt the excitement, not merely bombarded by the plethora of sights, sounds, and shapes.

A week before dress rehearsals Raul asked a favor, "I need my aunt's bar to do head balancing in Ring Three."

"You don't know how to head balance, you're a juggler." I wondered what was up.

"That's right, I don't. I can try. Pinito's bar has a beveled place for the head grommet. You can use your practice bar," he said pulling up the slack on a block attached to a guy line cable. Seeing me frown he offered,

"Ah, don't worry, I'm still here."

"Thanks...Raul. I appreciate your help." I turned and walked to the opposite end of the tent, admitting that Raul Segura was the real teacher for my act. Danny Chapman merely presented the idea. I rigged my comfortable practice bar in Ring One and decided to jazz it up for the show with silver paint. An aerial act, a loving father, and a faithful teenage coach made my senior Sailor Circus unforgettable.

Little did I know six years later that I would do my balancing trapeze on Ringling Bros Circus, the Greatest Show On Earth.

* * *

After I graduated in 1963, Daddy sat me down and explained finances to me. "You're going off to fancy Sullins College, and Mummy and I are doing without any extras because your school costs a lot of money." I nodded in agreement and he continued. "I want you to get a job. BeMent's Broasted Chicken across the Trail is hiring. They're holding the position for you."

"I know where it is. When am I supposed to go?" I complied.

"Today's a good day." I enjoyed my waitress job more than I let on to Daddy because he knew I wanted to work at the Off Shore.

One afternoon as I left BeMent's, Charles angrily called me over to his car. "Why didn't you see me?" he shouted his face fused red with anger.

31

I watch customers, not cars. "I don't know," I said frustrated, "I'm tired and want to go home. And I want to walk."

Charles confused and surprised me by doing things contrary to the person I thought I knew. One day he picked me up in a newer Ford and I asked, "Whose car is this?"

"Mine."

"Why didn't you tell me you were getting rid of the other one?"

"I don't have to tell *you*," he flashed back with contempt. It went the same way when I found out from friends he dated other girls, and smoked cigarettes. Charles neither nurtured nor admired me.

Maybe, I thought, *I should be different too.* Because I saw what happened to smokers and alcoholics at Daddy's bar, I knew I didn't want to smoke or drink hard liquor. I broke my "go steady" rule once and made a date with a junior who owned a '57 Chevy. We parked on a Siesta Key street and he asked for action beyond kissing. I refused. "I thought you were better than that! You're a prick tease!" he yelled jamming the tranny to leave. I made the right decision regardless of what prick meant. *Simple to back out... with anyone but Charles.*

One night with Charles at Turtle Beach, trying to fit into his paradigm, I put on a false bravado. "Give me the bottle, I'm not a baby." After a hearty swallow, I threw up immediately outside the car and never drank vodka again.

CHAPTER FIVE
SUSSIE

When the day to leave for college arrived, I quietly spoke to my father at the train siding, "I wish you were the only one seeing me off. Charles invited himself." Daddy didn't have to answer because he knew my heart was his at the time. There were no "Love you" exchanges so often heard today because parents and children didn't do that.

Pulling out of Sarasota for Bristol, Virginia, on an Atlantic Seaboard passenger coach, I was a young, mixed-up person. It was okay to leave my family for my education, but seeing Daddy standing there and gently waving hurt. At seventeen my life laid ahead, he was sixty-eight. Settling into my Pullman seat, I enjoyed the long ride. Further north in Georgia, Negro youth boarded the train in their marked car. I thought inwardly, *I wish I were with a group.* Searching for them, I ventured from coach to coach carefully crossing noisy, open-air vestibules noticing the surrounding hillsides covered with trees, pastures, and crops—mostly tobacco.

Sullins, a two-year liberal arts college for girls and a surviving finishing school had social rules that radically turned my life upside down. Did my mother encourage this relic for me to find a husband? Did she realize I was accountable for my appearance, whereabouts, classes, and homework, things she was remiss on during my upbringing. I felt foolish checking out to leave campus for town, church, or dates with boys.

* * *

Being away from Sarasota gave me plenty of time to reflect. I knew I manipulated my social life. On weekends, Charles played tenor saxophone with a band in bars from St. Pete Beach to Venice. I went most Saturday nights and joined the band's wives table where I wasted hours watching other people dance to roll and roll. When the bars closed, I eventually got home to get enough sleep before Episcopal church the next morning. I prided my perfect attendance and was a Sunday school assistant.

After church, I did homework until Charles picked me up at six o'clock to attend evening service with his family at the Church of Christ in Fruitville. A cappella singing and watching the sun go down behind gold tinted windows occupied my time. Released from church we drove twenty miles to Roller Coaster Road at Turtle Beach on the south end of Siesta Key. He wedged between sand dunes and sea oats, backed up once, and pulled forward killing the engine.

With the romp in the back seat done, we cleansed our bodies in the Gulf of Mexico. Kneeling in waist deep salt water and swirling my arms, I delighted seeing eerie phosphorescent pools of light around my torso.

"Charles, do you think it's wrong for us to do what we do? I mean, we just left church," I questioned.

"No, we love each other and that makes it okay. Just don't tell anyone." He pulled me close to him.

"I won't. Do you think other kids do what we do?"

"Of course! Why do you think their cars are here?" he mocked, removing his arms.

It was extremely important that no one found us with our clothes off. If he thought the usual beach patrol officer got too close to his car, he jumped in the front seat and took off driving wildly, clothes lifting off the seats each time the car dipped down and up room-sized ruts. When we got to the paved road, I knew he could outrun any pursuer. I can't say why I accepted these dangerous *Dukes of Hazzard* style chases.

On school nights, Charles expertly piloted the Ford to parking spots closer to home without using headlights. We often fell asleep in the parked car until three in the morning. Upon waking, he drove me home where I slipped inside my outside door.

I feared changing the relationships I had with Charles and my parents. I didn't understand it wouldn't have been the end of the world if I broke up with him or he dumped me. Wasn't I supposed to have a boyfriend? I didn't want to answer to my parents over my tryst. As long as I stayed in school and played the role of the good daughter, they seemed happy. A half of me wanted to break up the Charles/Sarah duet and the other half didn't. Besides, they never questioned my empty room, which meant they weren't checking on me.

I knew Mama's cursing mantra by heart: "All men are the same. They only want one thing." I thought there were kind and gentle men, comparable to Daddy. One night, I quietly stole into Mama's flowery purple room to share my love for Charles. I didn't tell her because our conversation ended when she reached for her mystery magazine. That left an empty feeling and I never tried to confide in her again. *Anyhow*, I thought, *my boyfriend will protect me.* I was kidding myself. If they had asked, I wanted to tell Mama, "You're right—I haven't amounted to anything," another of her taunts I knew by heart. I lived in a self-created vacuum with unfair rules and didn't see how to break them.

A voiceless part of me wanted to call it off with Charles a thousand times. I cringed when he disrespected his grandmother. While I couldn't see the present, I envisioned being old and knew I wouldn't tolerate a grandkid's scorn. I wished I never met him, and instead dated boys at school I liked who did things in common like sports and club activities. The right moment never came along.

* * *

Following my desire to be a County Extension Agent and lead 4-H programs, I majored in Home Economics at Sullins. My cooking and sewing skills saved my freshman college year. Except for food preparation, clothing, English, and history, other classes were weird. Exposure to centuries old literature, religion, philosophy, music, and art seemed useless at the time. My mind said, *I don't want to study humanities. Even PE is hard. I've never played tennis, soccer, or swum in an indoor pool.*

Sullins invited young men from area colleges to Friday night dances in the downstairs gymnasium. I met a red-haired linebacker from East Tennessee State University who asked me out. "Would you appreciate a country drive?"

"I think so. I can go Sunday."

"Good, I'll pick you up after lunch." Properly registered with the hem of my skirt touching the floor, we headed into the Blue Ridge Mountains' highways and byways finding a park setting to sit and talk on a blanket he spread out under tall trees.

"I'm glad you came," he began seriously, "I want to know if you are capable of running a household and accepting community leadership." He meant well. It sounded like he wanted to jump into marriage, something I couldn't fathom with him or anyone. I only liked him enough to spend an afternoon not a lifetime.

Staring at orange and yellow leaves lying on the ground and hanging limp in the trees I asked, "Why aren't the leaves green?"

"They aren't green because it's fall. You didn't listen to me did you?"

"No, not really. Will you take me back to Sullins?"

"Sure," he grumbled, rolling up the blanket with a layer of leaves attached to it.

Returning one hour late put us in much trouble. Grounded, I couldn't date him until the next semester. We both honestly appeased my housemother's inflated concern by admitting, "Yes, we're late. No, we did no evil." I wonder if he found his community-oriented wife.

Sullins wasn't completely repressive and provided good experiences from some of the teachers, programs, and modern facilities. The students were all classy including my roommate, Shelley Sue Sutherland from Dallas, Texas. She taught me how to study, a key that unlocked future academic doors. "Shelley," I confessed, "How did you know I never learned to study? I don't read much and make up book reports."

"I'll teach you how," she smiled at me. And she did.

A girl from New York City taught me kindness to others by sharing her family tradition, giving 'sussies' on her return trip from town. "Here's your sussie," she'd say giving out a pencil, bakery treat, gum, or other simple gift. I looked forward to sussies and shared her custom with all I've met since.

As time passed, I felt blessed going to Sullins despite having my grades drop each quarter. In early November, Daddy wrote, "You're costing me and Mummy too much money. Your charge account at Penney's is closed. From now on we're sending you $5.00 a week." Down $15 from my usual $20 weekly expenses, I called home collect.

"What about the bookstore account?"

"You can only buy classroom materials."

"That's not much to live on. Goodbye, Daddy." Quick thinking told me that laundry cost $2.50 a week leaving $2.50 for miscellaneous. *Hmm…several people commented on my muumuu. I'll make a few and sell them each for $5.00 plus material.*

Sewing muumuus on weekends replaced studying. On Sundays I went to Shelley's Bible church or visited a family from her church that lived within walking distance.

All Sullins students had the nickname Suzy Sullins. That I comprehended, but not the myth of the Southern Belle. *The picture-perfect lifestyle Sullins represents is a waste on me, a girl born and raised in a five-acre Tamiami Trail jungle.*

Over Christmas vacation, I took my first airplane ride from Tri-Cities Airport in Johnsonville, Tennessee to Sarasota. My body felt and looked porky eating more than my share of Virginia smoked ham. I had Charles cut off my waist length tresses. I learned too late that my classmates considered them a trademark of Martin Hall.

Hair bobbed chin-length and Sullins no longer a mystery, I relaxed on the return train trip to Bristol. In Georgia, the same Negro youth I saw in September boarded. I admired their composure and wanted to interact, this time stopping in their coach and asking, "May I sit with you?"

"Sure, right here." One of the girls motioned to an empty seat. I listened to their hopes, dreams, and future aspirations. My life seemed useless compared to them, after all, I made my problems, they weren't imposed by society. With dignity and integrity, they struggled against inequality. From my heart, I wished them my freedoms.

At Easter, instead of going home, I took a bus over the Appalachian Mountains and stayed with Mama's friends, Naida and Calvin Meyer and their three children in Mocksville, North Carolina.

Fun reigned in the Meyer household. They danced the Polka in the living room every night. Their children were close to my age, however years ahead emotionally. They used their heads and did chores responsibly. One morning I stumbled into the kitchen where high school sophomore Larry stood by the stove stirring oatmeal. I gasped, "You know how to cook?"

"Sure. My dad's an even better cook than me."

"I thought only women cooked."

"Not in this house!"

Naida's interest wasn't sharing recipes. Her objective was finding what made me keep the faith with Charles. Naida asked me where I went and what I did with Charles, things parents usually ask, but not mine. She was close to my mother and telling Naida was the same as telling Mama. By clamming up, I probably confirmed to Naida that I was up to something. I detoured my answers to other interests, "Your tulips and forsythia are lovely."

* * *

The final train trip home from Virginia was one of anticipation and reflection. I told myself, *My lack of self-discipline, not knowing how to put important things first, and inadequate social skills prevented me from succeeding at Sullins.* Taking home Ds in history and all the humanities would not make my father proud. Constructive thinking flickered away because, more than anything, I wanted my home. I wanted to hear crickets chirping in the night, I wanted to hug Oakairs large live oaks, I wanted to hold Daddy's chickens, and I wanted to hug my dog and never let her go.

My mind drifted to Daddy, who visited me at Sullins on a rare trip to his home state. He was a welcomed guest eating dinner with my suitemates. What was there about him that made him fit in with people and not my mother?

CHAPTER SIX
CONFUSION

Before the cypress house was ready for living, Mama bought a house on Padgett Avenue. She also bought a motel annex and relocated it to Worrington Street. Daddy lived in it while he worked on the cypress house. The annex was a one-room affair with a bath. In 1964, I reluctantly lived at Mama's house and drove fifteen miles to Manatee Junior College in Bradenton. They accepted my credits from Sullins and I enrolled full-time. This college campus differed vastly from Sullins—girls wore slacks and skirt lengths went unnoticed.

I saw friends from my junior and senior high schools. Charles was a second-year-engineering student. I asked him to take me to lunch one day and he informed me, "You're not my responsibility. I can't buy you food or provide transportation. You can use my car if you pay for gas." What annoyed me was he told me this in a corner of the hamburger joint where I couldn't respond. I wanted better treatment than that. Long time friends help one another not make it rough.

Driving back to campus my mind went blank. *That means I need money. My parents don't give me any and I don't have a job. Isn't going to school enough?* I decided on the spot that I wouldn't ask to use his car and I would take a lunch. Plus, I accepted I needed to look for a job.

The distorted Charles/Sarah relationship continued off campus, except my thinking crept ahead. A year earlier, we took a trip in Mama's station wagon with another couple to the Daytona Raceway and slept in the parked car on the infield. Restless and horny, Charles wanted sex. "No way! Not here! Not around people," I scowled and exited loudly slamming the car door.

Late in the 1965 spring semester at MJC, Charles mentioned, "You're invited to an afternoon beach party given by the engineering students." I joined him at the water where he separated us from the other swimmers and came on to me.

"Stop it. Don't do this." I snarled and swam ashore to mingle at the pavilion. What was once private between us was going public.

Charles imposed another distasteful chore. "I want you to douche within twenty minutes after sex. It helps kill sperm cells."

I thought,*Where does he get his information?* I felt guilty running water after a date. Douching reminded me of the childhood enemas Mama gave Merritt and me. I hated her control over us and swore I'd let my kids poop on their own.

My grades plummeted. I skipped too many classes, didn't turn in assignments, and attended too many weekend parties. Sometimes I sipped beer in order to blend in. I always went alone and left alone in my little Morris car my parents bought me to drive to school.

Living with Mama in a subdivision wasn't for me. My heart lay in the woods and with Daddy. Visiting him in the small rental unit told me I couldn't stay there. My father built the cypress house in 1940, added an addition in 1955, and had it moved in 1964. After the movers left he elected to rebuild all the steps, and restore the power and plumbing. Added to this were the same tasks for the annex. He was tired. I know he missed watching Saturday night TV and ballgames together. I tried not to look at the barren five acres behind the house. He did not ask me to help nor did I volunteer. Not having anything uplifting to say, I left feeling worse than when I went.

* * *

At mid-term the academic dean sent me a note. A divine light foresaw my appointment. Seated in his office, the polite dean looked up from his desk saying, "You're not doing well....the college has a waiting list to take your place."

Spontaneously, I dropped to my knees, folded my hands, and bowed my head. Deep in prayer I heard a voice saying, "Miss Wheeler, please take a seat. Miss Wheeler?" When I resettled, he inhaled deeply, "If you agree to academic probation, you can stay in school. You need to earn C's. Can you do that?"

"I know I can! Thank you!" came out of my mouth with easy determination. *The dean challenged me and now I'm challenging myself to make passing grades.*

That settled, ending the Charles mess was a priority. My strategy for him started on the phone, "Come see me and park next door. No one lives there."

I advanced alongside his Ford, stopped, and turned to him sitting in the driver's seat.

"Aren't you getting inside?" he asked.

"Not yet," I said making eye contact. "We've been together five years. Are we ever getting married?"

He paused to think, gazed through the windshield, and said, "I'm going to finish school. I don't know whom I shall marry." He turned his head back to me.

"In that case, good bye." His truth surprised and hurt me. I returned to Mama's house promising, *I won't look back.* A great weight lifted, yet I was bewildered. I wasn't a virgin and I didn't know anything about dating.

I cried rivers for days, always alone—always forlorn. Teardrops splashing on my unhappiness became a habit. I didn't confide in anyone. *How did my life get in such a mess?*

After a few phone calls to high school friends, I finally went on a double date. We spent a quiet evening sitting and talking in the living room of an apartment on Siesta Key. To me, a date meant sex. I waited and nothing happened. Finally, my date took me home telling me at the front door, "I've had a nice time. Good night."

That confused me—where was the sex? At nineteen was I fat at 145 pounds wearing a size fourteen? Part of the tears was for the extra weight gained at Sullins.

My crying spells continued yet when my mind cleared, I said, "Can't never could do anything." I heard it so often when Merritt or I whined that we couldn't rake any more, refused to work anymore, or wanted to quit for the day. Focusing on being a doer not a quitter, I created a new mantra. *I'm an aerialist. Practice will put me in shape.*

When spring classes ended, I was still on academic probation. I enrolled in World Literature for the summer and employed my new study techniques. This was my last chance and I didn't want to botch it up, as Daddy would say.

I put up the sixteen-foot rigging in Mama's back yard. During single trap practice Mama called me to the phone, "Danny Chapman wants to speak to you."

"Hello," I began. "You want what? A clown? Where? Maybe. Come by and we can talk about it. Goodbye."

"What did he say?" Mama chided.

"Danny wants me to clown this summer at the Circus Hall of Fame. He's paying me fifty dollars a week." I learned later that my job entailed four-shows-a-day, seven-days-a-week for thirteen weeks. Thinking positively and remembering my mantra, I said aloud, "I'll lose weight because I can practice my bar at the Hall of Fame."

* * *

Danny's word skills compensated for a lack of empathy. "You're amazing rushing into the Hall of Fame and changing your school clothes for that heavy-wool outfit, floppy shoes, and thick white-face make-up. One day you'll have a degree." I knew Mama's quote about me hanging myself if I had enough rope, but Danny encouraged me. The more praise he lavished, the harder I worked at my class.

He commented on my personal life saying, "That boyfriend of yours is a drag. He doesn't have your best interests at heart." It was none of his business who I saw, but Danny was nosey to most people. He let me decide that if Charles didn't advocate for me, then who did? Danny, of course, by offering me a job, and more. This wasn't logical thought progression, but it beat crying myself to sleep.

"I don't see him anymore," was my awkward answer. I fiddled with my clown wig and hat before assisting him in his featured European-style clown numbers. They surpassed the usual noisy fill-in spot gags. He worked delicately in pantomime with simple props, a broom, a soda straw, three balls, his hat, etc.

"Don't worry, you'll only remember the good things in life."

After that number Danny vented his anger at Bob who I replaced. "I wouldn't have asked you to join me if Bob hadn't left town. He stole my program coin purse from the Hall and appliances from my house. That's the lowest form of deceit. Robbing someone's home. Other than hiring him, I've only made one other mistake."

I learned he meant his first marriage. I was blind to the growing fleet of red flags. Shortly after I started the clown job, Bob picked up a prop during working hours. I noticed he was gay. Maybe that was why he took off. The fact presented to me was someone wronged Danny because Danny was never wrong.

"Bob's gone, Danny," I reassured him. "I'm learning his part."

Between shows, we polished our clown routines in the sweltering Pat Valdo Arena. Blissful, my clown persona, learned how to handle magic props, slap flat-leather clown boxing gloves, and clearly present dialog for the shooting gag. I also practiced my balancing trapeze out-of-doors under the blazing sun while ignoring planes landing at the nearby Sarasota-Bradenton Airport. I lost weight and gained strength, which improved my outlook and balance, as well as my appearance.

Often on my way in or out of the attraction gift shop, I paused near Ringling's huge, ornate Two Hemispheres bandwagon, admiring the gilded wood relief intricacies. *How would I feel riding this masterpiece pulled by a forty-horse team?* I fantasized.

Most nights Danny took me to dinner, sometimes we walked barefoot along the Gulf beaches. Anywhere near water pleased me.

One day he ordered, "Get in the car. I'm taking you to Tio Zacchini's machine shop on Lime Avenue." I guessed his intent because he told me that Tio made a bar for another aerialist. Her shiny bar with twelve-inch pivoting uprights and a removable bullet on each end was a design masterpiece.

"You wanta I maka one for you?" Tio asked in broken Italian-English.

"Yes, Tio," I said keeping my hand the showroom bar. "Leave off the head grommet. And, can you put grooves where I stand?" He brushed his fingers on the smooth surface and nodded.

"Thatsa good. Come back nexa month." I left with a $250 debt and no aerial job in sight. It didn't matter, I was an aerialist.

My new bar had the same dimensions as the old one: forty-inches long, two-inches wide, and forty pounds. And I had it chromed. The chrome filled the grooves and my bare feet felt slippery on a moist day. "Danny, I need the same traction as the old bar. What can I do about that?"

"See if non-slip tape helps." It did and I had a uniform texture in all weather conditions.

Danny took a chance the day he told my parents I had potential. Not everyone succeeds in aerial work despite the best of intentions. His belief in my talent helped him contribute to my rigging.

I spied him from a distance looking like a spider tangled in its own web; hair askew, reading glasses on nose tip, and shorts dampened at the waist. His muscular fingers manipulated multiple strands of stainless steel non-rotating aircraft cable as if he was making a gigantic necklace.

"What are you doing?" I asked as I advanced.

"I'm splicing your new cables. The old ones cut your hands."

"Yes, they did."

"Yesterday, at the gas station, you forced air into the clear plastic tubing while I pushed the cable into it. The plastic gives you a safer grip and keeps the cables clean. Hand me the fid."

"What's that?"

"It's a splicing tool used as an insertion wedge. I learned how to splice cables on Tom Mix Circus. This fid was given to me for helping repair the tent," he informed as he worked.

"Now I see. You're making an eye splice to hook it to the trapeze."

"Yes, you're getting chromed hooks and shackles. Everyone has them."

"It will be pretty," I said, glad for his talent and effort.

With the cables installed, my sleek bar glided effortlessly wherever my feet willed it. "The bar is wonderful, Danny. Balancing is much easier."

"Good. Make a routine about six minutes long. And, you can stop biting your lip."

"Sorry, I do that when I'm concentrating."

He tolerated my fingernails bitten to the quick and acned face but picked on my diction. "I come from Pennsylvania. They have the clearest speech in the United States. Your voice has a twang. Pronounce the words Harry, Larry, and Gary," he barked with authority.

"Hairy, Lairy, Gairy." I twisted my hands in a knot. Mama and Daddy wouldn't let us kids talk Southern or use Ma'am or Sir at home. I believed his criticism came for a good reason.

"There's no 'i' in any of those words. Do it again and lower your voice. Distinguish each vowel and consonant.

"Your grammar is adequate. I don't see you reading. I get all the words correct every month in *Reader's Digest* Word Power Quiz."

"Oh, I don't read. Only what I must for school and that's it," I retorted, letting him know it was hopeless trying to make me read.

Danny Chapman swore worse than Mama did because God damned so many more things. It seemed immoral. I asked, "God doesn't damn that object—why do you?" When it got too much, I'd put my hands over my ears, "Please don't swear in front of me." I never dared saying that to Mama.

Danny had strong opinions. "People respond to diplomacy better than brute force. A leader is a person who works alongside his employees and sets a positive example. Bosses just give orders." My spongy mind welcomed, rather than questioned, his tirades.

BALANCING ACT

I saw Danny as a forty-seven-year-old, divorced man with bluebird-colored eyes and a balding head of light-brown curls touching his collar. His well-proportioned stature wasn't threatening, he only stood five-foot five, 133 pounds, his hands and feet similar in size to mine. Mugs of creamy, sweetened, coffee, and lit cigarettes were his constant companions. Nicotine stained his teeth and nails a grimy yellow.

Danny's family included three children, a housekeeper, and his elderly mother. The two younger daughters, Deborah and Stephanie, were seven and five. His carefree fourteen-year-old daughter Dinah Michele, who went by Ringo, buzzed around Sarasota on her motorbike, and lived with her mother, Joan, Danny's first wife.

During high school, I practiced at Danny's house with other Sailor Circus kids. Whenever Joan entered the yard to speak to Danny, I saw her attractive hair framing an expressionless face. They divorced and he kept the house.

When he invited me there after work, he met me in the driveway with an old stooped woman with a satchel in her hand. "This is Olga Campbell, my housekeeper for my paralyzed and widowed mother, Patrnella. Olga also feeds and supervises Deborah and Stephanie when they stay home."

"Mr. Chaplin," Olga mumbled, always calling him Mr. Chaplin, "I won't be here this weekend. I'm going to my sister's."

"Right-o, Olga. I'm giving you a ride home."

When they left, I surveyed the inside of Danny's flat-roofed L-shaped house. Sliding floor-to-ceiling glass doors opened from the great room to the Phillippi Creek Bayou. Two of the three bedrooms also opened to the bayou. No one slept in one of the twin beds in the children's room.

When he returned, I asked, "Danny, my mom's been making things rough at home. My father doesn't have room for me. Can I stay here?"

"Of course you can. When do you want to come?" he spoke without hesitation.

"At the end of June, after my last exam." After the relocation, I felt closer to Oakairs—just two miles away.

CHAPTER SEVEN
TRUTH OR DARE

I took everything I owned to Danny's including my new medium-sized black-and-white dog, Lacie. Aging Mitzy stayed with Mama. A week later Mama called me and told me to go to Daddy on Worrington Street.

"Why did you want me?"

"Mummy says you're to give back the Volkswagen." I forgot I borrowed their bug when they sold the Morris.

"I think Danny will let me use his Alpha Romero. Oh Daddy! My grade came from my summer class. I got my first 'A' in college!"

"That's good news and deserves congratulations. Now, about the car…"

I wish Daddy wasn't the executioner that day. Instead of returning possessions, I would gladly have moved back home, if they had asked me to live with them in one house, instead of two. I knew my conditions weren't ideal. They never talked to me about my move to Danny's, nor did they stand in my way. Lamely, I tried to understand where my life was going.

Skin-deep thinking took me nowhere—*I'm a Christian girl with talents to offer this family. Danny sees I care for the children and sew clothes for them. I make clown shirts and wardrobe for him. I wonder what I'll make next.*

Not much later Danny solicited, as if he could hear my thoughts, "Why don't you make yourself a costume?"

"I'm not sure how to make a leotard." It was worth a try. I began with a muslin pattern and when completed, my $10 glittery red costume snuggly flexed around my streamlined 128 pounds.

With high spirits, I settled into the daily Circus Hall of Fame routine and living with the Chapmans. We didn't go out for dinner as much after I moved to the bayou. I made simple suppers when it was my turn to cook. I was considerate to Patrnella, but unappreciative of Olga's role in the family, probably thinking I was better for the children.

Danny taught circus skills to youth and adults at his home. They came and went after working hours. Bayou life was enchanting, easygoing, and Bohemian, often with music playing from the radio. Evenings we ate a late supper often inviting co-workers. Danny opened his kitchen to anyone who could put together a meal.

"Who's cooking?" I wanted to know.

"Cayetano Segura is making his famous Paella Valenciana," Danny sang out.

"Will I eat whatever it is? Is he related to Raul Segura?"

"Yes, you will like chicken and rice. Cayetano is a chef at the Plaza Restaurant. I don't know his family."

Later, licking my fingers, I asked the contented little Spaniard, "How are you related to Raul?"

"Raul is my son. You may call me Papa Segura," he expressed proudly thumping his chest.

On paydays we went to the Original Oyster Bar on the South Trail. I slurped both raw oysters and the special lemonades (Tom Collins, or a Daiquiri) Danny ordered for me. "You have a light alcoholic drink. I drink gin and tonic because the doctor in England made me drink one every day. A little alcohol is good for you."

When I finished my red costume, Danny insisted on act photographs. I yearned for a reflection of my soul and daringly posed for the still shots teasing the camera lens to close in on my grey eyes and bobbed near-black hair.

"Have the photographer make these into a montage," Danny advised, handing me several prints.

"Is this the right way?" I asked laying them out.

"Sure. Send it to New York and get 100 prints. It's cheaper."

When the pictures returned it was important for me to recognize my parents and the role they played in my career. Without Daddy's encouragement, I may not have continued from day one.

I signed and framed one action shot for them and presented it to Daddy. "My trapeze isn't as dangerous as it looks." He frowned and set it on a table. I think of us three kids, I was his biggest disappointment. The other two acted out so much, trouble with them was inevitable. Quiet Sarah needed a saner life than the one she choose with Danny. I couldn't comprehend any of that at the time and left Worrington Street that day feeling empty.

* * *

Between shows at work, Danny took extra time with me. He gently massaged my shoulders or my neck for a headache. We did some light petting and exchanged kisses, nothing more.

While he massaged, he explained human sexuality in many deviant forms including how same sex couples copulated. Awestruck, I asked, "Why do queens, dykes, and queers join the circus?"

"Because no one bothers them. When I was with the Bounding Gordons during the depression, several clowns approached me. It didn't hurt me to learn about their lifestyles." I didn't ask him his sexual preference.

I thought, *Sex might be better with someone experienced. A place I've never touched with my hands gives me great pleasure.* I rubbed there in first grade on a playground pole until a good feeling came and went. Danny told me that was masturbation. He said the good feeling is "the goal of intercourse" called a climax. *Hmmm, why didn't I ever have a climax with Charles? Or...after marriage to Danny?*

Returning one night from the Oyster Bar, Danny walked me to a corner of the screened porch. During dinner, he'd acted adolescent by laughing, teasing the wait staff, and giving a large tip. He was fun and not his usual attack-dog self.

"How am I going to live my life without you?"

"Are you proposing marriage?" I coyly asked.

"Yes."

"Why should I marry you?" I answered slipping my hands behind me.

"Because I make beautiful babies and you will be the second Sarah Chapman," he said quickly, as if he had prepared lines.

On the first point, I acknowledged his daughters were attractive and smart. Danny's laissez faire parenting style worked because the younger girls were well behaved. If they fussed at all, he'd hand them money and say, "Now go get lost." This wasn't parenting to me, but he was in charge. Both girls were physically active. The first Sarah Detweiler Chapman, a Pennsylvania Mennonite, was Danny's grandmother. The key words he used were 'beautiful babies,' nothing else mattered.

Danny waited. A simple "Just fine," would have worked for his original question sending my life on a different path.

My thinking teetered, *I want Mama to soften to my circus career. Daddy will be so proud when he sees me on the Ed Sullivan Show. A producer will see my act and send me a TV contract. Danny is making my circus dream come true.*

Instead, I said something like, "I'm holding you to that."

We talked about where and when and he said, "I'll work on it."

Expecting resistance everywhere, no one confronted me. Not one person. Moreover, I didn't ask.

When the news of my planned marriage got to my parents, the only thing Mama said was, "I want my sewing machine back."

* * *

"Don't worry. Let's go buy one so you can keep sewing," Danny asserted. The new Singer cost $99.95 plus 3% sales tax. I wasn't sure if it belonged to him or me.

About that time I felt childish calling my mother Mama and I started using Mother. Growing up, Merritt and I were supposed to say, "Yes, Mother," or "Coming, Mother," when she called us instead of saying "What?" We didn't do it because her name was Mama and Mother was too nice. Mama didn't soften with her new name.

"You got hired to clown and do single trap on Gus Bell's Texas dates," Danny blurted out rushing into the great room. He added in a softer tone, "You're legal age there." I felt like an adult yet acted childish running away to marry instead of getting parental consent.

In 1964 they signed for twenty-year-old Merritt to marry. Lucy married at age twenty-one. The last to leave home, I wanted to be a good spouse and parent. Stepchildren gave me a head start. There were good reasons to have legal age at twenty-one. I was one of them but I squirmed my way under it.

Danny traveled with a 1963 self-contained, sixteen-foot Frolic trailer, and needed a reliable car to pull it. He secured a loan for a used station wagon. Together we packed the little trailer for our trip. Stephanie, my youngest stepdaughter, and Lacie went too. Danny thought nothing of taking kids out of school to travel.

Danny explained, "The toilet has a waste-water holding tank. Take four squares of toilet tissue, fold them in half and then in fourths. Put the used tissue in the paper bag next to the stool. The baby lotion is for me, I need to clean up sometimes. There's pressurized water for the sink and toilet. Shower inside the building where there's hot water. I don't use the water heater. You can brush your teeth at the kitchen sink. Are you brushing every time you eat?" His rules gyrated in my head but he knew best, I did some and not others.

* * *

Instructions completed, we went "on the road" for all of September and October. Danny told me before we left, "You can't have alcohol because you're a performer now."

"I won't, I don't want to fall off my trapeze." I didn't miss drinking.

Our first stop past the Florida panhandle was Mobile, Alabama. The *Mobile Press* featured me, saying, "Miss Wheeler is three in one: a clown, college student, and future bride."

Danny quoted, "It's the best job in the world and the second oldest profession. Where else can you work twenty minutes a day?" I believed him.

My clown job in Mobile was a walk around with the snake-in-a-basket gag and the back half of producing clown, Chester Sherman's antebellum bustle. I strained running on the track bent into the skirted half of a heavy, hot, antebellum costume attached to Chester's rear end. His partner, Joe Vani Sherman was too old for that number. Gasping for fresh air when I came out from under the prop, Joe asserted, "Kid, you're doing great."

"Thanks. Anything…to keep…the show going," I choked out between breaths.

I passed the time driving westward sewing our wedding quilt made from cotton and wool fabric scraps. Seeing me cutting out small squares, Danny nicely asked, "What is the quilt backing?"

"Royal blue corduroy with an embroidery of me swinging on my balancing bar. You're holding the web and looking up at me."

I measured, cut, and thought, picturing myself in desperation. *What else can I do besides get married? I don't live at home nor have a regular job. I don't have money for college. I'm away with a divorced man. If I don't return married, people will gossip.* It was all or nothing.

* * *

Our forty-dollar wedding included license, blood tests, my gold ring, corsage, and flowers for the trailer.

When the third show ended Saturday, I relished the thought of joining as man and wife. "Danny, can Stephanie sleep next door with Carla Wallenda?"

"No, we're leaving after the show to catch the Cristiani Circus playing outside New Orleans."

Up-and-down and down-and-up bounced the car and trailer on every hill across Texas. My wedding night ended in fiasco. To worsen matters, the next day at a Laundromat our white clothes turned pink. I flubbed Laundry 101: separating lights from darks. Seeing Danny in pink shorts taught me to switch his underwear to dark colors.

Looking back, I subtly tried to change Danny. "Please let the hair on your chest grow out." "Wear a loose swimsuit at the beach." "Let me do all the laundry." Marriage was a serious business of domestic responsibility including managing the household with the available funds. Common sense told me to iron Danny's shirts and not send them out.

I shopped, cleaned the house, washed clothes, and cooked. Danny did some shopping and cooking, got the vehicles serviced, and did all the driving on the road. "When there's more money, we'll get a better car," he announced. I couldn't see into the future and blindly accepted his debts in life as mine.

Danny set the tone from the beginning of our marriage with rules, lots of them:

"I want you to pay the bills. Here's the checkbook."

"I want you to be quiet at home. Don't slam cupboards or doors."

"If a drawer doesn't close, ask for help."

"Keep the kitchen counters cleaned off."

"Don't leave any dishes in the sink—I don't want it looking like your mother's."

He wanted a clean organized house. In fact, he offered, "When you cook, I'll wash the dishes my way." What a deal!

He also dictated my toiletries, "It isn't necessary to wear make-up, except when you're working. You're naturally pretty."

I appreciated hearing his complement. "What make-up do you want me to wear?"

"Simple street make-up will do fine, no eye shadow or liner," he answered with authority.

"Leave your hair long."

"Your clothing should become a married woman."

"Wear tailored suits with knee length skirts and high heeled shoes to help your posture and show off your legs."

"Positively no jeans! They are for workers."

I didn't wear denim, and jeans weren't a problem, but in the next fifteen years, I missed mainstream American life. Danny isolated me from current events, namely the Vietnam War and national politics, not to mention popular music.

"Don't listen to that stuff!" he guffawed. "Listen to opera. It's on every Saturday. I'll get you good music." He bought vocal and instrumental albums. We also collected children's and holiday music. When we became affluent, Danny bought expensive stereos and cassette equipment.

Not having pop music annoyed me. He didn't ask me if I wanted to expand my musical library, enrich my knowledge of classical music, or listen to something he enjoyed and then leave it up to me to decide how I used my first amendment right. He talked to me as if I was unintelligent.

I didn't know marriage came with so many rules. I entered into an unbreakable contract practically saying, "Heap as much displeasure as you want on me." While Danny wasn't getting in my pants by his choice, he controlled that and every other part of my body and mind. My soul was still my own.

CHAPTER EIGHT
RULES

Our next engagement was a Miami Shrine circus. "Did you bring my blue suit for seeing Al Dobritch?" Danny asked, driving south on US 41.

"Yes, I did," I answered, then forgot about our circus agent appointment in Miami. Getting dressed several days later, Danny's instructions were precise; light street make-up, straight skirt, and high heels. I added a white tailored shirt. *Remember to say only the things Danny told me*, echoed in my head as I walked out of the elevator towards the door of the national talent agent.

Al waved a hand at Danny saying, "Have a seat."

"Al, this is Sarah," Danny introduced me to his Bulgarian friend.

"How do you do?" I smiled into his face, as programmed. While I gracefully sat, I noticed Mr. Dobritch briskly flipping pages in our photo album.

"Have you got any glossies to leave? I might have a date or two," the agent routinely said, with his head still down.

"Yes, you may keep these," replied Danny removing our original 8x10-inch prints from the album putting them on Al's plain metal desk.

I left Dobritch's office not knowing any more than when I'd arrived. Entertainment is a buyer's market with fees set by management and a hefty commission going to the agent. When I mentioned this to Danny, he quipped, "If we wanted to get rich, we should work in concessions or rides on a carnival and not perform in a circus arena." He had a point.

* * *

"Danny, when you introduced me today you called me Sarah."
"I did?"
"Yes and on the shows you do that. One of the Italian boys asked me out on a date. I told him I was your wife, not your daughter."
"Oh. That's why he asked me about you. Don't worry about it. Sarah is fine." Ouch, went my mind. *Why try so hard to get me to say the right thing when he doesn't?* At home or out in public Danny never referred to me as his wife, Sarah, or any other name. It was as if I didn't exist.

* * *

I think most people thought of me as charming, because I voiced no opinion on anything. I was an unknown with little experience and Danny nurtured me into a first class act, by keeping me quiet on and off stage. My publicity interviews always put the shows in a positive light. Danny told me I would lose my job, if I did otherwise.

* * *

The date ended, rigging torn down, trailers packed up, and everyone headed to their next engagement. We returned to Sarasota where I cared for aging Mitzy at the bayou.

I went to Worrington Street and presented Daddy a pair of pheasants we transported back from San Angelo. He looked at me and then at the birds. Eventually I said, "Daddy, you always wanted to hatch pheasants." The next time I went to what was left of Oakairs, the pheasant cage door was open. "What happened to the birds?" I asked Daddy.

"Oh, they got out and flew away." His hand hovered towards the Trail.

Expecting Daddy to accept my marriage was impossible, he wouldn't discuss it. His shadowy brown eyes revealed his frustration.

* * *

Circus people had other concerns, mainly finding work and they didn't care who Danny Chapman married. One fall night after supper, Danny said, "Get dressed. There's an AGVA meeting for performers at the Sarasota Terrace."

"What's AGVA?"

"American Guild of Variety Artists. Now get dressed."

Sitting in the top floor of the historic hotel with a room full of circus performers gave me chills. The energy expressed by members of famous circus families overrode their country of origin. The Zacchinis, Cristianis, and others proudly pledged to the US flag as naturalized American citizens. Ringling imported European performers as early as 1929. When American men were away fighting WWII, the Mills Circus imported notable British and French performing families to the US.

In 1965 both naturalized and American-born performers looked warily at the influx of Cuban, Central, and South American acts. The American circus made the transition from tents to buildings. Could it withstand the new wave of performers from Latin America and Eastern Europe? Could it accept lower pay, increased agent percentages, longer seasons, and more shows per week?

When the time came for closing comments, I stood and bravely said, "I'm not sure where to fit into this group. I want to make the circus a better place for the next generation."

At the end of the meeting, the steward passed out AGVA application forms for membership in a branch of the AFL-CIO affiliated Teamsters Union. Annual dues were thirty-five dollars. I signed with two new names: Sarah Kate Chapman alongside Sarah Katé (ka tay), my stage name.

"It's official Danny. I'm a real performer," Sarah Katé tastefully recited as we motored down the Trail to Phillippi Bayou.

Skipping my jubilation, Danny responded, "I forgot to tell you. I'm working Frieda Wriswell's Funny Ford dates. I'm taking the bus to Wichita and will be gone a week. You'll be fine."

* * *

Time passed quickly during his absence. On his return, my husband handed me a package. "Here's your sussie." I unwrapped a colorful Italian glass clown doing splits with a big smile on its face. I looked at Danny's matching grin, "It reminds me of you in your clown make-up."

I wasn't smiling when I cleaned out Danny's circus trunk and found his US passport and military identification card. Comparing them I thought, *The birth dates are different, I wonder why? The passport says June 5, 1918, the date he told me. His Army card says June 5, 1913. That's five years difference.*

I left the documents on the kitchen counter. When the right moment came, I pushed them in front of him asking, "Why are these birth dates different? Which one is true?"

Caught off guard, he jabbed at my face with steely eyes. Then his hardened complexion blushed when he revealed, "Oh, that little thing. I did that to protect my mother. She had me at an early age. You know how women don't tell their age." His ploy failed and he looked ugly.

"You lied to me! You're a liar! You're five years older than you said! You're older than my mother!" I screeched at him bug-eyed.

Giving me no response, nothing to reinforce our union, I ran to the bedroom, stopping once to blurt out, "You're not my confidant anymore!" I never trusted Danny after that. I was married one month.

Turning my rage inward, I brewed, *I want to pack up and leave. To where? I have no job, no home, and no work skills. I'm not cut out to be a secretary, stewardess, nurse, or phone operator.*

I didn't leave. I pouted. I felt bleak and irrational. *I want a baby. He won't throw me out with a baby.*

When I stopped crying and returned slowly to the kitchen, Danny promptly enforced his authority, "It's your duty as my wife to support and agree with me because I'm right. Don't question my motives and never embarrass me in public."

I accepted defeat. None of my familiar thoughts, words, or behaviors emerged. What remained was that I married a man over fifty, something I wouldn't have done in any circumstance. The Sarah I knew dissolved, gobbled by a cold hard ghost possessing my shell. Returning to calm, I solemnly resolved, *I'm a circus mannequin, not an ordinary housewife mannequin. Things could be worse.*

* * *

About the same time, the State of Florida settled the condemnation suit for Danny's land removed for the Phillippi Creek cut-through built to prevent inland flooding. Thrilled, I handed the check to Danny saying, "Look! Here's a check for $16,000."

Studying it and coolly passing it back, he said, "Good, make a check out to Joan for $15,000. It's the balance of my alimony."

I wrote that check, and another for the attorney, and one for court fees, totaling $950, leaving us fifty dollars. I felt humiliated. Joan got a good settlement for their fifteen-year marriage. I got Danny's debts. She and I weren't friends. We had nothing in common…or did we? We were both nineteen when he married us. She was a quiet person. Me too. Angry and hurt, I told myself, *Don't complain, no one pushed me to marry him.*

* * *

One weekend Deborah and Stephanie quietly played in their room. Deborah burst into tears and ran to Danny sobbing, "Daddy, Stephanie took my doll and won't give it back."

"Why are you crying?" Danny calmly asked his middle daughter.

"Because she hurt my feelings," she bawled loudly.

Losing his calm, he scowled at her tear-stained face gruffly saying, You shouldn't have feelings. Now go to your room. Awash in tears, she heard him shout, "People shouldn't have feelings!" I'm sure my face reflected horror at Danny's tormenting. My already repressed feelings sank as low as they could go. I felt stuck like a bird with wings in a crude oil slick. I knew of no one who would rescue, clean, and release me to clear water.

So I chanted, *People shouldn't have feelings. Get rid of my feelings. Feelings are wrong*, until memorized. Trapped in a marital cell, I felt the intense moment my usual Technicolor outlook changed to half tones. The worst freedom I lost was self-expression.

* * *

With my torn ego, I willingly left the bayou and drove with Danny to New Orleans, where he clowned at an excellent Shrine circus.

"I suppose you want to go to the French Quarter," Danny said at intermission of the opening show. Later Danny and I promenaded arm in arm to nearby Basin Street. Syrupy blues, the kind that slows me down, cascaded through wrought-iron-balcony railings romancing my dreaminess. Mutually in the mood for sex, we leisurely strolled back under hazy lampposts to the nearby hotel.

After he climaxed he pulled up his slacks, sat on the bed with his back to me, and took a couple of drags on a cigarette. He fondled a water glass saying, "If a married man puts a match stick in a jar for every time he has sex in the first year and takes one out for future sex, it will take the rest of his life to empty the jar." I pondered, *Is that the way it will be with us?*

Deep sleep overtook me until my shoulder wobbled back and forth. "Get up, you can't sleep. You're excess baggage and circuses don't carry dead weight."

"I'm not working, let me sleep," I mumbled hiding my head under a pillow. He jerked the blanket and sheet out of my reach. I sat up trying to guess what would happen next. I hugged the pillow to my chest, pulled my legs underneath me, and inched backwards to the headboard.

"What do you want me to do?" I asked as he paced the room.

"You have to practice. I'll ask in the building for a place to hang the single trap." His fists pumped, the air exploded around him, "People, all people, have to work and contribute a salary to the institution of family. There are no exceptions. I choose to work in the circus which means—so do you."

Whipped into his logic, I vowed, *I'll add to what Danny earns.* If he'd struck me, I would have gone to my parents because I knew that was wrong. All Danny's blows were mental. They took me down inch by inch.

***

Returning to our semi-tropical home, we decorated the house for Christmas. Danny strung colored lights from the rooftop television antennae mirroring reds, blues, and yellows in the still bayou. I took the girls on a cedar tree hunt to an undeveloped lot Daddy once owned on Siesta Key. On the way home I asked, "Where are decorations for the tree?"

"In with the nativity set."

"What's that?"

"It's a small stable and plaster figures of Jesus, Mary, Joseph, a shepherd, and animals. We put it on a table."

Unmentioned in Danny's rules, I attended Christmas Eve midnight service at St. Boniface Church. The next morning he baked a turkey for the combined Chapman/Wheeler families. My family came, except Daddy, who was ill from bladder infections.

I wanted to impress everyone that first Christmas. I spent too much money, and held future work accountable for charges to Danny's Maas Brothers credit card. I turned twenty the night of December 31, 1965. A hairdresser expertly styled my thick hair. While eating birthday cake at home, Danny presented me with a chromed single trapeze bar. Corresponding to my big bar, it had chic weighted bullets.

PART TWO

CHAPTER NINE
FIRST OF MAY

Early in 1966, Danny told me, "Wilson Storey, an agent for Clyde Beatty, Sells & Grey, and King Bros. Circuses, offered us the King Bros. season. It's under canvas, goes out later, and works smaller towns than the bigger shows. King Bros. will be your proving ground. You're an ingénue."

On the way to sign contracts at Mr. Storey's home, Danny said, "I'm clowning with another fellow and you can break in your trapeze. I think you'll like being on a little show. Before we go out on King Bros. we're doing Shrine dates in Detroit and Cleveland." A mud show wasn't what I had in mind to start my career and going to big cities was unfathomable.

As we cruised north in I-75, the Midwest winter freeze shocked me and Deborah, who'd skipped school to join us on this trip. Danny said, "You'll be working King show elephants. Rex Williams, a famous trainer, has the elephants on the Beatty show and he's teaching you how to work bulls in Detroit. I'll be in Clown Alley."

"What are bulls? Aren't you going to do any of your numbers?" I asked innocently.

"All elephants are called bulls," he explained. Then his voice fell flat, "I'm starting over as a clown. Other producing clowns in the business have done these dates for years. And you're just a First of May (beginner in the circus). We'll make just enough for expenses."

After the elephant lesson from Rex, I discovered something wonderful—elephants. Delighted to ride, I smiled to the audience after each trick. The *Detroit Free Press* printed a photo of me riding atop an elephant.

"Look, Danny." I exclaimed handing him the paper.

"Your exuberance shows in the ring. Make sure if the press ask you any questions to say general statements about the show and plug the time and location." It was easy giving generic show information and saving my personal opinions.

Halfway through the date, Danny surprised me, "I talked to Karl Wallenda's right hand man. He said the Shriners are letting you do balance trap in the aerial display. There's no money because you don't have a contract. The riggers are putting up your bar now."

I hadn't hoped for this break for my act. I also wondered why Danny didn't ask if I wanted to perform. Why should he? He didn't consult me for anything. I practiced the week before in Detroit but felt nervous and ill prepared. Even Danny coaching me after it was rigged didn't help. I looked like a girl right out of college doing a part-time stint that noisy Saturday morning matinee. To bolster myself I wore my best costume—the red one.

I stood on my bar after the short climb up on the web. It was level with the first-tier seating rail and near enough to talk with the audience. They were constantly moving and it was hard to find a focus point. Noisy barkers sold pink cotton candy, plastic blowup toys, and chameleons. From the live band, trumpets blared under drummer Boomboom Browning's direction. Children and adults gazed past me to see other acts in the display. It was a test of my concentration and power of focus, not a time for shaky legs. I only had time for the twist, handkerchief, and a side swing. I felt accomplished when a few faces of attentive circus goers descended with me on my web to the arena floor. When I returned to the dressing room, my status moved up a notch from elephant girl to aerialist. Doing my balance bar gave me overall strength that I would soon need.

Before we left Cleveland, a telegram arrived from Mother saying Daddy had bladder cancer and was at a hospital in Memphis, Tennessee. I raised my head after reading the news. Danny urged, "You can fly there on the way home. It will do you good to see your dad."

I spent two days with my parents and finally had a conversation with Daddy. As we talked I thought, *Daddy is my friend. He's so brave.*

From Memphis, I flew home to Sarasota, vomiting in a bag. Not feeling well for another month I went to a doctor for what I thought was a chronic cold. It didn't take him long to say, "Congratulations! You're three-months pregnant." Shocked, happy, and sad, the only one I wanted to share the news with was Daddy, and he was far away and dying. Telling Danny wasn't hard. He smiled and said, "I hope it's a girl." I never did tell my parents I was pregnant. I thought I would tell them when the baby came.

As we prepared for King Bros. Circus, Danny tightened the already snug money belt. He dictated which bills to pay and said, "I'll be giving you the cash. Send most of it home in a money order. Give me just $5.00 a week. Oh, can you cut men's hair? All shows need a barber and you can earn some money."

"The only hair I've cut besides yours was Daddy's and Merritt's. I don't have any clippers," I responded, and let it pass.

"We're trading in the station wagon for a new pickup truck. I'll look around for a used camper top." I gingerly signed joint loan papers, adding $2,000 plus interest to our already stressed economy.

"Remember you're packing the trailer for the next eight months. We need warm clothes for spring in Tennessee where the show starts," Danny barked at me as I toted pile after pile of belongings into the trailer. I needed help and knew not to ask him to carry anything.

"What about the house? Your mother? The girls?" I anxiously asked.

"We're leaving it empty for now. Patrnella's going to Burzinsky's Nursing Home in Fruitville. Deborah and Stephanie will live with their mom in Las Lomas and walk to school."

"Olga will be out of a job," I protested, carrying blankets to the trailer. "She cried the last time you took her home." Danny couldn't give a hoot what happened to Olga.

* * *

With no sentimental baggage, he lived in the present. That meant making the most of the King Show contract with a pregnant wife and new clown partner he hadn't met. A second family at his age took nerve. He chuckled to the other performers on the show. "Sarah didn't marry me for my money or good looks." I felt blank when it came to express anything about Danny.

Our weekly pay for fourteen shows a week with an occasional Sunday off was $125, free gas for the truck, and free cookhouse food. We ate lunch and supper there, prepared by the young lively cook, Tweety Bird. On frosty mornings, I went in after breakfast and poured extra evaporated milk into hot tea at the cookhouse tables. "Honey, I can do more than cook, you know," Tweety said, throwing dishwater out the door.

That season I was Miss Sarah Katé, featured aerialist in center ring. "Treat it like a practice. And watch out for the guy wires," Danny said helping me up to my bar twice a day. So I practiced, styled, smiled, and took a bow at the conclusion. When I couldn't pick up my handkerchief because my belly got in the way, I stopped my act and hid the swelling under long ugly skirts.

I sat on the necks of two old and lumbering pachyderms, Hattie and Mary, during their act. In another turn, I put Mary on a tub in center ring and lightly touched a pointed bull hook to each front foot. She reluctantly raised them to "dance" in time with a "Go-Go" recording. King Bros. was one of the first shows replacing a live band with vinyl records.

My big top acts weren't nearly as special to me as assisting Pietro Canestrelli in the sideshow where illusion prevailed. I sat in a customized wooden chair and placed an ordinary light bulb in my palm. It magically lit from the energy in my body. I stood in front of a wooden door and Pietro threw knives outlining my frame. Lying on my side in a custom coffin, Pietro wedged long swords past nooks and crannies. For a small fee, circus goers climbed stairs to see my tangled body. Most recognized the sword box as a sham and their faces reflected how the show gypped them out of a quarter. I didn't mind. Risk taking was part of a trip to the circus.

The show featured Danny's smooth solo pantomime. He prided himself not using his voice in the ring.

Everywhere else he was proliferate. Mornings in the Frolic trailer started with, "People don't need more than five or six hours sleep. Why do you sleep twelve? I never sleep more than four. Get up!"

Pulling myself out of a deep slumber, I didn't recognize my dewy surroundings. "Why is there a spoon wedged in the tea kettle?"

"Leave it there. Steam takes the chill out of the air."

Day after day he put a bowl of Cheerios with milk on the blankets. With half-opened eyes I raised up spilling the bowl's contents. Cleaning up the mess made me angry because I wanted to keep sleeping. He told me, "I want you to sleep next to the wall. I get muscle pain and cramps from my paralyzed leg. Oh, crack the window open next to you."

"The furnace doesn't work and cold air comes in," I said wrapping flannel clad arms around my chest.

"Then wear socks to bed. I learned to do that in the Army. If your feet and head are warm, you don't get cold." Danny had answers for everything.

I put an extra blanket on my side of the bed. Sometime in the night, Danny threw his blanket on top of mine making me sweat and wake up. I slid as an agitated bug over his bones to urinate in the adjacent toilet. Later that season, when his night cramps went away, I still crawled over his sleeping body. The honeymoon was over.

I needed $125, our portion after insurance, to pay Dr. Alfons Bacon when the baby came. I went into a hair-cutting partnership with the King Bros. waterman when he bought the electric hair clippers. At one dollar per cut, I gave him fifty cents on his investment. I sewed buttons, did mending, and gave free first aid bandages and aspirin to the working men.

When I thought about it, I called to see how Daddy was and to ask about Mitzy. I left her there when we went on King Bros. He assured me they were both okay.

Every Sunday Danny called his girls in Sarasota. He learned Joan's second marriage ended and she was moving. Asking and telling me at the same time, Danny said, "Joan's homeless and doesn't have a job. I want her and the kids to stay in our house."

That's what she did. I thought it improper, but couldn't change the situation by complaining, and I believed Danny when he said, "It's just temporary, until she finds another place."

Sarasota schools ended the first week of June. Michele and Deborah flew to join us at the King Show at Columbus, Ohio. Little Stephanie stayed behind in Sarasota.

We had them picked up and they arrived on the lot during showtime. I was in the big top at the sound wagon spinning records on three turntables. Danny stopped at the wagon door saying, "They're here."

We ate a between-show-meal and I showed Deborah and Michele to the truck camper to unpack their bags. When it came time for bed, we closed the camper door. Fifteen-year-old Michele left the lot the same day she arrived. Dealing with a willful, troubled teen wasn't in my marital job description. Listening to my husband's wailing was.

Frantic with fear, he left the lot each night to find a pay phone and call Joan in Sarasota. On the fourth night, he decided to call the Ohio Highway Patrol and report a missing person. Then he phoned Joan with me listening by his ear.

"Is Michele there yet?"

"Yes," Joan said wearily, "I'll put her on."

"Hi, Dad. Now don't get excited. I was just escorting Deborah to the show. You didn't expect me to stay, did you?"

"That's a dirty trick," he shouted. "I reported you missing."

"I was fine. I left the show when it got dark and hitched a ride home."

Michele's foolish behavior caused anguished grief making Danny's usual expletives explode beyond reason. He felt someone was at fault for her delinquency and it wasn't him. I was the target for his verbal tongue-lashing. It penetrated enough for me to remember the situation.

Back at the lot Danny explained to Deborah, "You can relax. Your sister is safely home. Think you want to work concessions?"

Deborah stayed for the rest of the King Bros. season. She performed single trapeze with strength and grace, blithely went in the paint gag as a little person, and sold circus programs. A circus fan gave her one dozen red roses on her ninth birthday. What a trouper.

I cared deeply for the younger girls, especially Deborah because she was easy to get along with and we were comfortable together. I was just a child myself with no parenting skills, except what lingered from my childhood and I was pretty sure that wouldn't work too well. Step parenting was far harder than the other roles I was currently learning in life.

On the King Show I got to know my neighbors, learned the lot with and without mud, and watched the big top center poles creep from prone on the ground to tall ship grandeur. Consistency and efficiency are circus keys. At night, the canvas dropped with a whoosh and the electrician killed the noisy light plant. Hattie and Mary gently pulled their stout necks up yanking sidewall stakes from the earth. Chain jiggled free from wood or metal making rustly clinking and the handler moved on to the next stake.

The route took us to northern Minnesota where Mother's siblings and cousins too numerous to count came to the show. They said nothing about Danny, hugged gregarious Deborah, and wished me well with my pregnancy.

On our Sunday's off, Danny exchanged his bayou gin and tonic for a drink from a bottle of cheap whiskey stored in the bottom of the trailer clothes closet. Sometimes he shared his bottle with other performers. When I suggested a picnic on a warm, sunny afternoon, he refused to sit on a blanket on the ground, and found a picnic table instead. "This isn't a picnic to me," I said disenchanted and tired of giving in.

He and Deborah toyed with the new twelve-inch black-and-white television adjusting the antennae several times a day for weather and news broadcasts. He safely drove our truck-and-trailer from town-to-town and set us up with lights and water, if available.

* * *

Danny surprised me when we went to St. Louis, Missouri. "The baby is coming in four weeks. I want you to fly back to Sarasota and stay with your parents."

"Why? Can't I stay on the show?"

"You need your mother."

I flew to Sarasota on September 1. "Where's Mitzy?" I asked pulling into the driveway.

"Talk to your father," Mother casually said looking at her nails.

"Where is Mitzy?" I demanded from Daddy.

"Mummy had her put to sleep."

"Where's she buried?"

"Mummy told the vet to bury her at their office."

"Daddy—why wasn't I told?"

"Mummy didn't want you to get upset."

"She was old Daddy. I don't blame you." My anger turned to grief. Mother was Daddy's caregiver and she did it well. Still, it seemed sometimes, I was the only clear thinking person in my family. What I thought then was that my mother was cruel and untrustworthy.

Our baby came six weeks later in October. Assisted by Dr. Bacon, I birthed naturally a plump, pink, baby girl. Lying in my hospital bed, just forty-five-hours after I arrived, I worried about the bill, rang for the nurse, and told her, "I'm leaving."

I went from the hospital directly to Dr. Bacon's office where I handed the receptionist my hair cutting money ($85). "I'll pay the rest as soon as I can," I promised.

Against my wishes, Mother invited friends over to see and

handle my newborn. Both Daddy's weakening health and I needed peace and quiet. With an unknown inner faith, I silently spoke, *God is going to take care of Daddy*. The mother in me took charge and told me to forsake my old house in its new location and ask Danny to come get us. We remained on the circus for the rest of that season. I learned that the bayou, not Oakairs, was my home now, and I tolerated Danny's rules somewhat better. He was mistaken about me needing my mother.

* * *

Ivy Anastasia Chapman's baptism took place on a Sunday in December, at St. Boniface Church on Siesta Key. The new pastor told me, "Ivy is my first baptism."

"That's wonderful. I'll make sure the photographer sends you photos."

Deborah, Stephanie, and our neighbor, Emerich Moroski, Ivy's godfather, were there. Ivy's godmother was absent.

My parents missed the baptism too. Daddy was in Bay Pines Veterans Hospital. After the baptism I loaded Ivy and Lacie into the pickup and drove to Bay Pines.

"Look, baby Ivy, Uncle Merritt's here." I met Merritt at Daddy's bedside and he gave me his chair. Daddy rallied, reaching out his ashen hand to meet the tiny one of his granddaughter. Merritt and I didn't say much to Daddy. Our hearts were too heavy.

It was hard returning to Montclair Drive. "Please take the calls, Danny. I don't want Mother telling me Daddy died."

"I understand," he obliged, and left me alone in the dimly lit bedroom.

The inevitable call came two mornings later. The new pastor administered two sacraments for us in less than a week.

Accepting Daddy's death was impossible. Nothing would bring him back to erase the feeling of complete desertion. The wrong parent died.

CHAPTER TEN
OBEDIENCE

My loss overwhelmed me. Daddy was one of a kind and I was special to him. I knew that since I was ten when I rescued a carbon copy of a letter he typed to a family friend. Daddy wrote:

Sarah Kate. Here is the practical one of the family, the worker. The one who makes it possible for everything else to be done. She collects butterflies, shells, feathers, and plays the piano. That's Sarah Kate.

* * *

With closed eyes, I pictured a time when Daddy reprimanded Merritt and me for behaving like monkeys dangerously climbing up and bouncing mature stalks of bamboo right to the breaking point. Without his usual baseball cap, sunbeams had exposed thinned, salt-and-peppery hair. A wrinkled short-sleeved cotton shirt held his reading glasses in one pocket and a pencil and a flap from a cigarette carton stuffed in the other. His faded rayon trousers, leather belt and worn canvas shoes, all some shade of brown, completed his apparel. I accepted his saggy look, drooping shoulders, swayed back, and small protruding belly. Sixty-year-old weathered skin covered his hands and face and chestnut-brown eyes peeked out from short, straight black lashes. Tiny white whiskers grew through a vapor of his morning Old Spice aftershave. That was my dad, and I was his little monkey.

Reality brought me back to my darkened bedroom on the bayou. I brooded while Ivy slept. *The Ed Sullivan Show doesn't matter anymore. Daddy won't see it. Twenty is too young to lose him. Why did Mother and Lucy squabble? I know, so I could make decisions for the funeral. Charles had nerve saying hello to me at Daddy's grave. Oh, if only the cemetery bells would stop ringing. Please let this day end.*

"Whaaa, whaaa," broke through, into my dark cocoon of despair. *Crying, I hear crying; my baby is crying.*

"Mama's coming baby, Ivy," I whispered, picking her up from Stephanie's hand-me-down crib. I slipped through full-length curtains to sit and nurse on the screened corridor in my antique Boston rocker. The carillon bells, several hundred paces away, continued ringing for Daddy, and for me.

Annie Edelston, wife of Danny's longtime friend, Willie Edelston, watched Ivy while I went to the funeral. Distracted again, I thought, *Dear Annie, showing me how to fold cloth diapers, fasten safety pins, and pull up plastic pants. She's had lots of practice with her four children. What do I know about life?*

Annie and Willie were the youngest members of the athletic Sommerton Gang, a group from Philadelphia. The Edelstons joined the circus as aerialists and later moved to Sarasota to live in Monticello Subdivision.

The first thing anyone noticed about diminutive Willie was two muscular arms poking out from cuffed short sleeves of his blue mailman shirt. Annie was the keenest listener I ever met and probably stashed scores of secrets from her numerous friendships. Always patient and understanding, this couple practiced what some preached: faith, hope, and love in each other, their friends, and the community.

Grandmother Wheeler busied herself with her three preschool grandsons, one each from Merritt, Lucy, and my foster brother, Roy Soul. She treated little children well and the boys amused Daddy. Ivy was my responsibility and I couldn't see the need to leave her with Mother or anyone. I was enamored with my baby and considered her a precious gift.

Despite the hardships I endured as a child, I thought I turned out okay and headed in the right direction. Unlike my siblings I didn't take loans from my parents, I went to a bank. I kept my house clean and worked for a living. Was I not worthy of approval for my accomplishments? Mother saw some good in me part of the time, but no "well done" type of comment uttered from her lips. For the time being, I focused on my newborn, leaving the rest of my family to themselves.

* * *

Danny invited John Seaton, a towner from Owensboro, Kentucky, to join us on the 1967 Carson & Barnes Circus season. A few years older than me, he had an average build and light complexion. If Danny could do aerial work, we wouldn't have hired anyone.

John had one finger shorter than normal due to a game of chance on King Bros. where he was a working man. He took a dare to insert his index finger between sledgehammer strikes on the top of a metal stake and the game ended when he lost. The hospital couldn't fix his smashed finger other than fold skin over the wound and prevent infection.

I questioned Danny, "Why did you choose John?"

"That's easy. He didn't leave the show when he got hurt. You need a partner for the ladder and I need him for the boxing and clown gags."

John and Danny did many chores in the three months before leaving in March for Hugo, Oklahoma. Danny's revolving ladder rigging that he fell from in 1959, was sanded, painted, and put up in the yard. John and I practiced a two-person act with the single trap and comedy. Danny designed and manufactured the ladder rigging and performed this first class act with a variety of partners, including Davey Seidel, for ten years on East Coast fairs and throughout Europe. "I called us The Aerial Chapman's," he told me. "After the accident, other people took the act out and it was never the same."

"Why did you fall?"

"Something slipped from the girders, knocked me off, and broke Davey's leg. Sandy, our female partner at the time, wasn't hurt." Danny talked vaguely about his accident and questioning him further was futile.

Danny made the metal ladder twelve-feet-long, weighted at one end, and supported by a central axle and two lighter-weight metal-tubing ladder uprights.

I thought about the show. I contracted for the free act, my featured act, the swinging anchor number, the elephant act, and finale. "Danny, how is my balance trap supposed to improve when production wears me out?"

After a moment he formulated, "We don't do cherry pie."

"What's cherry pie?" I raised my eyebrows.

"You know, setting up seats, taking tickets, ushering, tearing down the tent, general usefulness."

"I know now. We get less money because we work less. That makes sense." Satisfied, I forgot my original question. His diversions worked every time. Before we went on the road, I had plenty to do making new wardrobe, practicing two aerial acts, cooking, and minding the baby.

Colicky Ivy spent two hours every afternoon wailing loudly with me close by. I checked on her in her crib but couldn't help her despite gently rubbing her tummy or cheerfully singing, "Little baby Ivy, I love you. Yes! I do. I...love...you." *Poor baby, she'll never know her grandfather.* That thought saddened me and I said, "Come little one, let's sit and rock in the sunshine." *Daddy knows we're here.*

* * *

Danny found us on the porch, "I want your trap routine polished. Gena and Lolita are helping you."

"Thank you." I said and thought, *Hmm...wonder what Gena will say.*

Two of the finest women performers were my nearest neighbors. Appearing first, Gena Moroski watched my practice and gave me encouragement and a demonstration. "Position your arms and hands like classical ballet. Keep your legs straight, point your toes. Here, watch this." She flexed thigh and calf muscles taunt, then arched one foot to a perfect point.

The Polish-born woman teaching me, a former prima ballerina with the Ballet Russe, was married to well-known horse trainer, Charlie Moroski. Admiring Gena's thick accent, I thought of Madame Skylarsky, the ballet instructor at Sullins College. I copied Gena's positions. "This way?" I asked.

Nodding her head, Gena gracefully returned to her yard to groom shrubbery.

My other neighbor, a petite Spaniard named Lolita Perez, did a tight wire act. She often watched me practice from her screened porch. "Lolita, Danny says you'll help me with wardrobe. I'll come by when I'm done."

"That will be fine, lovey. I'll be in the kitchen." Later, watching the preparation of paella for their evening meal, I listened to Lolita tell me about fabrics and wardrobe styles.

"You can have a theme costume. Mine was a matador outfit and I didn't take off my hat or cape, because I worked on a wire. Do you want a taste?" she asked handing me a bowl and a fork.

"Yes, please. I know it's delicious by the way it smells. I never saw your act."

"That's all in the past. I make draperies now and take care of my husband, Frankie," she purred. I ambled away, wondering what to cook for dinner and not fantasizing of a future when I got out of the business.

* * *

Sleeping late for me ended with Ivy's birth. My body also dramatically changed, shrinking to a mere 115 pounds on my 5'5" frame.

"Great! You'll live longer. Be glad!" Dr. Bacon declared at my six-week checkup. I couldn't wait to tell Danny when I got home.

"Where's the old figure?" he pried.

"Gone, and it's not coming back." I pouted, not expecting his rude comment.

*　*　*

Before we left on the road, I asked a few high school friends to a potluck picnic under the live oaks. They arrived with their spouses, children, or friends to renew old times and discuss future Sarasota jobs or college graduation. "Do you enjoy traveling?" someone asked.

"Yes, I've never been homesick for Sarasota. Although, about August, I miss the warm Gulf beaches and saltwater seafood."

*　*　*

The next day, Danny, still concerned about my act had more advice. "I'm taking you to Max Weldy. He makes wardrobe for the Ringling show and has a true flair for design and color. When can you be ready?"

"As soon as I put on a dress and heels." On the way downtown to Max's wardrobe shop, I thought, *It will be nice getting professionally fit for a new costume—one that I'm not making.* The prim, well-groomed Frenchman entered his foyer wearing a long-sleeve oxford cloth shirt, tie, and light-colored wool cardigan. Wrinkle-free tailored slacks complemented polished leather loafers.

"Please, stand up," Max asked politely then walked around me with fingers tucked in armpits and thumbs lightly tapping pectorals. "Pink, Madame. I believe pink is your color." I smiled and glanced down into Max's warm, friendly face. "I'll have some things brought out to you," he told me, then exited the door where he'd entered.

I quietly asked Danny, "How much does he charge?"

"Plenty."

"Then I guess used costumes are what I can afford," I whispered as the assistant entered, her arms clutching a huge wardrobe bundle. I tried on many leotards, capes, and rhinestone headpieces. The final purchase included three leotards made of stretch fabric decorated with rhinestones and sequins. I picked matching green and red feathered capes and headpieces making two complete outfits. I asked Danny, "May I also have two rhinestone tiaras?" He nodded. Sadly, none of the pink costumes fit.

I now had decent act wardrobe for $250, even if it wasn't new and didn't quite fit. Going home I thought, *We spent one week's* salary on my wardrobe. I hope the show can store the feathered capes and headpieces.

* * *

Before leaving Sarasota, Danny told me, "Davey Seidel's here. Show him exactly where you want the cabinet for baby clothes and costumes in the trailer. I'm on the phone with the new renters. They want to know when they can move in."

"When we're set up in the trailer," I called out, folding clothes and feeling smug about my transient lifestyle.

Packing the trailer for the third time included making room for three adults, one baby, my dog, and later on, a place for stepdaughters. Between loads of linens to the trailer, Danny told me, "Put anything of value left in the house into the walk-in closet. The renters, a retired couple, will leave it alone."

Another detail needed attention. Circus women told me, "You can't nurse your baby and work." I didn't ask why, I just stopped nursing Ivy. I thought Danny and I would resume intercourse. He told me earlier, "I'll leave you alone as long as you breast-feed. By the way, you can't have another baby until this one is out of diapers." I thought, *Have sex, just don't make babies.*

* * *

On the trip to Hugo, we took John Seaton along. He slept on one of the cots in the camper before moving into the working man's car, a special semi-truck made into sleeping berths. "The show hired you as a working man," Danny told him, "Your salary includes clowning and aerial work. Does that suit you?" John grinned in approval, it beat being a towner.

Danny enjoyed feeding his new, jolly daughter in the morning and let me sleep. "Eat your egg like Daddy," he said, dipping buttered white bread into the yolk of a fried egg and holding it out for her bite. He changed her diaper and gave her a bottle filled with evaporated milk, water, and white Karo syrup. She sat up and played opposite him at the dinette where a crib railing kept her securely in place.

He took pride in his intellect. I know he missed reading the *Sarasota Herald Tribune* and solving the daily bridge hand. To compensate, he read *Billboard*, a show business magazine, and typed letters to the editor.

* * *

Danny grinned at the first muddy lot that had show trucks stuck up to their axles. Parking our rig out of the way he entreated, "Watch what happens." The mighty Carson & Barnes elephants pulling chains hooked to their wide harnesses, made of flattened fire fighting hose, appeared with handlers. These beasts pulled equipment out of the goop onto dry land alternately grabbing clumps of fresh green grass to push in their mouths and then sucking up muddy water and shooting it over their backs.

"Aren't they something?" Danny asked when the handlers poked treats into their pink mouths and whispered sweet nothings. "I brought you on a tent show so you get the full experience and feel of sawdust under your feet." Instead of sawdust, sharp stalks on rough-mowed fields jabbed my ankles. I witnessed severe weather warnings and 'hey rubes'—a show term for fist fights—usually between the working men and towners. My fancy feathered wardrobe, stored in the costume truck, went unused that season.

Other performing families on the show were Joyce and Pietro Canestrelli, Grace and Peter Ivanov, and the Alfonso Loyal family. I fell in love with Papa (Alfonso), Mama, Luciana (Lucy) and Luciano (Joe) Loyal. Eighteen-year-old Lucy lovingly followed me around the lot. Outspoken, she had guts and grit, saying what was on her mind. Unlike me, who kept thoughts internal. Silence was my peacekeeping tool. Lucy Loyal was the spirit of the Carson & Barnes Circus that season and many more to follow.

There may have been other people in my life up to that time that spoke frankly, they just didn't impress me as much as Lucy. Perhaps I wasn't listening.

John Seaton worked out well. I mainly saw him when we performed the ladder act, which we did for the free act on top of the marquis truck. Paying customers bought tickets at the truck and walked through the semi's belly to the midway.

* * *

Early in the season, a surprise waited for me when I returned to the trailer after the free act. I boldly screamed as loud as I could. "Get your trunk out of there! Don't hurt my baby! Help! Get out! Back! Someone help me!" No amount of fist pounding and yanking moved the leathery elephant from the opened screen door of my tiny trailer.

The adrenal surge got results. My yelling told the trainer where to find his lost pachyderm. "Come here, you rascal, don't you know when to leave things alone?" he chastised in a fatherly voice, gently guiding six tons of lumbering flesh back to the herd. Peeking inside, I saw little Ivy sound asleep.

Was this female Asian elephant up to no good in my trailer? I don't know. I also don't know where my strength came from compared to all the other times I felt powerless. We never parked near the marquee again and ever after when we left Ivy asleep, we closed the metal outer door. And we parked in the back yard along with the other trailers and closer to the curtained back door where we went in and out of the big top.

* * *

Deborah and Stephanie joined us toting their schoolbooks at the beginning of April. "Come. Let's make a classroom in the camper," I said, encouraging them to contribute. I found it simple teaching circus children—traveling is a classroom in itself. "The show's going to Minnesota, Stephanie. It's your turn to meet relatives."

The spring route zigzagged north deep into Tornado Alley. Danny feared violent wind and rainstorms to his core. Each time the sky turned black, he listened intently to the radio or TV and decided when it was time to load in the pickup, hook up the trailer, and pull off the lot. Frantic searches located each child, the dog, and Ivy's bottle. Packed tightly together in the cab, clothes clung to damp rainwear. We left the circus's tent, stakes, equipment, and personnel to its own fate. Because of Danny's aloofness to that show, when the warnings lifted we never went back to the lot.

Danny's mission, escaping harm from tornadoes, was similar to dodging bullets in field maneuvers. We sped to the nearest town and tentatively parked next to the largest building in lee of the wind. It took patience sitting in the truck entertaining Ivy until he decided if we moved or stayed. Some nights, we moved three times before the storm left and we could lay in our beds. If tornado sirens went off, we descended the nearest shelter until the townsfolk said, "It's safe to leave." Jack Moore managed the circus that season; Danny Chapman controlled the weather fear factor.

CHAPTER ELEVEN
BLUE SKIES

When the storms diminished, Mother visited us at the lot on her way to Minnesota. Little Ivy thrived, and walked by herself at six-months. Her half-sisters were constant playmates. Life went rather well on this big three-ring circus.

I picked at my toenails and the inevitable happened when both big toes were infected and stayed that way. "Danny, my toes are worse…they have proud flesh…They need to be seen." I wanted his comment, not deaf ears. He said nothing. I went to a country doctor.

"Your toes will heal with antibiotics and daily saltwater soaks," said the doctor.

"Thank you." Tentative but needing to know I found the courage to continue. "I have a question. Can I get pregnant while I'm nursing?"

"No. Women can't conceive during lactation."

I was enlightened, but didn't understand why Danny hadn't touched me for the past year. *I stopped nursing three months ago.*

People are around us most of the time and quarters are tight. Aren't married people supposed to share each other's bodies? Not having sex concerned me, but not Danny. I pictured the few matchsticks thrown into our imaginary jar and drearily accepted a sexless marriage along with everything else. My sense of justice warped. *What in this world is fair?*

* * *

Stephanie celebrated her seventh birthday in early May. It was a warm, memorable day and we scheduled a party in the big top between shows. All the kids ate cake and ice cream and pinned the nose on the clown. When the time came to get ready for the second show, I took the remaining sheet cake on its flat open box to the trailer, placing it on the table adjoining Ivy's crib. My older girls took the gifts to the camper.

Danny and I went in and out of the trailer to change wardrobe. We checked on seven-month-old Ivy. "Keep your hands off Steph's cake. You'll get some later," we told her. The lion act came after opening and, after it ended, working men slid the heavy iron cage sections up into a semitrailer.

Costumed and waiting for my aerial display cue, Danny appeared and shoved a disheveled youngster, perhaps age fifteen, inside the trailer "Help this man, his leg got caught between the cage sections."

Looking into the boy's ashen face, I quietly said, "You will be fine." After helping him sit on a cushion at the dinette, I reached behind me to the closet, fetching Danny's whiskey bottle, poured a little in a glass, and handed it to him. "Drink this." *I bet he's never tasted whiskey*. Working fast, so I wouldn't miss my next number, I grabbed scissors and cut his pant leg open below the knee.

"I'm going to pull your boot off." Blood spilled on the floor making me wish I'd sipped the whiskey too. After wrapping his torn calf in a towel, pinning it tight, and elevating his leg I said, "Your boot protected you. This could have been worse."

Danny poked his head inside. "How is it?"

"He needs stitches. Get someone to take him to the hospital. He's staying here until his ride comes." I stuffed the working man's boot in a paper grocery bag, handed him the bag, and looked into his youthful face saying, "You'll need this when you walk again." I left to work in the aerial display where six of us women gently swung back and forth on metal anchors while doing ankle and hand loop positions.

An even bigger mess occurred in the trailer while I was gone. Ivy, forgotten during the first aid emergency, pulled the cake box into her bed and sat on the cake grabbing fistfuls to her mouth. Then she messed her diaper, and whimpered about her dilemma.

"Oh, dear baby, I don't know whether to laugh at you or cry myself. Mama will clean you after I wash blood from the floor. That's the end of Stephanie's cake."

The hospital sutured the boy's leg wound. He returned to the lot on crutches, got his things, and quit the show. I wonder if he forgave me for ruining his new jeans his first day on the job. And I wondered if circus life hardened my hide or was I strong only in the right circumstance.

* * *

When sunshine finally warmed lakes, rivers, and pools, I took the children, Lucy and her friend, Roxie Null, and others swimming.

"I don't approve of you going to unsafe water," Danny growled.

I went anyhow. I looked at those excursions as a small victory, a momentary freedom from Danny's rules.

He bought a Kodak Super 8 movie camera and filmed movies of the circus, side trips, and family. "I'm taking these for posterity. Some day you'll enjoy watching them with the grandchildren."

Typical teenagers, Lucy and Joe Loyal listened to music on the radio out by their truck. "Papa keeps it on for the horses," Lucy said.

"Good. I like it too." I didn't tell her it was verboten in the Chapman chalet. "There's a snack for you at the Frolic. Come by."

* * *

Carson & Barnes paid our gas and allowed us cookhouse privileges, but we didn't eat there. Danny encouraged me to cook. I made breaded pork chops, creamed spinach and whipped potatoes. I even mastered fancy crepes Florentine on our day off.

When it was Danny's turn, he made his famous fried chicken and milk gravy, and always invited Joe and Lucy.

His culinary challenges paid off and I gained confidence and improved. He invited show people for family meals, sometimes even for leftovers.

At that time, I didn't cook baby food. "I'm sorry Ivy your food comes from bottles, cans, jars, and boxes." Danny wanted me to excel at cooking for him, while I did it for myself.

* * *

As for sewing, I knew the mechanics, yet compared to other circus folk, felt unskilled in fancy decorations. With limited time, basic trim appealed more than hours spent adding frills.

The cotton handkerchiefs I picked up in my act perplexed me. I stained all of them with bright red and orange lipstick. The marks came out when I soaked the hankies in dish soap. After ironing, the twelve-inch squares folded into a two-inch square with a tail off one end. I pulled the pointed tail out from under the elasticized leg of my costume. Concerned, I asked Danny, "What if I drop the handkerchief?"

"I'll tie it around the web and you can pull it up." Luckily, that rarely happened.

* * *

The purpose of the smaller tented shows was to develop my act under a variety of conditions. I think I exceeded Danny's expectations by balancing confidently on my bar above his head. I know it helped me having him down below. I stood on my bar, balancing away while increasing winds prior to storms bellowed the thin faded canvas like a sea of ripened winter wheat. Outside the big top, teams of working men adjusted the slack on stake line ropes between each exhale of the canvas. Inside the big top, multiple quarter poles rose up and down tugging at tie down ropes. Patrons watched the featured aerial act unaware of the encroaching danger. Eight-inch-diameter aluminum center poles rose from the ground straining my fixed crane bar, guy wires, and stakes. The center poles returned as gently as they lifted, and balancing in mid-air became the norm.

***

We left Carson & Barnes in late August on a technicality. If I'm correct, Danny felt the show wasn't paying in the unemployment taxes for us and the other performers. He knew we worked enough weeks for unemployment and were entitled to draw out half our salary during the unemployable winter months.

"We're leaving the show before it heads to Kentucky. We don't owe them anything. John's staying because Kentucky's his home state. I've got his address and phone number," Danny said, convinced it was the right thing to do. We drove home to Florida.

Enriched with vagabond memories, Danny's girls returned to school and living with their mom, now only two houses away. Our renters vacated early and we moved back to spaciousness.

Our first unemployment claim failed, was appealed, and then awarded.

One of the things I wanted to do in Sarasota was attend Incarnation Catholic church because Patrnella went there before her stroke. "Please take me to Mom's church, Danny."

"If that's what you want." We went to Mass and I found it unpretentious. Babies cried, people shuffled about when sitting, kneeling, and rising, and parishioners walking forward in long lines quickly received communion hosts placed on their tongues. I felt like I was there many times before and easily sang along with the congregation.

"That was rewarding. Can we go again?" I asked.

"We'll go next week. Don't sing aloud. Your voice isn't in tune. And, don't stand the baby in your lap."

Always rules, I thought. *I won't sing. However...Ivy can stand in my lap anytime, anywhere.*

Moscow Circus 1967

In October, Art Concello made Danny advance man for the United States segment of the Moscow State Circus touring North America. Concello, a former flying artist turned producer gave Danny the job as a favor.

"I'll send the money home," Danny said in parting. I was too young to realize the sensibility of me in Sarasota and, as a faithful dog told to stay, I followed my master anyhow. Secretly, I wanted to see the Russian performers.

Neighborhood children helped celebrate Ivy's first birthday. I made a cake with one candle. Robust and strong, Ivy smiled.

Full of energy, I packed food, clothing, baby, and dog in the pickup and drove north. I stayed the first night out with the Meyers in Mocksville, North Carolina. Both Calvin and Naida sensed a change.

"You've grown up since Sullins," Naida commented. "It's cold where you're headed. We'll help set you up with food, a bed, and blankets." I thanked them for the improvements and continued onward to meet Danny's chilly welcome in Baltimore.

* * *

He didn't appreciate me coming but didn't reprimand me in public or in the hotel room. Maybe he didn't know my driving skills or figured I would stay home. I didn't pack a trapeze so I couldn't practice. Danny was popular on the show and acted professionally wearing a white shirt, dark pants, and a sweater for work.

The Moscow Circus performers were wonderfully genial to the audience and those backstage. Each aspect of the performance captivated my imagination. *I'm glad I came*, I thought more than once.

"You're coming to the party after the show aren't you?" Danny asked on closing night of Baltimore. He wore his blue suit.

"I am? Who'll watch Ivy?"

"She has a sitter," Danny said, knotting and positioning his tie.

"I'll meet you there," I answered, knowing I hadn't brought fancy clothes. Glass after glass of vodka lifted to eager lips, except Danny's and mine. Each Russian artist possessed romantic and mystical qualities, reminding me of Old World fairy tale characters.

* * *

I met Danny's Philadelphia friends when the show played the Spectrum. "I've called the gang and they're having a family dinner, we're invited. It's at Phil and Ecky (Eleanor) Schneider's house in north Philly." As he chauffeured us to dinner, instead of telling me how to act and what to say, Danny told me his friends' names, jobs, and backgrounds. That made me more nervous than learning an interview script.

"Welcome, welcome," Phil and Ecky said, smiling and greeting us at the door. "May I hold the baby?" Ecky asked, taking Ivy from me. Looking at a picture on the wall, I noticed they had children my age.

That evening I told Danny, "You have nice friends." He smiled and I thought, *But none compare to you.* I learned their names, got their addresses, and never forgot their warmth and generosity.

* * *

Riding in the pickup to the Philadelphia engagement Danny told me, "I want you to go to Hahnemann Hospital. They'll know what to do about the questionable Pap smear you got a few months ago." At the Hahnemann Clinic, a doctor took a tissue biopsy and gave me pills to regulate my hormones.

* * *

Danny's job as advance man for the Moscow State Circus was to leapfrog ahead of the show and set up an identical set of ring curbs and horse stalls in the next town before the animals and performers arrived. He also checked out hotel and dressing room reservations. Lastly, he bought horse feed and dirt.

"I'm having trouble finding the right dirt for the European circus ring. One of the riding act Cossacks feels the soil between his fingers. If he thinks it's appropriate for the horses, he says '*Da.*' If it isn't he says, '*Nyet*,' and every cubic yard gets hauled out and new dirt is delivered."

* * *

At first, Danny traversed ahead. I didn't mind joining him later with the pickup. The show played Hershey, Pennsylvania, then Cleveland, Ohio, before heading out to California. For the cross-country trip, Danny rode with me because the equipment went ahead on a freight train.

Passing through Utah in December, just west of Salt Lake City on the flats of the Great Salt Lake Desert, the pickup burned out a front wheel bearing. Danny, frustrated and worried he'd miss set-up in San Francisco, abandoned me. "I'm taking the bus. Stay here until the truck's fixed."

"Wave bye-bye to Daddy," I told Ivy. I felt scared and alone with a dog and a child stuck in a foreign hostile environment. Setting Ivy down, we walked with Lacie to the ailing truck and gave thanks for the bed in the camper.

Day turned into night. I drove the repaired truck forty miles to Wendover. The next morning, driving far too fast through a mountain storm on roads littered with tree limbs, I pushed on. Uncharted territory lay ahead, namely, stunning San Francisco and all her charms.

The breakdown plus gas-credit-card charges pushed us into debt. The trip taught me the meaning of dead weight. Had I stayed home in Sarasota, the expenses wouldn't have happened making me feel better economically, but I would have missed the sights and experiences I encountered, like attending hockey games and seeing the Pacific Ocean.

After San Francisco the show headed to Los Angeles. "We need to conserve money. You're staying here," Danny ordered. He put Ivy and me in an older hotel in the Watts district and left us. He seldom checked in, leaving me to my own devices. Keeping myself busy by sewing little things by hand for Ivy, I wondered, *Why does he leave us? Does he want us to go away?*

* * *

One day in the room, I made stew in the pressure cooker on a hot plate. BANG! The pressure valve exploded, erupting stew clear to the ceiling leaving dirty emerging stalactites to enhance the dingy decor. Cleaning up the mess reminded me of the 4-H motto, *Learn By Doing*.

"You can come to San Diego. Its 125 miles down the freeway. I've got us a room," Danny announced by phone, inviting me back to the show. I packed in minutes.

Driving south to San Diego, I smiled at vivid flowers resembling a huge grill of burning briquettes. "Look out the window, Ivy. See the red in the hills? It's thousands of poinsettias. We'll buy one for Christmas." Arriving at San Diego's waterfront park, it reminded me of Sarasota.

"Can we go to Tijuana?" I asked Danny, wishing he would give me a tour. I wouldn't go by myself.

"Yes, I'll take you there. Then we're leaving for Portland."

* * *

Seattle was the last date for the American service crew. The 1967 Moscow State Circus US tour was a successful venture for promoter, audiences, and me. Danny documented their exquisite acts on film.

"I'm buying a super eight movie projector and teaching you how to splice five-minute films into 400 foot reels," Danny said during our ride back across the desert.

Gazing across the empty skyline, I gave no thought to where we worked next. That was up to Danny.

CHAPTER TWELVE
RED LEOTARD

We were broke and out of work in January 1968. Danny went to Concello and returned home saying, "You've been invited on a Russian exchange circus. It's a wonderful opportunity. Ivy has to stay behind, no children are allowed." The decision was up to me.

"Then I'll stay here too. I won't leave Ivy with Mother." I didn't doubt my performing ability, but no telling what would happen to my daughter. I passed on performing in Europe. "We can work in Sarasota, can't we?"

"I'll tell Concello, and find out what's available around town."

A few days later, he had a plan, "The Circus Hall of Fame needs an aerialist for the spring season. I'll sit web for your balancing trap."

A web is an untwisted cotton rope covered in cotton tubing that performers use to climb up to riggings. Mine was custom made to fit my hands. It was the standard thirty-three feet long—the length needed to hang from the flying act frame to the ground. I wrapped my legs on the web and pushed upwards while Danny held the bottom of the web steady and tightened and released pressure on the web to aid me climbing. Danny faithfully sat my web for twelve years and, if necessary, made affirmative comments on my act, without me ever saying, "Thanks."

The Circus Hall of Fame let us park the Frolic trailer in the back lot. Most days Danny made coffee and read the morning paper. Ivy napped while I worked on new leotards using the 1965 pattern.

One time between shows Danny found me in the trailer. "Come outside. Simmy and Peaches are here."

"What are their real names?"

"Searle and Ruth Simmons are retired aerialists. Simmy's short for Simmons. Her nickname, Peaches, comes from her velvety complexion, strawberry blonde hair, and she's from Georgia."

I greeted them, "Hello. How are you?"

"We're fine Sarah. Peaches wants you to have this," Simmy said, handing me a bulky bag.

While Danny chatted with Simmy, I examined several pieces of jewelry. Then I pulled burgundy and aqua coque trim (pointed rooster feathers) from the bag and stroked the smooth feathers. Looking up at Peaches, I asked, "Can leotards be made of velvet?"

"Be as creative as you want. Take the jewelry apart and use it for trim. It's leftovers I don't need anymore," Peaches said smiling at me.

"Thank you, Peaches. For everything." My striking burgundy velvet costume used the coque feathers three ways; draped as a skirt on my hips, wound into a fluttering head piece, and twisted into a long boa. To complement the aqua feathers, I chose aqua/gold brocade and placed feathered epaulettes on each shoulder matching the aqua skirt. In both costumes, feathers fluttered back and forth adding a new dimension during swings. I ordered a rubber stamp saying *Simply Sarah*, printed my logo on satin ribbon, and sewed a label into original designs.

Danny's contribution at the time was appropriate. "Why don't you use silk handkerchiefs to match your wardrobe?"

"Lend me one of yours and I'll see how it works." The wafer thin silk pulled out of my costume smoother than rubbing talcum on skin and was so light I practically inhaled it. "The silk's great, Danny. It floats and glides. Do you have a fifteen-inch square?"

"No, but you can sew one." *Leave it up to Danny to tell me to make something*, I silently complained.

"No thanks, I don't hem silk well enough. I'll buy magic silks."

* * *

As the short Circus Hall of Fame season came to a close, I turned my thoughts to the future. "I'm taking Music Appreciation at Manatee Junior College, making up my 'D' from Sullins." Three months later I drove home in a tizzy.

"Guess who got recognition for the most improved student?" No answer from Danny.

"Guess!" I was practically hopping for joy. "There were eighty students in my class." No answer.

"Me! I did," I exclaimed, finally grasping the meaning of words written more than once on my grade school report cards—Sarah can do better.

Danny glossed past my victory, turning it back to him. "I was smarter than all my teachers, even when I took a class at Temple University. A lot of good it did me to graduate from high school."

On Sundays, we attended Incarnation Catholic Church. Yearning to learn more, I practiced saying the Hail Mary prayer in front of a statue of Mary. Curious about the Rosary beads Patrnella kept by her bed at Burzinsky's, I asked her about them. "The Pope gave those beads to Danny." I'd heard the story how he and a movie star had an audience with Pope Pius XII towards the end of WWII. As they left, the pope reached into his drawer for souvenirs.

After mass, we brought Patrnella home for the afternoon. "What's for dinner?" she chirped.

"Baked chicken, whipped potatoes, vegetable, and dessert."

If it was someone's birthday, I made the Chapman family's famous sugar cake trimmed with pink frosting and sliced fresh strawberries. Everyone, including drooling neighborhood kids, watched the decoration and cutting of the strawberry cake. It disappeared in minutes.

In August 1968, Art Concello produced the Thrill Circus in New York and gave us a contract. "You and John are doing the ladder seventy-feet up. It's a thrill circus, so do a short routine and work out some kind of fast revolving finish. We're using all five upright sections," Danny told me. "I'm clowning."

"Can Deborah and Stephanie come?"

"Sure."

John scraped rust and painted metal. Danny cut and spliced new support cables. He asked John to overhaul the ratchets. We packed a lot of steel up the East Coast to Shea Stadium in Flushing, Long Island.

Dismal heat and humidity didn't stop sightseeing. We saw the Statue of Liberty from the Staten Island Ferry, viewed Manhattan from the Empire State Building, stretched at Rockefeller Plaza, and counted flags at the courtyard of the United Nations Headquarters. Finally, we zoomed on the famous wooden rollercoaster at New Jersey's Palisades Park. Another day, I took all the circus children to the Bronx Zoo. These excursions were as important to us as performing. We thrived on variety, on the new experiences.

"We don't perform for three days next week," Danny advised. "Take the bus to Massachusetts to see your relatives. I'll watch the kids."

"Okay," I answered tentatively. I'm not sure why he did that, maybe because it wasn't my mother's Minnesota family.

On the trip I wondered what to say to the aunt and uncle I knew so little about. How did they look? Act? In Great Barrington, I met Aunt Hazel and Uncle Robert Wheeler for the first time.

"Sarah, we're delighted you're here. Hazel has planned the day and we'll meet at the Red Lion in Stockbridge," Uncle Robert told me, in a voice that sounded like Daddy. *Oh, I've missed a treasure all these years.* Aunt Hazel and I breezed through two dress shops. Then we viewed the duplicate Lincoln Memorial sculpture at Daniel Chester French's studio, followed by tours of Tanglewood and the Norman Rockwell Museum.

Uncle Robert owned the Red Lion Inn where Hazel and I joined him for lunch. Afterwards he and I went to his office at Wheeler & Taylor Real Estate and Insurance in Great Barrington. Both aunt and uncle prepared our simple evening meal.

"No one could have had a better day than me here with you. Thank you," I said to them and thought, *I love you both. I have my own Auntie Mame.*

I returned to Flushing on the bus and decided to go alone to an Episcopal church, not far from Shea Stadium. I wore a new dress from Aunt Hazel. The Wheeler part of me was still Episcopalian. Walking into the church, I saw only African-Americans inside and almost turned to leave until a few white faces came up the steps. When I kneeled at the altar rail for communion, I prayed, *Dear God, help me to love all people. Please forgive my doubts.* I left church dumbfounded at my race sensitivity and blushed because I knew better.

At the Thrill Circus I worked with a pack of performing daredevils. I wandered the lot and talked with anyone I liked. The Yerkes Flying Act from California included blonde, muscular Bobby Yerkes, his dark-haired wife, Dorothy, and a young Hispanic named Donny Martinez. Danny and Bobby were old friends except for one glitch. "Don't pay any attention to Bobby. He's a Jesus preacher."

On the lookout for the preacher man, I found a group of performers socializing. I reached out and shook the speaker's hand, "Hi, Bobby. I'm Sarah Chapman." *The circus is lucky to have Bobby and his Bible.*

Danny announced during breakfast, "I've got someone to watch the kids today. I'm taking you to the city to buy you a Konica 35mm camera. I made an appointment at J.J. Krigsmann's studio for a professional portrait. You'll like it there."

Euphoric at days end I softly voiced, "Thanks for the camera, Danny. I'll take more pictures." He looked pleased gazing at my Krigsmann proofs lined up on the table.

"They don't need retouching," he whispered. The poses flattered me. The gifted photographer captured a Sarah different from the one I saw in the mirror—a rested and composed woman—with grace and beauty, which didn't correspond to my past. I had deep inner flaws I felt responsible for. Still, it wasn't hard giving a friend one of my Krigsmann's photos looking my best.

* * *

Back in Sarasota, I enrolled as a full-time college student. Danny and Mel Miller toyed with the idea of adding clowns to Ringling Bros. Circus. The new Ringling owners created a second unit and needed thirty clowns. Mel Miller, then curator of the Ringling Museum of the Circus, hired on for the clown alley expansion.

Danny, Mel, and I enjoyed each other's company. Sometimes we went to the Asolo Theater at the Ringling Museum or met for lunch in town. Handsomely tall, dark-haired, and articulate, Mel Miller attracted me. "Mel's a dreamer. He pays attention to detail," Danny warned.

On a warm September evening, when the jasmine wafted sweetly through screened windows into the great room, Mel came over at the end of his working day. After putting Ivy to bed, I sliced a freshly made apricot jellyroll and took it and dessert plates to the dining table.

"Sarah, we want your input on an idea. Danny tells me that most clowns are old men," Mel began.

Danny interrupted, "Yes, that's right. You should have seen her running behind Chester Sherman in Mobile. Those old clowns know the routines, but they can't move."

I listened while Danny boasted. "It's an opportunity for young men to work and travel."

"It's gambling to say you can find thirty new clowns," Mel countered.

"Why don't you teach them what you want them to learn?" I asked.

"There are several young men in town that might be interested. Students from 1962 when I ran clown alley at Sailor Circus," Danny said.

Mel the detail thinker, wrote on a scratch pad, stopped and tore off a page, handing it to Danny. "Clown School. Congress of Clowns. College of Clowns." Danny passed it to me.

No one spoke.

"That's what you have to do Mel...convince the new owners to start a clown school and call it Clown College," Danny finally exhaled. Plates emptied, coffee cups and minds drained, both jasmine and evening spent, we bid, "Good night," to Mel at the door.

"Mel resigned his museum job and opened an office in Venice at Ringling Winter Quarters," Danny told me when I came home from class. "He's handling promotion and paperwork, the school application, and advertising. I'll teach and direct clown gags."

A week later Danny gave me the local paper, "Here, read this. We're getting applications from around the US." In the classified section, a small ad read, "Ringling Bros. and Barnum & Bailey Circus is establishing the world's first and only school for professional clowns . . . . Young men interested in the tuition-free program should contact Mel Miller, Box 967, Venice, Florida."

The eight-week clown school opened in Venice on Oct. 21, 1968. Danny told me to stop at the Clown College office located upstairs in the arena. A friendly woman, older than me, with two young girls at her side, stopped stirring sloppy joe mixture in an electric frypan, "Mel and Danny went to town for something. I'm Marty Scott and these are my girls, Linda and Mary. We're here from Michigan. I'm getting lunch ready before the clowns come up from the arena to watch Charlie Chaplin movies."

I looked around the unusual office. "I'm Sarah. Danny wants me to read some of the applications."

"They're over here." Marty helped, guiding me to Mel's desk. I recognized a few names of my friends from Sailor Circus, then left to do an errand for the six new clown dogs that Danny picked out earlier at the Sarasota Humane Society. Lou Jacob chose a small white dog from the pack, named it Knucklehead, and led it to stardom.

Two clowns, Joey Matheson and Louis De Jesus, lived at our house during Clown College, because they were minors. Others stayed with us when they were broke. Danny's Clown College salary was $100 per week, yet he loaned out several hundred dollars to some of the thirty hopeful students. "Danny," I asked, "when will they pay us back?"

"When they graduate and get a job on the show."

"I'll cross my fingers."

"I'm a producing clown. We'll have more money if we both get contracts. Mel told the new owners about your trap act."

"Good. I hoped he would," I slowly answered, reflecting on Danny and Mel discussing where Sarah fit in.

* * *

On a steamy October afternoon, on the banks of the Phillippi Bayou under the live oak limbs, my vision of myself on Ringling Circus came closer to reality. At twenty-two I auditioned my single and balancing trapezes for half-a-dozen circus bigwigs: Richard Barstow, Trolle Rhodin, Lloyd Morgan Sr., Max Weldy, Irvin Feld, and Allen Bloom. They were director, talent agent, general manager, wardrobe genius, show co-owner, and corporate business consultant. Leaving suit coats behind in air-conditioned cars and seeking shelter from direct sun, the men slowly spread out in the tree-clad lot, each with a different view of the rigging and me. Neither seats nor beverages were available.

"Which act are you doing first?" Danny asked beforehand.

"Balancing, because I work barefoot. Then single trap, because I'm wearing tights and opera stockings with my red practice leotard. I don't want rope burns."

After my last swing on the single trap, I bounced to the ground where Allen Bloom addressed me. "Are you always out of breath?"

Wiping perspiration away from my face and looking directly at him, I puffed in segments, "I usually, practice in the morning, when it's cool." He turned away joining others in closed cars.

I headed inside to change into shorts and hailed Danny on the way. "What did they say?"

"I didn't ask," he sheepishly responded. No job that day for me, nor the promise of one. Irrationally I thought, *He should have talked to Feld.*

* * *

The media descended upon Clown College, discovering what makes a clown. *Newsweek*, December 2, 1968 described Danny in Life and Leisure as "an instructor with a vengeance." "We only teach the mechanics. We can't teach you that indefinable something that is your personality," Danny was quoted. A former clown turned Ringling official also made the magazine. "The show got streamlined . . . but the clowns . . . were allowed to grow old . . . the show has sixteen clowns, four are at retirement age." This created an urgent need for younger clowns.

The *Floridian,* weekly magazine of the *St. Petersburg Times* reported…"A small, broad-shouldered man in a green jersey is supervising their efforts, using a training harness suspended from the ceiling high above. Danny Chapman . . . is teaching the would-be clowns the fundamentals. The atmosphere is serious. This is a business, being funny."

In the same article Clown Otto Greibling, who started tumbling for Poodles Hanneford in 1913, said he thought Clown College is, "A helluva good idea . . . The old-timers are all gone. We never had this many young guys before."

Clown College graduation arrived and along with it a diploma, each neophyte clown received a contract to the Blue or Red unit providing eighteen clowns to each unit. Danny, the school's head clown, hired on as Producing Clown on the Blue Unit with an unknown salary. After a one-month rehearsal in Venice, he was going on the road in February.

My unmentioned contract made me uneasy. "What should I do, Danny?"

"Go to rehearsals like everyone else. You're not the only one without a contract."

I spent the rest of 1968 enjoying the weather, my toddler, college classes, and new friends I met on campus. Occasionally my good-looking, six-foot three-inch brother popped in at Montclair Drive. "Merritt, why not go on the circus?" I teased, "They need responsible animal people. That way we can be together."

"No, I'd rather stay in Venice." He definitely possessed star qualities—richly tanned body, flashing brown eyes, even pearly teeth, thick-black-curling hair, and a killer smile. I loved him very much.

* * *

When I was six Merritt was seven and a-half. We were cockfight assistants. Our job was fetching Daddy's lean, powerful pit-game birds and holding them outside the ring until he called us forward. The fighting cocks lived in individual wood-sided cages, with the fronts and backs made of inch-square wire. If they accidentally got out, they chased us.

Daddy summoned Merritt and me after Sunday lunch, "Outsiders are coming today. I know you both like to go without shirts but, I want you to cover your chests." Shirted or bare skinned, we never thought of getting scratches or bites from his sleek headed cocks because he tied the legs of the mean birds with a string. We found them lying down in their cages and inserted our middle finger between their legs and avoided sharpened metal spurs held in place by leather straps wrapped around powerful avian feet. We tucked flapping wings next to the bird and pulled the contender to our waist quieting it for the walk to the bout.

Our sentinel post was twenty-feet away from the men gathered inside the big fenced chicken yard. Betting ceased, the men stepped back forming a ring, and Daddy summoned us to present the birds. We slipped in on opposite sides glancing up at the men. Some we knew as regulars at Daddy's bar, most were strangers.

Daddy caught our attention, raised, and then dropped his arm. We released the birds who eyed each other immediately. The men crowded in, voiced a dissonance of bets and threats. "I've got a winner." "This bird's a fighter." "Stay back—they can hurt you."

Before the birds stretched, crowed, and made eye contact, Merritt and I rushed to Daddy who pressed silver quarters in our palms. Dashing away to the house, we stripped off our shirts, chattering whether to save or spend our loot.

* * *

With Mama, we went hunting. Merritt and I knew the difference between all the nighttime sounds at Oakairs. We ignored screech owls and mimicked whippoorwills. Grunts and growls meant it was mating season. Screams told us something was after

Daddy's free-range cocks roosting in the treetops. That's when it came time to hunt critters.

Mama stored her 12 gauge double-barreled shotgun in her clothes closet. Beside it on a narrow shelf was a box of shells. From our beds, we heard her push shells into the chambers, click the gun shut, and press the safety button. Placing the gunstock on her shoulder, she turned away from the closet walking out of the darkened room. I'd grab a piece of her cotton gown with one hand and Merritt's hand with the other. Our procession stopped for Mama to pick up the flashlight.

We preceded barefoot into the pitch-dark jungle to locate the poacher, be it possum or coon. It didn't matter to Mama. She'd shine the light up into the face of the offending animal. Sometimes it released its prey, sometimes we were too late. Passing the flashlight back to one of us, she'd aim the shotgun barrel upward to the marauder and pulled the trigger. BA BOOM! Craaack. Thud. Bump, bump. WHUMP! Layers of small, dried brown oak leaves scattered and rose up, resettling into a camouflaged carpet, with some landing across the furry gray and brown lifeless carcass.

After verifying death, Mama unloaded her gun, passed the spent red shell to us. We enjoyed sniffing the warmth of heated gunpowder. Victorious, we marched back into the house returning to quiet slumber. I think Mama thoroughly enjoyed those shadowy hunts in the woods.

CHAPTER THIRTEEN
THE BIG ONE

1969 RBB&B Blue Unit

Among circus performers and fans, Ringling Brothers Barnum & Bailey Circus is simply The Big One, Big Bertha, or RBB&B. While it is big, it isn't always best because every show is a blend of acts and talents. A teeny-tiny tent show in the wilderness may have a first class act, one exciting enough for a patron to go home and tell his neighbors. A colossal sized circus can be full of top acts, yet still leave that same patron with emptiness. That's show business.

The Big One was the epitome of shows and we wanted to be on it.

Ringling's Red and Blue Units were identical in size and strength, making circus history, because no circus had two equally large units running at the same time. The Big One was in operation for ninety-seven-years when John Ringing North, sold his shares in 1967 to two brothers from Washington DC; Irvin and Israel Feld. The Felds took a partner, Houston investor and judge, Roy M. Hofheinz. Economy was the driving force behind the sale;

the same reason in 1956 when North switched the show from playing under canvas to buildings. Circuses have tremendous overhead and need full houses and high concession sales to stay afloat.

It took entrepreneurial foresight to buy a circus. The Felds already had concert contracts with many of the buildings the Ringling Circus performed in each year. They were familiar with tour routes and well established with the media. Irvin and Israel planned for the future, with bigger, better shows.

They split the existing management between the two units, added new staff, and relocated the corporate offices to Washington DC. The property in Venice, Florida, leased from Sarasota County, became a winter quarters, where acts practiced and the trains were stored and repaired. Daily rehearsals took place in a makeshift arena.

The first year of the twin shows, the Red Unit, enjoyed considerable ease on the road, with a continuous route, longer dates, and no backtracking. The Blue Unit split a week, performing in two towns. An example opening in Knoxville, Tennessee, for a Wednesday matinee (a show was two-hours and forty-five minutes long) and closing on Sunday night, followed immediately with a 518 mile, overnight jump to Mobile, Alabama. After four performances in Mobile on Tuesday and Wednesday, the show took a one-day move to Lafayette, Louisiana, for the Friday weekend opening creating a hectic schedule for performers, working men, animals, staff, and concessionaires.

The AGVA contract stipulated a maximum of thirteen shows a week and when possible, we did them, with a minor exception. The Saturday morning show, we performed a shortened version with a few acts deleted. After each finale, the parking lots emptied and quickly refilled, seats readied, and props reset for the next show opening.

Act women doing the aerial ballet got substitution on Saturday morning, something I wanted too. The ballet director, Miss Antoinette Concello, a holdover from the John Ringling days, had assistants on each unit who monitored the showgirls and scheduled rotations. When her assistant skipped my name, I thought there was a mistake. "May I have the morning off like other act women?"

"No, you don't get substitutions." Ouch. My six numbers never varied. It tainted my view of the assistant and I avoided her, rather than challenge my fate.

* * *

Money was a big issue…we didn't have any. Danny's meager $100/week Clown College checks whittled down the credit card and truck payments leaving little left to spend on a day-to-day basis. Looming upon us was a one-year $1,000 promissory note with interest to W.E. Lawson, a show person I never met. I knew he shipped beef and horsemeat to lions and tigers.

Danny got that loan after we went on the Moscow Circus saying, "Use this until work comes around." I wanted to pay Lawson back in full, not his annual fee. I also wanted the same for Danny's $5,000 house mortgage. Two Ringling contracts meant a better life, free of debt.

* * *

"Sarah, we have to decide if we're going on the train. Go have a look," Danny told me during rehearsals.

"What did you think of the train today?" Danny queried me.

"Oooh, they're awful and the compartment is tiny. Can't we live in the trailer?" Danny nodded. We went overland in our sixteen-foot Frolic at our own expense. Trailer life was healthier for Ivy, our energetic two-year-old—a no-fear kid with Chapman-blue eyes and straight-light-brown hair. Overjoyed at having Ivy with me, I forgot about the train.

I was afraid we might loose our job by taking her on the show, but determined she went along. Danny warned, "Ringling doesn't like kids."

"That was old management, maybe the Felds will be different," I replied hopeful. They were and Ivy was one of several circus children. Her physical and emotional strength surpassed mine. Speaking her own special language that only I understood, her three main words were ellalas (elephant), doka-dola (Coke) and Nora (for her same age friend, Laura McMurray). The word "No" didn't deter her most of the time. If others considered her a pest, she behaved for me and usually took her afternoon nap.

"We're not taking her bottle on the circus route," her father informed me.

Ivy impressed us when she toilet trained herself at nineteen-months. Danny's words about having another child flickered, then faded in my mind. We kissed briefly on the lips and said, "Good night," when I went to bed. He watched one more news and weather broadcast.

At twenty-three, the Ringling show exhilarated me. Vicki Unus contracted to Ringling after her Sailor Circus debut. Hard work trimmed her figure to muscle and bone. Her featured Roman Rings made her the second circus star in the family. Her father, Franz Furtner, called Unus, stood on one finger. Blonde, blue-eyed, and smiling, Vicki greeted me during her Red Unit rehearsals with, "Welcome to the show."

"Thank you, Vicki. You look great!" was all I could think of to say. I wanted success…a contract too.

One week into Blue Unit rehearsals, Danny informed me I had another audition. "Do I have to?" I pleaded. *This is impossible—two auditions for the same people for the same job. Everyone's going to be watching.*

"Yes, and this time it's backstage at the arena. I assume you're wearing the red leotard." That meant I had to wear it.

My stomach went liquid prior to the audition. "They're all waiting," griped Danny to me at the restroom hallway. In spite of doing well and not panting, I didn't net a contract, though I never auditioned again for the remainder of my Ringling career. I believe I made a name for myself as a reliable performer.

* * *

The first season with the Blue Unit opened my eyes. Performing, cooking, traveling, laundry, shopping, and sewing left me with no time for thoughts. I missed church services. The Ringling season was a huge commitment whether you were a captive beast or an independent contractor.

As Producing Clown, Danny was in charge of every aspect of Clown Alley including routines, props, wardrobe, attendance, animals, and make-up. He tried to keep everyone satisfied and never gave enough of his time to please anyone. He also had a habit of giving unspecific answers. This left a number of people who depended on him to make their own decisions, prominent among them, his daughter, Michele, age seventeen.

"Do you want to go on the circus route?" he asked at her grandmother's home—her court-ordered residence due to truancy and leaving Joan's home the year before.

"Yes, Daddy. I don't want to go to school anymore. Sure, I'll go."

Michele Chapman was on her own for the past three years with minimum contact with her father and none with me. Her overweight and out-of-shape medium frame held no outstanding features except some muscle tone.

Danny pleaded with me to groom his unruly teenager. "Please take her shopping for try-out clothes and help her with make-up and style." I reluctantly taught Michele the Spanish web routine, some elementary ballet moves, and a little about managing her thin, light brown hair and applying basic make-up to highlight her oval face. Somehow, Michele passed Miss Antoinette Concello's try-out and became a 1969 showgirl. Amazed, she tightly clutched her ticket to freedom from authority.

"Daddy, I can't live in the single girl's car," she complained a week into the tour. "Let me use your compartment on the train." She moved in without our consent, annoying the hell out of me.

Danny soothed my ruffled feathers. "We should keep our assigned compartment just in case the pickup or trailer breaks down on the road." That made sense at the time.

Our two-person compartment was six feet wide, eight feet long, with bunk beds, a sink, and a closet. It cost us each $7/week, a total of $336 for the time we paid for it. When I saw the deduction on my check, I seethed, more so knowing Michele lived there and not in the girl's car. She paid $7/week for her vacant berth. The train fee needed closure.

* * *

During rehearsals, circus director and choreographer, Richard "Dick" Barstow, discovered that I didn't dance. Most people won't know him from Adam, but anyone on that show has him locked into their memories. Barstow directed the show for decades, could make or break a career in a matter of seconds, and with positive words, he gave recognition equivalent of an Oscar. The production numbers were opening, aerial display (web), spectacle (spec), ménage (European name for animal act), and finale. I danced in four of them.

During spec practice Barstow was at his best...with me!

"You there, your right foot, not your left. Somebody tell me her name. Put out your right foot. NOOOOOOO. For Christ's sake... the right foot. WHY do I have to work with these people...?" I couldn't take his humiliation and couldn't stand in front of him anymore. I ran to Danny.

"Did you (sob) hear him (sob) yelling at me? He's worse than a wicked witch." I sobbed blowing my blubbering nose into a tissue.

"No, I was out back," he answered. "You'll get the hang of it. Just do what he says."

"No! I'll never be able to dance. I don't even put the right foot out." I wept louder looking for any sign of sympathy. Nothing. Dealing with Barstow was my problem.

Occasionally Barstow showed a dance step to a cast member. When he hovered near me with his wispy-grey hair and dusty-blue eyes, I always felt he was an insect, i.e., a praying mantis in expensive, yet gaudy clothing. Besides choreographing Broadway shows, his claim to fame was staging the Ringling Bros. Circus. A once a year job.

No amount of Dick Barstow's humiliation or my tears of frustration made my feet dance. My heart simply wasn't in it. I wasn't afraid of elephants and wanted to ride them not dance in ménage.

* * *

The elephant master, Hugo Schmitt, assigned me Siam, a large, mature Asian elephant. Predictable easy-going Siam and I worked together in the center ring with four other elephants of descending sizes. Donna Welsh Gautier, the assistant elephant trainer's wife, also in center ring, did the leg carry, full body cover, and foot-on-face tricks. "I went to school with your sister, Lucy,"

Donna said, smiling at me. "We were in Sailor Circus together." Donna and I became friends.

German-born Hugo Schmitt trained elephants for the Ringling show since WWII. His concern for his four sons and wife, all living in Sarasota, impressed me. He was somewhat of a substitute for my dad's attentions. Noticing his need for a trim, I told him during rehearsals, "I cut hair, Hugo."

"Ya. Gut. Kum after elephant practice. Ya?" Infrequently getting off the lot, stocky built Hugo was a satisfied two-dollar customer.

* * *

I gave no thought of where my act costumes would go until Danny ceremoniously presented me a small black-and-red Taylor trunk during rehearsals. I followed him under the bleachers to where he stopped at one of the rectangular trunks that came from our house. He told me earlier that Taylor, a locksmith, designed a flat recessed lock for a flat-topped trunk that stacked evenly and outdated round-topped trunks.

"Fix it up for the season with oil cloth (vinyl) and paint on the lower left hand corner of the lid the letters WDR for Women's Dressing Room," I opened the trunk and saw a tray with compartments and below that, a storage area.

"Oh, thank you, Danny," I responded with affection, patting the opened trunk lid.

"I'll get you a key," he said, walking away from the trunk and me.

I put make-up, costumes, towel, and soap in my trunk along with a blanket and pillow for Ivy's nap. It was important to me to glue a small picture of a sailor steering a ship in a storm on the inner lid of the tray. I'd had it since Palm Sunday in second grade when my church teacher gave it to me and said, "Jesus is helping pilot the ship. Jesus gives hope and love." *Guide me, Jesus, through the Ringling Circus*, I prayed in silence looking at the sailor's hands firmly gripping the ship's wheel. If life was a storm, then I needed to let Jesus calm me when I worked. Unlike some performers who crossed themselves and kissed their St.

Christopher medals before they worked, my trunk was my sanctuary and I cared for it tenderly.

Danny came back during break saying, "Here's your key. And a trunk rack to hang your costumes. Unscrew it at the joints and make a canvas bag to carry it in."

"Do you want a bag too?"

"Nah, I don't use one," he said, disappearing again.

The trunk set me apart from showgirls, despite dressing in their common area. Initially, I slid quietly next to my trunk at least until Araceli Baumann, a showgirl and Charley Baumann's wife, insisted I loudly greet others with, "Hello everyone!" or "Good night all!" at least once a day. Not having learned common courtesy words from my family or the Chapman's I wondered, *Can't I just appear and disappear as I've always done?* I didn't see the need for it at the time, but thanks, Araceli, for your socialization tip.

* * *

After a month of rehearsals and dress rehearsals, the Blue Unit opened in the bleak Venice Arena. The happenstance building painted a dull blue inside and out, missed simple creature comforts like adequate restrooms, dressing rooms, and heat. Despite that the Greatest Show on Earth opened in Venice since 1956.

My trapeze act in the second half of the show followed Charley Baumann's tiger act and preceded Evy and Franz Althoff's riding tiger act.

"The show wants you on single trap." Danny advised me. "You'll have three ladders on either side of it and it will bounce. It's the best they can do," he said, leaving me no voice. We went to the rigging. I looked up at the single mainfall holding the 3"aluminum tubing outrigger 33' off the arena floor. One guy wire at each end of the outrigger steadied the well-loaded beam. Six short-chromed ladders used for the aerial display dangled from it in two equal groups. Between them hung my web and my red single trap on ten-foot manila ropes making me 23' off the floor. Thankfully, heights never bothered me.

"I'll do a still routine and a little swinging," I mumbled discouraged with the set up.

A week later, I thought differently. Every move had an outrigger countermove making the trap jerk in dangerous unpredictable aftershocks. The more it jerked, the tighter I gripped the bar and ropes. Numb with pain I hated it. *Single trap is harder on me than the balancing bar. My calluses tore open, my calves hurt from shin splints and rope burns. I don't care if I do a trap act.*

"My rigging isn't safe. I wear bandages and undertights. These ugly sores are not healing," I complained to Danny.

"Don't you know? Stars are made not born," he cryptically replied, through tightened clown lips. He turned his back saying, "I'll be in Clown Alley."

Alone at the back stage curtain, I felt helpless with the all-or-nothing situation. One dismal thought repeated through my anger, lodging in my brain, *It's not easy being married to Danny.* Lost and confused, I headed to wardrobe.

Circus wounds are promptly treated. Years before, Lucy mixed powdered sulfa with petroleum jelly and packed it into torn calluses. "Cut away any loose skin with cuticle scissors," she explained, bevel trimming her palm. "New skin starts growing in two or three days. Wrap with adhesive tape for shows and soak your hands in soapy dishwater at night. Rub again with sulfa and let it air." Her formula worked.

* * *

"We're signing the contract after finale," Danny told me prior to pushing me up my single trap web for the last Venice show. I was instantly angry. *He tells me now? In the arena?* Angry throughout my act, I slid down my web, and my lid came undone. "I have to sign a contract? It's closing night," I groaned through clenched teeth squeezing the web until my knuckles whitened. Every muscle in my body ached from four grueling weeks of rehearsals and the opening shows.

"Yes, it's fixed. They need you to sign. Meet me at the office upstairs."

Clowns and showgirls waited ahead and behind us in line, in the darkened office stairwell. Danny quietly explained the offer. "Our contract is made out to The Aerial Chapmans. We're getting

Hans Hermann on the show as a clown. He doesn't have a green card. Pay is weekly: I get $250, producing clown salary; Hans $155; and you have $135. That's the beginning salary for clowns and showgirls."

I stomped my foot on the wooden stairs and bit my tongue while doing the math. The alternative was screaming and running away. Taking a deep breath, I held my anger in check when I answered. "Our joint salary is more than a two-person act, but less than a producing clown and an aerial act combined. You and I don't do a comedy aerial act. It's a false premise."

"The show is overlooking that. Just sign the contract. That's all you have to do," Danny ordered angrily as if I was a robot. We both knew all the standard clauses regarding general usefulness applied and any omissions in the standard AGVA contract were included in the RBB&B Rider.

"I'm an act but only getting showgirl salary AND doing production," I whispered, as we approached a desk where Hans waited for us. With heavily weighted breaths, I scribbled my name and briskly left the office without looking at anyone, especially Danny. *It's fixed, he said. Robbery is more like it.*

* * *

In Knoxville, the first road date after leaving Venice, I was miserable. I missed having Ivy with me during the long performances. Danny's "No kids in the building" rule forced me to accept Bumpsy Anthony's wife, Eva Mae, as her baby-sitter. I adored Bumpsy's clown persona—an easy going, long-necked sidewalk superintendent. His equally patient partner tolerated Ivy's terrible twos.

Looking back, I would have earned as much being only a showgirl on RBB&B. My body would have suffered less. When the rope burns on my lower legs turned bright red, I finally told Danny to ask about substituting my balance trap.

"Just move the clamps from the outrigger to the frame."

"I'll talk to Jack," Danny warily replied.

Jack Joyce, Blue Unit Performance Director, looked the part of a trim executive. He wore a black tux, and gold wire-rimmed glasses, his grey hair groomed to perfection. Danny huddled with Jack and the boss rigger leaving me out. I heard the boss rigger's objections, "Her balance trap weighs too much and has to be hung from the flying frame on top of the tiger cages."

Jack nodded his head, listening to them both. "No one should be working over the tiger cages." Then he waved me over to join the group. "Show me your legs," he said in a fatherly tone. He winced at the cherry red abrasions. "Can you substitute your balance trap?"

"Yes, I can. Thank you, Mr. Joyce." Triumphant, I realized I'd won. *It's okay to talk to bosses. Not everything Danny tells me is true.* My legs and hands healed quickly after the switch. Fate, with a push from me, landed my balancing trapeze on The Big One. Eight years perfecting an act on a two-by-forty-inch metal bar paid out.

* * *

In Mobile, the next town, Danny took charge of my new act. "Your rigging's up. You'll want to practice." I climbed the web and stood on the bar. Danny bantered while I surveyed the arena. "Try out the new location; become familiar with the setting. Look around the seats. Find your focus points. Get acclimated to the height. I told the lighting man to keep the spotlights out of your eyes. You get two of them."

I choose to look straight in front of me and to my left shoulder with both points at least 100 feet away. I knew I'd be looking directly at one person or an empty seat in each direction and hoped they understood my staring. Satisfied, I felt confidence settle on my shoulders and in my feet. *Hmm...I've come along way since clowning here in 1965.*

I slid down the web to the arena floor. "Can I have yellow and pink spot lights? Those colors make me feel warm." White spotlights strained my eyes and bleached my skin.

I adapted to my graceful trapeze and found focal points in each new building. Balancing took total concentration with all the music, moving tiger cages below, and arena noises blocked out of my mind.

* * *

Danny smoked three packs of cigarettes a day during Clown College and everything about him reeked of nicotine. A non-smoker, it wasn't hard to distance myself. I noticed an unopened pack of Pal Mals on the trailer countertop for several days. "Are you going to smoke these?"

"Haven't you noticed? I quit smoking when we left Venice," he replied, a smug grin on his face, coffee mug in hand.

"No, I haven't. I see you eating sunflower seeds when we travel." Not smoking on the long road trips was hardest for him. Grey and white sunflower hulls never bothered me as much as second-hand smoke.

CHAPTER FOURTEEN
SECOND HALF

"The show asked me to go to Louisville because I'm the producing clown. They're doing a feature story on one of the clowns," Danny told me in Tulsa, three months into the season. "We can take the train and have the trailer dropped off in Little Rock, the date after Louisville. I've asked Michele to sleep in the girls' car while we're in the compartment. She said she would put her stuff in the closet."

It was a hard lesson learning the conditions for the majority of people on the train. First was taking the show bus back and forth to the building. Working men, performers, clowns, and showgirls all paid the fare. Occasionally a group of friends pooled together and hired a taxi. Certain staff and performers had the luxury of the show transporting their cars overland on the train. Others paid clowns to drive their car from city to city.

After the last night show, Danny, Ivy, and I boarded the bus to the train carrying clothing to last four days. Our compartment had nothing set aside. "What shall we do?"

"Put Michele's stuff on the top bunk. I'll sleep below and you and Ivy can have the floor," Danny said unplugging her stereo and TV. As he worked, I changed Ivy into pajamas and headed to the toilet at the end of the car. I screeched like a fishwife, "There's no running water and the donniker (toilet) stinks! We're stuck."

"You brought a bucket, didn't you?" Danny asked, sounding tired.

"Luckily, yes."

I was immensely unhappy camping on the train those four days. When the incoming Louisville circus train arrived in Little Rock, the pink and white Frolic never looked as good as when I unlocked the door. "I'll never stay on the train again," I said to myself and wondered, *Why do we pay for a compartment we'll never use?*

* * *

From Little Rock, we journeyed to El Paso, Texas where I found an authentic Mexican restaurant. Daddy spent two years in El Paso during WWI. Looking at the colony of adobe homes surrounding the building, I didn't think much had changed.

I reported to wardrobe to adorn my sequined go-go dress for ménage. "You're not riding today," the wardrobe mistress, Mrs. Joe Hodgini said.

"Why not?"

"Your elephant has a sore leg."

I went directly to Hugo. "What's wrong with Siam?"

"A groom pushed a hay fork in her foot. A vet kum. When she goes gut, you can ride."

"Poor, Siam," I said, turning away and wondering if she got Epsom salt soaks.

Siam suffered irreversible blood poisoning that crept up her leg and into her left ear. Lack of circulation slowly decayed the bottom half of her ear lobe. Grooms rubbed thick petroleum on her rotting skin for several months. It made riding dangerous because my left foot slipped on the oily mess and I couldn't use the toehold onto her ear.

"Donna, what shall I do?"

"Hold on to her halter with one hand. And show Mrs. Hodgini your tights," Donna offered. The wardrobe mistress had vinyl boots waiting for me and advice, "Here are extra tights because you'll be washing them often."

* * *

Our Ringling contract rider included the phrase general usefulness that included publicity when asked. Neither Danny nor I minded talking with media, in fact, I felt it was a privilege.

In a casual interview in the 1969 Amarillo *News Globe*, Gloria Denko paints my domesticity. Denko talked to Danny while he put on clown make-up and watched Ivy. I was out with the pickup doing errands.

Denko wrote, "During our conversation about clowning, Chapman's two-year-old daughter, Ivy, had been a sometimes-silent observer to us, offering only an occasional whoop to their dog, Lacie. The television set had been playing all the while, but we hadn't noticed until a shriek from Ivy told us that a film of the circus was on TV. 'Mama!' she shouted, when her mother, Sarah Chapman, appeared in her act high on the trapeze.

"Just then, a car came up behind Chapman's trailer and Sarah, an attractive dark-haired girl, jumped out, excitedly telling him that she had planned 'the best meal for him—lamb chops and broccoli and rice, and we have clean clothes for next week.' "

Each town, including Amarillo, had a circus animal parade from the trains to the show arena including clowns and showgirls riding a variety of vehicles. The one in Amarillo featured vintage cars and I had my camera ready when they passed the lot.

"Wave to me, John! You look nice in your popsy suit. It matches the car." He waved and I pushed the shutter button. Four days later an Amarillo hey rube ended our partnership.

Sunday night as usual Danny and I slept in the Frolic along with the other trailers at the back of the building. When the trailer was hitched and ready to pull off the lot Monday morning, Danny told me out of the blue, "John's in the hospital. Do you want to see him?"

"Yes, I do. Can we go now?"

"I'll take you there," he said, adding, "John's a carouser and bar-hops. He probably got in a knife fight over some woman. I'll stay in the truck with Ivy."

John was in a private room at the hospital. "I'll find my way back to Kentucky. The police didn't press charges." I didn't question or pry further.

After a farewell kiss on his bruised cheek, I gave him the circus parting, "See you down the road." I haven't seen John Seaton since.

* * *

For the next thirteen weeks in Houston, with no days off, the Blue Unit performed at the new Astrohall, a smallish performance building alongside the huge Astrodome stadium. Mel Miller flew in from Sarasota for the show's grand opening party held in the Astrodome. I mingled comfortably with the Hofheinz family. When the party quieted down, Mel lingered with clown after clown and lastly Danny.

He joined me as I dipped a large pink Gulf shrimp in cocktail sauce and said, "Don't you love this seafood, Mel?"

"I do, yes." He looked serious. I stopped shoving food in my face. He patted my hand and continued. "I'm leaving the circus to restore old merry-go-rounds in Savannah. You and Danny are visiting."

"We'll do that," I smiled into his tanned face.

Danny and Mel discussed the future. "I don't want Mel's Clown College job. I don't have control. I'll remain as producing clown. Management can handle discipline," Danny told me later.

In old circus tradition, the producing clown controlled his joeys (clowns), not management. When Mel resigned, both Danny and Mel recommended Bill Ballantine to replace him.[1] Bill stayed with Ringling for the next eight years as Clown College Director.

* * *

My stepdaughters, Deborah and Stephanie, flew to Houston to join us that summer. "We're loaning the trailer to Levoie Hipps,"

---

[1] For 1968-1976 history of Clown College, see *Clown Alley*, Bill Ballantine; 1982; Little Brown and Company. ISBN 0-316-07958-8

Danny said, "His wife is coming from Sarasota. We'll get an apartment in the trailer park." The park closest to the Dome had ancient one-room efficiencies with wilting air-conditioners weakly fending off 100-degree heat and humidity. I lay awake at night hoping a condemnation notice would prompt Danny to find better Houston housing. As I tossed and turned, hasty flights of huge airborne palmetto bugs performed stunts equivalent to Flying Aces, reminding me of Oakairs.

Mother came for a week and stayed in a modern motel room. Our three girls spent all their time with her, swimming in the pool, and seeing the sights, including a visit to the Houston Zoo. Mother never made it to the Astrohall to see the show or witness my act.

* * *

To my consternation, another mother joined the show in Houston, Danny's ex, Joan. She stayed in our train compartment. Michele and other showgirls moved off the train, sharing apartments in Houston. Joan worked in Ladies Wardrobe zipping up show costumes, including mine. She spent minimal time with Deborah and Stephanie.

"None of this makes sense to me, Danny," I angrily spat at him, tightly wrapping my arms around myself. When he didn't respond after several attempts to communicate, I hissed, "If Joan isn't removed from the show, I'll jump off my trapeze!"

My foolish threat motivated Danny to talk with Lloyd Morgan, Sr., the Blue Unit General Manager. We stood in silence outside the makeshift office located in one of the show's metal wagons. Danny got the nod to enter and contrary to his nature he pushed the door open for me.

Not waiting to sit, Danny blurted to Morgan, "Sarah's uncomfortable with Joan here. Did you have to give her a job?"

Morgan finally answered. "The show doesn't limit employment because of relationships with other employees. You can leave the show." Considering our economics, we weren't in a position to leave. The taste of reality hurt me more than Danny.

There was a compromise. "You pay the show for the compartment. Don't approach Sarah when she's in Ladies' Wardrobe," Danny told Joan. I wondered, *Where are Danny's loyalties?*

At the Astrohall, Danny and Ivy posed for a Father's Day photo picked up by the Associated Press. Houston's *Post* magazine featured me in an article. Boldly printed in red letters, *Mama Is the Pretty Lady on the High Trapeze* splashed across a photo of me resting on my knees before I picked up the handkerchief.

Carol Spencer's article accurately recorded the outlook I held at the time: "I'm married to a wonderful man. He was in the ring long before I was. He advises me on the moves and steps I should make. He is the one behind me."

"If Sarah Chapman was not in the circus ring, what would she do?" Carol asked.

"Continue school and take home economics to become an extension agent. It's true that the circus gets in your blood. We both like this business. When I haven't been performing, and go to a circus, I get tears in my eyes when I hear the applause. I want to be out there too, performing with them."

Spencer's introduction was, "Not yet in plumes and sparkling clothes or with a trace of her glamorous make-up on, Sarah Chapman, 23, was about to disappear through blue-curtained dressing room doors. Scissors in hand and a robe thrown on, she looked as though she had just seen a clock. 'I forgot to mention I cut hair. I just finished giving two haircuts.' It was 20 minutes before showtime.

"Without her make-up, Mrs. Chapman with long-black hair and grey eyes, is as naturally pretty as she is glamorous in the circus ring. She also seems to be naturally herself—wherever she is and especially in the ring. . . ."

Nothing could have been further from the truth. I kept my secrets, telling no one of my inner turmoil, telling no one what I really wanted. I didn't tell her I was under a doctor's care, advised to eat bland foods and get more rest. I didn't tell her Danny put every word in my mouth. In addition, she didn't know that no matter what the conditions, Danny coached me with his familiar sentence, "Do the best you can." I never knew if he said that from his heart or mocked me. His old-school ways meant 100% effort all the time. Literally, I was well-oiled human machinery.

* * *

Hot and miserable Texas Gulf Coast weather in July, plus the strenuous daily grind, sapped every ounce of my energy. *I wish I lived inside the building, enjoying the air conditioning.*

Pretty Spanish born, Araceli, was full of life. She cornered me at my trunk with her English girlfriends.

"Don't you think your skirts could be a bit shorter? After all, its 1969," Araceli mentored the others nodding behind her.

"Well, maybe. I'll think about it," I answered slowly, fond of Lucy's hand-me-downs, expensive suits, and dresses. *If I cut six inches off my skirts, they are ruined.* However, before the end of summer, my knees stuck out below all my skirts.

Bill Pruyn, the show's musical director, studied my act. He understood and accepted input from the performers.

"Bill wants to see you about music," Danny mentioned one day between shows.

"I have a song for you. It's *Bess, You Are My Woman* from *Porgy and Bess* the George Gershwin musical. Here's the melody," Bill said playing his backstage portable keyboard as politely as he spoke.

I listened. "Why don't we do it in the show and see how it fits? If anyone can work to the blues, it's me."

Heavy and moving *Bess, You Are My Woman* was better to work to than *Somewhere My Love* or *Spanish Eyes*. Bill was right about the *Bess* music—it added depth to my act, and hence the entire aerial display.

* * *

The occurrence on July 21, 1969, made circus tricks seems minuscule. We don't walk on the moon.

Following a brief announcement, the afternoon show stopped for five minutes while the audience excitedly talked among themselves. Many acts, clowns, and showgirls reverently gathered around a television set up backstage. Young and old, we watched the live transmission of the astronauts planting the American flag on the surface of the moon. The *Houston Post Sports Final* added Moon-Day to the date.

"Tweeeeet," shrilly blew the ringmaster's whistle calling the show back to order.

*　*　*

My husband flippantly quoted facts about our relationship for *Tempo* magazine, a section of the *Houston Post*. "Just my charming personality and the fact that I'm rich—that's why she married me." *Tempo* continued the story, explaining Danny's background. "Danny was an aerialist himself until a fall in Belgium broke his back and grounded him. He first met Sarah at a school for aerialists he was conducting in Florida. Then a gawky teenager, she developed into his star pupil. Four years ago, they were married.

"Now while Sarah soars in the spotlight, Danny is down there in the darkness below, ready with the safety rope (web) if she needs him.

"To the Ringling family, any rival circus is just a 'mud-show.' Even among European circus people, this is 'Big Bertha' or 'The Big One.' Svoboda, the Czech acrobat, may mutter about how much harder he has to work in the American show—the opening, his troupe's act, the spectacle, and the finale. In a European show, he just does his own act and that's it. When he goes home though, he will be able to brag that he has performed with The Big One. It's not a lazy man's life." I, too, felt prestigious on The Big One.

In our third month in Houston my acts changed yet again. "Jack Joyce wants to see you between shows," Danny told me.

"What for?"

"I don't know. Just go."

I was afraid I'd done something bad. Fortunately, I was wrong. "Sarah, you've been taken out of opening and finale," Jack calmly said. "See me before the show and I'll put you in the performers' lineup."

"Thank you, Mr. Joyce," I mumbled, not sure I heard him right. Dazed, a voice inside of me gained strength—grew louder—shouting up to my Daddy. *I'm an act now, not just a showgirl!*

I liked wearing the pink, sequined, European clown-suit and cone-shaped hat for the opening because I carried Danny's oil portrait painted on a circular canvas lashed onto a forty-inch hoop. The patriotic theme and music for the finale were fine too. It was repetitive dancing, an ill-fitting hat, and the stupid umbrella I detested. Now for the opening, I wore my burgundy velvet costume and stood with the other acts behind the curtain. Jack Joyce eyed me, motioned with his arm, and said, "Follow this person." I was last in a long line of performers up the back track. When the line halted, we faced the audience with a two-arm salute. I heard applause. The line continued to the front of the house where we saluted again. I heard stronger applause. My inner voice warmed me, *No dancing Sarah, just smiling*. No one guessed the reason for my smiles and waves to children on the way back to the curtain—*The last shall be first.*

After a few days, the elation I felt over my promotion plummeted. I still worked six numbers. Wearing my personal costumes for the opening and finale was more of a hassle than wearing the show wardrobe. To lift my spirits, I schemed. *I'll make separate costumes for the opening.* Sewing additional wardrobe to keep up with the Ringling stars burdened my schedule. *In time*, I thought, *I'll have elegant gowns, feathered headpieces, and flowing capes.*

* * *

At the end of August, the Blue Unit packed up to continue the rest of the route in Northwestern states and Canada. My stepdaughters and other circus children and non-performing wives flew back to their homes and schools in Sarasota. Joan stayed on the show.

Facing west from the stage door of the Albuquerque, New Mexico arena sat a picturesque mountain. It was there the elegant Austrian-born performer, Evy Althoff, befriended me prior to performing. We chatted and posed for pictures with Tiger, her spotted horse. Evy's groom, Roy, constructed Tiger's thick riding seat and matching neck shield in leather. Protected from claws and teeth, sturdy Tiger allowed a Siberian tiger to jump on and off his back several times during the act.

Smiling, Evy requested, "Please get the mountain in the background."

Between camera clicks, I said, "Roy finished the leather case for my trapeze bar and cables. He did a nice job."

She nodded politely.

I trusted Evy's comments on my wardrobe and wore a new yellow velvet leotard. "How did I do on the headpiece?" I made it from orange, yellow, and gold feathered pom-poms.

"Hmm. Hang yellow ribbons from it. They will flutter."

"Thank you! Who creates your beautiful wardrobe, Evy?"

"Ah, thank you. My sequined dresses come from shops. The show made my white gladiator costume."

Hearing my musical cue, the end of Charley Baumann's tiger act, I bid Evy adieu and proceeded into the arena quickly glancing backwards at the mountain.

* * *

"I asked around about a magic shop in Portland, Oregon," Danny informed me. "The Lloyd Center Mall has one. While I'm shopping you can take Ivy ice-skating in the mall commons. It's where Olympic skaters practice."

Happy to expose Ivy to new things, I rented skates at the rink and laced up hers and mine. Danny took pictures of us on the ice then rudely commented, "Seeing that neither of you are skaters, how about lunch? Someone told me about a country club." He didn't waste a putdown.

Before we left Portland Danny calculated, "We get less money in Canada. The Rider reads: 'Artist to receive 50% of salary in Canadian funds and 50% in American funds.'"

He flopped the contract on the dinette and concluded, "There are a total of twenty-three days in Canada and three pay days. Send the American portion to the bank and keep the Canadian funds for gas, food, and gold."

"Great. I have gold fever. Bill Pruyn collects coins and he told me about some pretty ones. Aren't you glad our debts are paid and we have extra money?" He didn't answer. Besides their beauty and sound investment, the lure of coins added fascination to my nomadic lifestyle.

* * *

An active nightlife existed for the majority of the young people on the show. Going out eluded me for security of husband and home. While the party hardies loosened up, I sewed on new wardrobe, wrote correspondence, parented Ivy, or slept. However, one night Danny and I joined a group of performers at Lulubells, a gold rush-style saloon in Vancouver, British Columbia. I observed my peers playfulness. *What keeps me from dancing, guffawing, and joking?*

* * *

After the Canadian dates the Blue Unit headed south to Duluth, Minnesota playing the new Duluth Entertainment Convention Center (DECC) built alongside the Duluth harbor. When we arrived, Danny and I kept our noontime TV talk-show date.

Later, when I went to the building to set up my trunk and make-up table, several members of a group of male performers Danny called the Mickey Mouse Gang, taunted and threatened me. "You shouldn't have said bad things about Charley Baumann on TV." I knew they liked playing practical jokes but this was going too far.

"I did what?" I asked, perplexed. *Danny prepped me as usual.* "You better go to the studio and see what I said about Charley's act." I glared at them plunking both fists on my hips. I never ad-libbed and slanted all my statements towards marketing to the viewing audience. As Danny's puppet, I provided ordinary information, an upbeat sales talk—nothing more.

I sought out Danny inside the building. "What do they think I said?"

"That Charley's tigers had no teeth or claws."

"Then how do they eat raw meat?" I didn't lie about his cats. The gang rushed to the studio, returned with sour looks, and dropped the malicious rumor. Somewhere hidden in me was a line—crossed by the wrong person I defended it rigorously.

"I'm glad that's cleared up. The show will still use you for publicity," Danny jovially announced.

"Yes, it's an honor doing publicity, even if it takes time away from travel day. I'd never say anything bad about Charley. I think he has a classy act," I said warmly.

***

There were two chases in the show. The tiger chase ran after Charley's act and the skeleton chase went in the first half. Young clowns that liked to run did the chases. One Milwaukee reporter considered the circus' skeleton chase a death warning. It could be if the runner was in poor health. In this fast run-around, done only in spotlights, Joey Matheson encircled the arena chased by a dangling fake skeleton attached by a harness the audience didn't see.

Miles McMillin stated in his *Hello, Wisconsin!* column in the *Madison Journal,* "It (the skeleton chase) was ingenious, it was hilarious, and it was cleverly executed. It had a deeper theme, which I think the kids sensed. For in the circus, death is always hovering about, being taunted by the participants. The circus is where the defiance of death is made a way of life."

I performed perilous work for nineteen years. In response to McMillin's statement, our main goal is to entertain not subconsciously court death. The skeleton chase is pure whimsy. We are entertainers, practiced at our craft, and wouldn't ever endanger our lives or others.

Another Madison columnist saw the circus in a different light. Rosemary Kendrick's article quoted, "If you're a kid, you're likely to be alternately giggling and shrieking, and if you're an adult, you're apt to have several near heart seizures…because of the sheer danger of it all."

***

I didn't hesitate signing my new contract in Portland. An AGVA stipulation gave showgirls a five-dollar-a-week raise making my total $140/week. A second year on the show meant financial security for us, but more importantly, it was the 100th Edition of The Greatest Show on Earth, the Ringling Brothers Barnum & Bailey Circus.

Special productions planned a circus-sized birthday party. It fulfilled me being part of the Ringling show especially the 100th Edition. The past season's hardships slipped away and I dreamed of future glories.

Danny was jubilant too. "The Blue Unit gets the better route including the new Madison Square Garden." Even I knew MSG was the mother lode of buildings. A chill of anticipation ran down my spine.

Most of the 1969 acts, clowns, and showgirls signed up for 1970. The novices were now seasoned veterans. *Next season will be fun.*

The 99th season ended November 16, in Detroit. The 1969 Blue and Red Units were unparalleled in circus history because at a time when the Ringling Circus was in crises, it rose like a golden phoenix bringing renewed energy to staff, performers, and audiences. Our last performance was no different from the first. The show broke down rigging, packed trunks; loaded and carted everything to the train in preparation for our next season.

Rehearsals started December 8 in Venice after a three-week layover.

On the day before Thanksgiving, Danny and I, along with several Ringling Circus performers from Sarasota flew to New York City. Thanksgiving morning thousands saw us on the RBB&B float in Macy's Christmas Parade. I didn't feel as though the season officially ended until the plane landed back in Sarasota.

It was, after all, better than a nine-to-five job.

CHAPTER FIFTEEN
RINGLING YEARS

The many hats I wore for the 100th Anniversary Ringling Circus were performer, mother, wife, cook, barber, and seamstress. Comely photographs hid the continual exhaustion from the performance grind. Weekends don't exist on the circus route.

Just the same, during Venice rehearsals, I stole two hours of winter sunshine and took my active three-year-old to Sarasota's Crescent Beach on Siesta Key. Ivy wiggled down a narrow path, amber-colored sea oats gracefully arching over her head. Following a pace behind her I thought, *I can soften my heart towards Ivy, she's unique. If I'm angry with Danny, I won't victimize her like my mother did to us kids. She has personality, strength, determination. And she's cute.* Sitting together in the white-crystalline-sand revived a childhood rite from years before. I scooped up handfuls drizzling the tiny grains between our legs. She smiled and pointed at the waves washing in and out.

"Okay, we can go to the water." Brushing sand aside I stood up, grabbed her hands, and pulled her to her feet. "Come," I said and walked straight to the water assured she would follow me like a duckling.

We returned to the car holding hands, the sun warming our backsides. I gathered her in my arms at the edge of the pavement and glanced one last time at the water. *Little girl, you are my friend. I'll do my best to guide and enjoy you.*

Ivy's medical check-up came in Sarasota at the end of each season. One year earlier, I asked her pediatrician, Dr. Norman Goldstein, "How do I deal with Ivy? My patience is at an end. I don't want to hit her as my mother hit me."

Dr. Goldstein's solution: "Count to ten. Wait until you cool off. At naptime and bedtime, read her stories. All she needs is time and love."

"Thank you, Dr. Goldstein," I laid my hand upon his sleeve in gratitude. "What would Sarasota do without you?"

I nurtured Ivy with books, time, and love. I gave my stepdaughters gifts, seldom disciplined, and asked for nothing in return. I hoped they would help at home when they were older. That didn't happen. However, step parenting made me a better parent.

1970 RBB&B Blue Unit
Venice Rehearsals

Ringling Brothers Circus edged both Red and Blue Unit route cards in gold. They also minted two collector coins. One was aluminum, the size of a quarter, and given away free. "How many uncirculated one-ounce silver coins are you buying?" Danny asked.

"I bought one—number fifty-four. I'm hanging the aluminum token on my charm bracelet."

Danny identified some changes when we started Venice rehearsals. The Centennial Show motif spanned old-fashioned to modern acts. Irvin Feld contracted the King Charles Troupe from Harlem, the Poldi's from Czechoslovakia, clown Otto Greibling, Antalek chimps, Stephenson's dogs, Rogana, Fattini, the Petrovs, and Venice's flying family, the Gaonas to the show. Mario Gaona performed in my display on his trapeze dangling over the back track. He juggled hoops, swung back and forth, and finished with a revolving spin all while balancing on his head. I've never met a more genial man than Mario Gaona.

Feld revamped the production numbers. Hugo's Blue Unit elephants danced to *Those Were the Days* and showgirls draped gold necklaces on pink and blue Gypsy-style ankle-length dresses with matching coin-decorated hats. Festive tambourines accented the music and styling cues. Elephant riders donned knee-length dresses and rose-colored ballet slippers. Siam's ear healed and I didn't wear boots.

Hugo searched for me in the damp arena and said, "Kum. I show you som ting."

"What is it, Hugo?"

"You see." I followed him alongside to the sunlit barns. There in a hay-bale-crib no bigger than a card table stood a thin, hairy, baby Indian elephant. Axel Gautier protectively stood up when we approached.

"Axel, I show Sarah the baby," Hugo told his assistant. Turning to me he gestured toward the small animal.

"Go ahead. Pick her up. One day you tell your children you pick up an elephant."

"She's so delicate," I said, not wanting to disappoint Hugo, awed with my special privilege.

Axel spoke, "She was orphaned. They flew her from India in a wooden crate." He stepped aside. "Bend down and grab her legs. She's heavier than she looks."

"I'll try," I said, stepping into her crib and lowering myself next to her tepid frame. With one surge of muscles, I lifted the petite pachyderm an inch or two from the ground. "That's enough, little baby. I want you to grow big and strong. Axel, what does she eat?"

"We'll bottle feed her as long as possible," Axel stood at a table measuring drops into a blender pitcher. His eyes sagged with lack of sleep like a new father. "Bananas, cereal, vitamins, and formula. Her appetite's improving." He poured the mixture into a quart bottle and attached a long rubber nipple. "I've been by her side since I picked her up in Tampa." That meant he slept next to her and hadn't been home.

"Oh thank you, Hugo, for letting me meet her. What's her name?"

"Her name is Karen, after Mr. Feld's daughter. Yah, we call her Baby Karen."

"Welcome to the circus, Baby Karen." I said touching her fuzzy skull and letting her sniff my forearm with her trunk. "You're safe here. I'll visit you during rehearsals."

Karen soon followed Hugo around the lot and in the arena.

* * *

"Stop! Everybody stop! That darling baby is making her first appearance anywhere. Hugo, bring her to me." Barstow cooed. Karen sniffed his hand and patted his chest with her nose. He was a rehearsal god and we did what god wanted by waiting until he said, "Okay, back to work. Now, where were we on the aerial ballet? Oh, yes, bicycles built for two…"

We were at the point where twenty-eight of us women dismounted our bicycles, peeled off green and white-stripped pantaloons, jackets, spats, and hat; then climbed the short distance to chromed ladders. The show assigned Leon McBride, a new Clown College graduate, to sit my web. He easily pushed me up the web and even smiled.

I didn't miss Hans Hermann's putdown, "You feel like a sack of potatoes." Danny told people I was big and fat, but not in front of me. I didn't need Han's negative input too.

The centerpiece of the aerial display was Elvin Bale's elegant swinging trapeze, topped off with his forward rollover heel catch. The Bale family hailed from Venice, Florida and, except for Elvin, they were all horse trainers including his twin sister. Elvin and I shared mutual admiration for each other and our aerial work and more so when we discovered we were the same age.

The spectacle parade ending the first half was a living 100-year history lesson of the Ringling Circus starting in P.T. Barnum's day when circuses had sideshow freaks-of-nature and human oddities including exotic dancers and royalty from foreign lands, like India.

***

"Sarah," Richard Barstow called me over to him before I ducked under the bleachers to work on my trunk, "I've picked out something nice for you in spec."

"Oh...really?" I warily responded.

"Yes! I'm not telling. You'll have to go to wardrobe and see for yourself." He crunched up his mouth, dipped both knees, and pranced off with microphone in hand. Maybe he admired my contribution to the show—I always smiled.

"Sarah Chapman, report to wardrobe," blurped the loud speaker. I imagined myself in a ridiculous outfit.

To my wonderment, Mel Cabral said, "Hold out your arms. We didn't have your measurements. I had to estimate." He transferred a jewel-encrusted floor-length dress to my arms. Astonished, I guessed the weight at nearly twenty pounds.

I lugged the gold brocaded dress and the attached underskirt to a changing room. "Someone, please, zip me up," I hollered. Mel whisked in, zipped up the form-fitting bodice, and threw the curtain aside.

"Lovely, just lovely. I want Don to see," Mel murmured. He grabbed my wrist and led us to the worktables where Don Foote had his arms and hands spread out on a thickly jeweled elephant blanket.

Don righted and seeing me lost his frown. "You're our maharani and your maharaja will be here anytime. There's your hat and you carry a feathered fan." He wagged his finger at me. "Your white egret feathers weren't easy to find." He leaned over, picked something up off the table, and held up a shimmer. "Would you glue a red sequin to your forehead, please?" Don, the fussy new costume designer helped me bond with the show.

"You sit in a howdah. I thought you could wave to the audience. Let's see how you do that." I showed him my 'regal' wave.

Emil Svoboda joined us, as my maharaja. I thought his height and proud demeanor perfect for the part.

"Let me see you and Emil." We stood together in character. "Ooh, nice! Mmm, great." Don inhaled, placing one hand to his cheek and the other at his waist, while comparing our live modeling to his nearby design sketch.

The tight bodice and long sleeves prevented me from raising my arms higher than my shoulder. "Will you let this out a little?" I asked Mel gingerly.

"We don't have any extra fabric for that dress, do we Don? Don?" Mel's question was lost to his partner, who was absorbed in conversation with Hugo over elephant blanket fastenings.

I removed the queenly garment thinking, *I'll alter the dress myself. The sketch showed a third elephant carrying a jeweled chest. What an honor representing the show in the India section. I'm not dancing! Goodie.*

These two designers from Brooks-Van Horne Costumes gave their all to the show like us performers. They didn't give any thought to me getting in the elephant howdah in the bulky dress. It didn't occur to me either until I went to mount the first time. Kudos to Don, the show, and probably Barstow for making me queen for a season, a role I loved playing.

* * *

While it was hard to see my position in this massive circus, I recognized the importance of other acts like the Gaonas of flying fame. Tito, the triple-revolving son, stole the heart of countless young female and male fans with his broad smile, gestures of manliness, and muscular physique. The Gaona flying act was really a lofty symphony highlighted by the blindfolded passing leap and Tito's encores. It was a pleasure watching their graceful turns and twists high in mid-air with the security of a safety net below.

* * *

Once the opening, aerial ballet, spec, and ménage went without snags, Barstow worked the glitches out of the elaborate show finale, a circus-sized pink and white birthday celebration with a mechanical cake sporting enormous sparkle-shooting candles.

During rehearsals, Jack Joyce's wife, Ethel, shared, "We're cake decoration."

"Yes, I don't mind wearing finale show wardrobe because I

stand next to you. Anna Matarrese is on my other side." The costumes were pink—a plus.

"Oops," Ethel shushed between closed teeth and a false smile, "Dick won't see us talking this way."

"Now. All you ladies and gentlemen are going to leave the arena and the cannon comes in. Cannon! Cannon? You can come in now. Oh, finale is not going to work. I can't do this job if no one cooperates with me," Dick yelled fretfully pacing back and forth. He stopped, made fists at his sides, closed his eyes and took two deep breaths raising his shoulders each time. "Ten minutes everyone. Take ten minutes until the people, who are supposed to be helping me, get this straightened out." Frustrated he swung the microphone into the belly of his assistant, Bill Bradley, plopped down in his director's chair, dropped his head back, and assessed the situation as only Dick Barstow could.

Presented after the birthday cake, the Zacchini cannon act stretched the show to three hours. When the arena was set with the huge net, my Sailor Circus buddy Emanuel "Lolly" Zacchini and his vivacious red-haired wife, Linda, walked in together to the double-barreled cannon. White leather suits and helmets simulated astronauts. When Papa Zacchini properly positioned the cannon, he gave the all clear signal for Linda and Lolly's descent into their respective cylinders. The ringmaster stressed ear protection to the audience before two simultaneous deafening booms ricocheted in the building. First Linda, then Lolly shot out in graceful arcs to the waiting net and cheering circus goers. It was the consummate conclusion to the Centennial show.

* * *

Before rehearsals ended, my brother Merritt stopped by the arena to give me a present. "Here, you can make something with this. I got it on my property," he said, handing me a tanned five-foot-long rattlesnake skin.

"Thanks, do you want a belt?"

"No, I'm wearing my favorite belt. Why don't you make one for that man who made you cry last year?"

"Mr. Barstow?" My eyes couldn't help squinting.

"Yes. Make him a snakeskin belt with the rattle on it. That way you're biting him back," he said with a wink.

"Good idea. I'll buy purple leather and glue and stitch the snakeskin to it. Purple is his color."

About a week later, I handed a wrapped gift to Dick Barstow. He gazed at it cautiously, and then said, "Chocolate covered cherries?"

"No, I wouldn't give you candy," I said, and left him.

When I arrived at rehearsals the next morning, I heard a familiar voice clear out to the parking lot. "Sarah Chapman! Sarah Chapman! Sarah. Sarah. Sarah. Where are youuuuuu?" Dick careened into the microphone.

"Dick wants you. You'd better get out there," Danny warned, not knowing the director's fuss.

When I presented myself front and center, Dick looked at me as if I was dessert, and he was going to take a bite. Instead, he cooed, "Look, Sarah," and flexed his hips side to side shaking the rattle. "It's my birthday, and I'm wearing your present." I was speechless.

We did first half and second-half run-throughs of the show, then followed that with a full dress rehearsal. Barstow seemed pleased over the opening shows in Venice and returned to his home in New York.

* * *

The Blue Unit hit the road in nearby St. Petersburg where crews filmed the annual television special. I wanted new silks. "Please take me with you to the next magic shop," I told Danny at the curtain to Clown Alley.

"You gave up trying to sew silks?" I nodded. He acknowledged it without an argument. "There's one coming up in West Palm."

"Thanks. I need white, yellow, pink, orange, and green."

Up the east coast we went refining the show in several Southern cities before the Madison Square Garden opening. With the excellent additions to the Blue Unit, the 100th Edition was as close to impeccable as any circus ever presented.

In Jacksonville, Florida, one terrifying detail tarnished that perfection. Danny saw me several times throughout the show, so it was odd when, in the dressing room after finale of the first show a woman called out, "Danny's here for you." I threw on my robe and went to the door. I saw his face under his clown makeup. It looked crushed.

"Emanuel hit Linda in mid air. They're both hurt. I saw it happen," Danny whispered pulling me to a side-entrance of the arena where emergency crews frantically worked safely lowering two immobile bodies to the arena floor. Linda and Lolly resembled bugs on an automobile grill.

"Where is the audience?" I asked, looking at the empty seats.

"The show told them to leave and they're not letting anyone in until the arena's cleared. I went out to work the crowd, but it was hopeless. Emanuel hit Linda when she bounced up from the net. There's been a miscalculation."

Together we stood watching our friends carted to separate ambulances.

"Ivy! We have to check on Ivy!" I gasped.

"I'm staying here to be of help," Danny said, casting his eyes down, mimicking his tramp persona.

At the end of the evening show Danny explained, "The net the cannon act uses was left outside the building. Because it wasn't at room temperature, the webbing was tighter and bounced Linda higher than normal. Lolly's shot didn't allow time for either of them to adjust."

"Something as unseen as the air can make or break your act," I murmured.

"That's right." Danny nodded. "You have to know everything that can go wrong."

Within a week, friends of the Zacchini's shot out of the cannon. Lolly, badly bruised, fared far better than Linda. She broke her neck and leg, her recovery took all season.

* * *

The show hired an experienced publicity staff. Some assigned to us became part of our extended family. We exchanged holiday greetings and followed their media careers. These men and women obliged my children and me, ushering us in and out of television studios, radio newsrooms, and newspaper interviews at the lot.

When the media asked, "Do you practice a lot?"

I memorized a reply, "Not any more because balance doesn't leave my body. My daily show is my practice. I check my rigging at each building for an unusual focal point. That depends on where the spotlights shine on me."

One article expounded; "An aerialist in flaming red tights twined her body in a rope high over an end ring and went through various twists and turns. The aerialist came down and made a big loop in the base of the rope. Her three year-old daughter, Ivy, sat in the loop and swung back and forth."

CHAPTER SIXTEEN
TOURING

The Felds included a traditional sideshow at the Madison Square Garden run. Mel Miller helped assemble several human oddities, including a fire-eater, sword swallower, midgets, and a tattooed woman, all of whom displayed their skills in an area near the animals and on the same level as the circus.

I dressed early for the elaborate show opening wearing a new burgundy velvet floor-length gown, with my matching coque-feathered headpiece and boa. I wandered back to greet Siam. On the way, I noticed a lineup of horse drawn carriages not belonging to the circus. Each carriage held a well-known celebrity. I spied someone I recognized from watching television and knew exactly what to say.

"Hello Mr. Sullivan. I've always wanted to be on your show. Now you're on mine. It's great having you here." I smiled broadly, shaking Ed Sullivan's hand. His size and posture reminded me of Daddy.

Walking ahead to the next carriage, I stuck out my arm. "Mr. Armstrong, may I shake your hand?"

"Call me Satchmo, young lady. I want you to meet my wife."

"It's an honor. Thank you both. My father introduced me to your music. Good-bye now. Enjoy the show!"

Our ringmaster blew the opening whistle and the 100th Edition got underway.

Each performer lightly stepped through the opened back door to perform for 14,000 circus goers, all eager for the famous Ringling Circus's new offerings. That included me. Briskly smiling and waving to the audience, I thought, *I didn't make the Ed Sullivan Show, but I'm on The Big One.*

* * *

Prior to working the Garden, the publicity department chose me from the Blue Unit women to present a Spanish web routine for the annual Ringling mini-circus filmed at the NBC studio in NY. Blind to the significance of it, I treated it like any other publicity even if it was for *The Tonight Show* starring Johnny Carson. I asked Hugo which elephant he was taking.

"Baby Karen, she fits in the elevator," he replied like a proud papa.

On filming day I was distressed then elated. "I can't sit your web at *The Tonight Show* because I'm taping a show with Betsy Palmer at CBS," Danny told me. "Another clown is sitting for you in his clown suit," I squirmed at the thought, preferring Danny to anyone.

A low ceiling put my routine about six feet from Johnny's desk. Lingering backstage afterwards, I heard Johnny say something allied to, "Do all circus women have those legs?" His comment then and on re-runs brought a grin to my face.

My main interest at the NBC Studio was Graham Kerr, Johnny's guest. "Mr. Kerr, I watch your television show daily. I love it. I want to meet you. Please," I said for the third try at his dressing room door, wanting his agent to let me in. The door didn't open.

* * *

We parked the Frolic in an Esso gas station at West 38th Street and Eight Avenue during our engagement in Manhattan. "The show says we can move to the trains near the river's edge. The security won't be as tight," Danny announced.

"It's good here. The Garden and shopping is near, you go to the Italian bakery for round loaves of bread every day," I said.

"In that case, we'll stay. No one else wants to go either," he replied, moving out of my way as I made breakfast for Ivy and me. I didn't tell him I often gazed at a red neon publishing house icon atop a nearby skyscraper. "*Sesame Street* is on," I gently told blanket-clad Ivy. Those enchanting words roused her from deep sleep for thirty-minutes of intent television watching. Later, Danny supervised Ivy's outdoor play and I watched Graham Kerr's delectable show, *The Galloping Gourmet*. At the end of each show, he invited an audience member to share the tempting cuisine. Alone, in front of the TV, my mouth savored each bite without sitting opposite Kerr. His message was enjoy the food when it's ready and forget the mess in the kitchen.

Later in the season, a newspaper article quoted me. "You get authentic recipes at the circus; goulash, couscous, spaghetti, paella." Besides preparing daily meals for my family, I enjoyed certain snacks in each city. After trips to Macy's, the closest department store to the Garden, I'd pick up a marvelous calzone at a tiny storefront near the building. In all my exploring, I've never matched the same taste of sauce, bread, cheese, and meat.

* * *

"You'll like Boston," Danny told me on the next jump. "We park by the trains in the North End. It's the elite area of Boston. I'll take you on a walking tour."

Ivy and I followed him on historic trails to Old North Church, the USS Constitution, and The Boston Common.

He announced another mission, "I want you to have lunch in a tea room and go shopping in Filine's Basement."

"Do I have too?" I said wrinkling up my nose afraid of going on my own.

"Yes, it will be fun. Ask a girlfriend to go with you. Maybe Olga or Anna Matarrese."

They weren't available and I went alone. Later I insisted Danny take Ivy and me to the Union Oyster House for baked stuffed lobster. He preferred steamed blue crabs and cod fish cakes from street vendors.

On travel days we often stopped at landmarks and historical sites. "The show's going south to Hampton, Virginia, and we're taking the Chesapeake Bay Bridge, it's located at the end of a series of islands and barrier reefs protecting Chesapeake Bay. The seafood there is famous and you get to pick out a place for lunch," tour director, Danny explained. "If we order something good, try to guess the ingredients so you can make it at home."

We stayed overnight in a Chincoteague trailer park and explored the next morning. "Chincoteague is intriguing and quaint. Marguerite Henry wrote *Misty*, a book about a wild pony from Assateague Island. Can we drive there to see the ponies?" I asked.

"Yes, let's have lunch first. Nothing compares to Chesapeake Bay oyster stew."

* * *

During our Philadelphia engagement Danny said, "We put 14,000 miles on the pick-up truck last season. It needs replacing. I found a dealer outside the city and arranged to buy a heavy-duty model with my specifications." I agreed it was better to buy a new truck and be problem free than fix the old one. I didn't even question how much it cost or think I had a say in how we spent our money. My role was writing out the checks, balancing statements, and occasionally reporting to Danny. I hadn't begun to think I belonged in a freedom march and wouldn't have known equality if it came to me on a platter.

"The new truck is good Danny. I hope to have a camper for Deborah and Stephanie when they come this summer. It's important they have their own space." He took the hint and ordered a custom camper for our ghastly mustard-yellow truck, a popular color that year. I welcomed the girls' arrival in Nashville and felt the warmth of family intactness.

Danny drove south as we jumped to hot Dallas, Texas. Mrs. Sue Sutherland, my Sullins College roommate's mom, invited us to dinner at her home to meet Shelley's family. She also arranged a *Dallas Morning Star* article documenting a typical day unfolding for the Chapman family.

When Mrs. Sutherland came to the show she asked for a favor. "Sarah, I know you sew. Will you make Shelley a wool outfit and take it to her when the show goes to Denver?"

"Yes, give me an idea of what you want, please." I replied. I pondered a moment before continuing. "I love Shelley. I admire her for finishing her education. While she's in school, I'm raising a family in show business. That's an education of sorts, isn't it?"

"Absolutely," Mrs. Sutherland responded, returning Ivy to me.

I saw friends or family in a variety of states, correspondence making it possible. Danny, on the other hand, generally immersed himself in the day-to-day circus action.

"We're spending half of July and all of August in California. I've arranged for us to go to the Magic Castle in Hollywood with a group of clowns. The kids aren't going; I'll get a sitter," Danny told me looking at our new route card. He continued, "The menu is different, and I want you to keep an open mind."

"Okay, I'll try."

My place that night was Mrs. Danny and not Sarah Chapman. Indulging myself, I tossed bra aside and wore an emerald silk mini-dress slit down the front to my diaphragm. I pulled my long hair into a bun at the nape of my neck, added gold earrings, black heels, and black purse. The castle, really a Victorian house surrounded by trees atop a knoll, turned out to be a restaurant and tourist Mecca for wannabe magicians and clowns. Mostly it enthralled anyone star-studded enough to go there.

Glazed eyes of warm bite-size snails looked at me from an appetizer plate. "Dip it in garlic butter," Danny whispered stabbing one with a cocktail fork, hoping I followed his example. "Well?" he looked my way after I swallowed.

"They're chewy. I prefer raw oysters," I said, to his relief. We enjoyed the next course, cheese fondue with meat kabobs, better.

"How did you like the castle?" Danny asked, removing his necktie after we left.

147

"It was so-so. Touring with Katie Zacchini on Hollywood Boulevard will be more fun," I replied nonchalantly. That said, we slept 'til morning.

* * *

The show played the Los Angeles Forum, Long Beach, Anaheim, San Diego, and San Francisco. Then most of the circus children returned home for school. Before Deborah and Stephanie's departure, we enjoyed San Francisco's sights: Golden Gate Bridge, Fisherman's Wharf, and Chinatown. All five of us leaped onto a trolley car.

With the girls gone, Danny announced, "Everyone's going to Finocchio's after the Friday show.

"What's Finocchio's?"

"A stage show where female impersonators sing and dance."

"You mean it's a bunch of men dressed as women?"

"Yes, they're in drag."

"I'll go. I might not want to stay." The show was better than I expected. I know Danny liked it, but I'm not sure why.

* * *

Our Midwestern city stops included a ten-day stand at Chicago's historic International Amphitheater, located next to the stockyards. The 11th Ward Democratic Organization bought out one show and hung political banners from every balcony rail. The highpoint of the night was guest of honor, Mayor Richard M. Daley.

"Danny, its hard working to this crowd. They're unruly and don't sit still. I won't be able to concentrate," I said, concerned for my act.

"Just do the best you can," he jeered, disregarding my comment.

I buried my face in my boa. *Urrr, I hate it when he says that. Why do I bother to tell him what I think? Maybe this noisy show is how it was for the Christians fed to the lions.*

The agonizing contract signing for the upcoming 1971 season took a toll out of me. Standing in line at the Amphitheater and waiting our turn, Danny prepped me, "Hans doesn't want to clown anymore. He's working concessions and his name won't be on our contract."

"Right," I said. I walked with him through the open door of a gray room with a single light bulb dangling above a well-worn-wooden desk and four-metal folding chairs. I signed quickly when I saw the $35 raise for me, giving us a total of $450 per week.

Staying alongside Danny, I advanced him to a vacant corner and hummed, "I got a nice raise."

"All the showgirls got the same raise. Its part of the union contract," he grumbled, not knowing I wasn't aware of the increase.

"You mean I got more money because of the showgirls?"

"That's right."

"Then why do you get $275, producing clown salary, when you're not the producing clown?" I asked, running out of patience and feeling cheated with the concocted contract.

"So I get the maximum amount taken out for Social Security. It's important to pay FICA taxes the last seven years before I retire."

"Oh," I backed off knowing no circus offered pensions or retirement plans. I forgot my salary frustration for the time being. *There is much to Danny I don't get.*

Two years on the Ringling Blue Unit breathed life into Danny and me, enhancing our creativity and enriching our performance endurance, flexibility, and determination. The 100th Edition fulfilled what management envisioned, due partly to new enthusiastic clowns, spicy productions, sparkling wardrobe, jazzy modern music, thrilling acts, and breathtaking daredevils. An example of the latter was petite Elizabeth Andrekov, sweetly standing on the flying-act pedestal board at the beginning of the second half of the show. Her startling, yet graceful twenty-foot plunge into darkness below ended in the waiting arms of her strong male partners. No matter what circus magnet pulled all the individuals together, the heartbeats of the Blue Unit performers kept it running.

CHAPTER SEVENTEEN
CLASS ACT

1971 RBB&B Red Unit

Returning to Sarasota in December 1970, Danny summarized two Blue Unit seasons. "In '69 we hit twenty-eight cities in fifteen states and three provinces. This year we did forty-four cities in twenty-one states." Then he primed me for the change. "I've heard scuttle butt that we might be transferred to the Red Unit. That means we'll be in the Garden again." He seemed pleased. I was silent. "And you get to see your friend Dick Barstow."

"Who says he's my friend?" I snarled, "Who else is changing units?"

"Joey Matheson, Judy, and Laura McMurray. Placing us there strengthens an excellent show. The Felds need it to compete in the business."

"I suppose they want publicity?"

"Of course." He widened his eyes. "You and I are articulate, and with Ivy, we represent a typical American family."

I thought, *We made the show's circuit. I've drifted from education to circus. We're gone all the time, rent our house to strangers...* "Rent? Rent what? We do rent the house," I tried to catch up with Danny who was still talking.

"We need another income besides the circus. I'm going to find a family to fix the building I own on the Trail and Creek to turn it into a restaurant. It's been empty too many years. Vandals broke the windows."

He put an ad in the *Herald Tribune*, and in between Venice trips, interviewed potential restaurateurs. He chose a family who closed their Indiana ice cream stand and wanted to open a brew and sandwich shop in Sarasota. The rent was $100/mo plus property taxes.

"What about the vacant filled property along the Creek?" I asked, wondering what would become of it.

"That too, will be developed."

In a way, running off with the circus was easier for me than facing the legal scrapes Danny embraced. He relished court appearances, maybe because he thought he won something.

* * *

The transition from Blue to Red went well for us. During the opening shows of my third season, Barstow bumped into me when he pushed through the red-and-white striped curtain where I waited for my act to go on.

"Here you are. I want you to know how much your act improved. You make it look too easy," Barstow purred.

Startled and alone with him in dimmed light, I weakly replied, "Oh? I don't feel better than last year."

"You are. Be proud of yourself."

"Thank you Mr. Barstow," I responded and curtsied. "It takes time...to learn balance. I've had good teachers."

He tilts his head like that wasn't what he expected to hear, waved goodbye, and headed towards the sewing room.

Obediently I waited backstage at Ringling Brothers Circus debut in 1971. Waited to exercise on my swing where I flapped arms and legs and smiled for applause and a weekly paycheck. I was a submissive bird in a cage and knew it.

Ringmaster Harold Ronk's smooth tenor voice introduced to the aging, yet apprehensive Venice, Florida, audience the World's Greatest Animal Trainer of All Time. The one. The only. Gunther Gebel Williams.

Colored spotlights burst onto center ring revealing a spandex clad earth angel commanding seven Bengal tigers. A stimulating band, only a few feet away, played show music.

Stepping back from the curtain, I started my final grooming by hooking the clasp on a rhinestone bracelet and squishing panties under leg elastic of a velvet leotard. A hot pink handkerchief slipped from a pocket, was folded, and inserted next to my right thigh leaving a two-inch tip sticking below burgundy coque feathers. Lastly, out of habit, a swish down suntan opera stockings reminded me they were seamless.

Six years of mute swan silence earned each facet of my wardrobe, subservience, and ambivalence to the tramp clown waddling up to me—my husband, Danny Chapman. Setting my robe aside, I began warm-up squats, high leg kicks, and the usual chatter with Danny.

"Guess who was just here?"

"The Pope?" he replied with sarcasm dripping down the words.

"No, more important. Dick Barstow. He said I'm a good performer."

"You are. First class. I hope you told him it was your instructors."

I plopped my right ankle in his palm and avoided rolling my eyes. He firmly stretched my extended leg. I wanted to retort that my effort into my act is far more important than teachers. Danny would only laugh at my naiveté. His sly comments directed at others were hidden lessons I learned too late.

Tiger cages clanked shut simultaneously with Gunther's final chords.

Quickly, I wrapped my coque feather boa around my shoulders, loaned my fate to the unknown and strode confidently into the arena repeating, *I'm off to see the wizard.*

Front and back spotlights catered to the aerial display I was in for three minutes. Ronk introduced over lyrical music, "Aloft in Ring Three, Miss Sarah Chapman."

With no net, just Danny below, I scaled my thirty-three-foot web and unfurled my limbs into an arabesque disguising a quick glance at my shackles on the hinged uprights. They were erect and tightly bolted, leaving me confidently plunking two bare feet on the cold iron slab.

A ritual began when toe-to-heel flesh embraced under gravity's securing wings. Not a bird then, but a butterfly, I repeated this five-hundred-times a year.

In the opening stance, I placed the balls of my feet shoulder width apart on my two-inch-wide bar, and released my hands from the supporting cables. I bent my knees and riveted my eyes straight ahead focusing on a man in the audience, I fluttered unsteadily, a warning that I'm free standing. Slowly shifting my weight from left to right and back again, the bar started rotating. *Good job. Keep twisting. Raise my arms. High. Higher. Careful, don't over twist. Drop my hands to my waist. Smile over each shoulder. Done.*

I swung my right leg opposite the rotation of the bar until the bar hung motionless. Turning to my left, I arranged my right foot behind the left then picked a focus spot straight out from the line of vision. In Venice, that was a faded blue metal wall above the bandstand and less than thirty feet away. Thrusting weight forward and backwards on alternate legs, the bar gained momentum until it couldn't swing any higher without buckling. At this point I lowered down on my right knee, grabbed the front cable, then kicked my right leg high, and smiled front and back.

Danny looped the web into my right leg helping to still the bar. Then he placed the web to one side and looked up at me for the handkerchief trick. I pulled out the preset silk, gave two attention-getting swishes, laid it across the shiny bar, and gingerly kneeled as if on a pew. With arms held straight and bending forward a bit, my eyes located the same person I studied for the twist, this time intently focusing on just his face.

Alternating my glance between him to the silk between my knees, I slowly compressed my body. My head bobbed and I collected the pink silk, and paused long enough for the audience to see it in my lips. *Good girl, they're clapping. Stand up. Style. Fling the hankie.*

Danny caught it down below while I wrapped my leg around the web. He gave the web three forward pulls and I released my leg on the last pull. Free from the web, I pumped the swing higher, higher than children do at playgrounds. Turning to the wall, my left foot centered on the bar and my right leg pointed off to the side, I zeroed in on the focal point, raised my arms past my shoulders, and stayed on top of the bar for two exhilarating swings.

I styled (paid compliments to the audience) briefly and changed the direction of the swing to a large circle by stationing my right foot behind my left. After focusing, I bent my knees and flexed, and feathers fluttered for three circumnavigations. Moving rapidly, I grabbed the cables, sat down on the bar, and conveyed to my onlookers—Whee! What fun! Still in motion, Danny threw the web between my separated legs and I clung to it. I descended quickly to avoid the circling bar and glanced down the arena scrutinizing the finish of the other acts. Daintily placing my feet on the textured rubber mat on the arena floor, I bounced front and back styling with arms out, palms up, and a broad smile.

The spotlight gone and standing in darkness, my adrenalin flowed from sparkling Lepidoptera to lonely avian. I searched out Danny at the curb and held his hand as I stepped into high heels and scooped up the boa. Exiting to the curtain, he laid the silk across my extended palm. We separated behind the curtain—he to clown alley where our four-year-old daughter waited, and I to wardrobe.

"Easy," Dick Barstow's word echoed.

"First class," Danny uttered. I didn't feel first class. My brain continued the conversation: *I might be first class if I balanced on my head. What I really need is not to be a showgirl. Then I wouldn't be so tired. First class acts don't do production. Stop complaining, you're a featured aerialist on the Greatest Show on Earth.*

* * *

"You're riding elephants for Gunther," Danny informed me on the way to the building for rehearsals. I'm not sure why this information came from him, not management. I suspect Danny consulted with them about this and other things, i.e. contract wording and salary prior to telling me. I didn't have the option of negotiating with him or management.

"I am? What if I don't care for his elephants?"

"You'll have to dance."

"Then I'll ride. I miss Hugo and Siam already."

There was one immediate difference—red elephant halters, not blue. In addition, Red Unit elephants didn't go in groups into rings, they squatted on tubs around the track and performed simple tricks yelled at them in German from Gunther Gebel Williams. Congo, Gunther's male African elephant, provokingly waited in the center ring raising his trunk high in the air at weird angles making his huge ears flip about lopsidedly. Congo's turn with Gunther came after the herd ran out of the arena.

Tina Torres rode a fast elephant next to mine. Smaller in proportions to me with fine-fawn-colored hair and almond-shaped blue eyes, soft-spoken Tina was ideal for the show and expertly complemented her beauty with make-up and hairpieces. Her smile in the ring conveyed confidence. Late at night in the back yard, she often tapped at our trailer door borrowing an item to finish cooking the evening meal for her partner Peter and her. She never returned what she borrowed, and I never asked, just having Tina nearby was enough.

"We don't get to ride the big elephants because we're new riders," she explained. "I rode Topsy last year and she's grown enough so I can hook my feet under her ears."

"I've ridden before," I whined, "and my keester hurts."

"That doesn't matter to Gunther. If you feel you're falling off, hang on with one hand." Tina's gentle words didn't help. I never bonded with my Red Unit elephant nor learned her name. Riding elephants lost its allure.

Gunther Gebel Williams had two Ringling seasons under his belt and had a set routine. For Danny and me he was a new entity.

"Gunther's something else, the way he flies around the arena," I commented to Danny. "He works horses, cats, and elephants and he never seems to tire."

"Yes, he's quite a performer in his tights. But stay away from his whip," Danny teased. "Gunther Gebel didn't have it easy in his life. He came with the Williams family package. Their animals contracted to the Ringling Show. Williams hired him when he was young and Gunther had a knack with horses and tigers.

"It's nice working with Lou Jacob," Danny commented on the Red Unit Clown Alley. "He's doing the last five minutes of Come In. I'm spotted before him."

"That's great, Danny."

The Red Unit aerial ballet routine wasn't done on a short metal ladder but a traditional Spanish web with hand-and-foot loop routines ending with a fast spin. Without the ladder supporting my body, I had to cling to the web using more muscle power than I had available. Also, without Saturday morning substitutions, my performance slacked off in the aerial ballet and no one asked why.

The number was a sparkling pink-and-orange hootenanny. I arrived to my web under a haystack pulled by genial Costa, my Bulgarian web sitter. Once aloft I performed simple tricks while keeping an eye on the center ring where my friend, Vicki Unus amazed the audience with her Roman rings strength. Fifty lithesome, one-arm swings concluded each performance. Vicki was aerial perfection in motion. Her sunny offstage disposition always brightened my day.

* * *

The clowns and showgirls planned a side trip during time off between two North Carolina dates. Jim Howle and his friends handled the itinerary. "They want to go skiing at Sugar Mountain in Boone and need help getting there. I want to ski, please say we can go," I pumped Danny.

"You know I don't approve of you doing extra things. We'll go and be good sports, but that's all," was his final answer.

"Goodie!" I squealed, not knowing what to expect other than sixteen of us camped in one cabin. That part was fun compared to two days of treacherous skiing on ungroomed runs in cold, windy weather, and Danny's uncompromising torture.

"You're not going to ski are you?" Danny grilled me the first morning, away from the others. *I wish Danny supported my adventures instead of battling me.*

"Can't I try?" I quizzed already geared in boots, skis, and poles.

"Don't break any bones," he ordered, setting his eyes and jaw hatefully.

"That makes me more nervous. I'll be careful." I anxiously caught the lift. After dismounting I looked down the icy slope and immediately sensed fear. Without instruction, I promptly fell on my butt and decided to carry my skis, walk down the side of the hill, and grumble. *I'm bewildered. How do people have fun skiing? Maybe one day I'll zip down a mountain but not when Danny's watching. I hope he's satisfied my legs aren't broken.* Several people did learn to ski, all without injury. For everyone else it was a fun time.

I couldn't see that a tyrant controlled me. I didn't know how a husband was supposed to act. Inside my mind, I was Danny Chapman's wife, easy mark for his periodic verbal vengeance. Outside of it, I was Sarah Chapman, aerialist, mother, and student. The inside identity, the good person, tolerated his rules, while the other, still a good person, didn't want any part of his rules. I never questioned Danny's tactics, I just slumped down deeper into humiliation.

* * *

Not learning to ski wasn't the end of the world. I excelled elsewhere. I took sewing projects home at night and sewed in bed, attaching a few more rhinestones or tacking snaps by hand. As I sewed, I judged my craft. *My handmade creations equal Ringling status. I wear feathers; velvet and satin; custom jewelry from Las Vegas; and good high heels and hairpieces. It's fun choosing wardrobe.* One difference from my wardrobe and that made by a costumer was the price—home made costs much less. That meant I could throw out a leotard if I didn't like it, make another, and still be ahead.

When my eyes got sleepy, I set my sewing aside, pulled up the covers, and slept all night. I lazily woke most mornings, except for Saturdays, when I didn't sleep well the night before; afraid the alarm clock wouldn't ring. I started the first of the next five shows yearning for sleep that never came until Sunday night.

* * *

Besides being a wardrobe junkie, food was a big part of my life and I enjoyed cooking for Danny. Little Ivy helped me in the kitchen, sometimes patting breadcrumbs on pork chops and eggplant slices, or stirring ingredients for pumpkin pie. On long trips, I read books to her, did finger games, and we all sang songs as we traveled.

To Danny I pondered, "I wonder which German restaurant we'll celebrate Ivy's fifth birthday in October? Mader's in Milwaukee is my first choice."

"Speaking of food, we're going to Baltimore's Lexington Market soon. You can stock up," Danny told me, as he drove a constant 55-mph to the next destination.

"Ummm. One shop has the choicest dark chocolate creams in the country. I'm buying twice as many as last time. I ran out far too quickly."

Improving my culinary skills challenged me more than the show. In the arena, I did the same thing day after day, whereas creating a new dish contained the element of success or failure. Besides, picking up fresh ingredients got me out and about in the cities the circus played.

* * *

By 1971 male circus fans, reporters, and circus publicity staff starting coming by our tiny trailer or our home in Florida. Everyone knew they were welcome at the Chapman's and if it was suppertime, all the better, because no one was ever refused a plate of food. They came even when Danny wasn't in the trailer. My cooking wasn't that desirable to keep them there for hours. I was a host who offered tea, not coffee. More than once at night after the show, I pushed them out the door begging, "Sorry, I need sleep."

I asked Danny, "Why don't you tell them to go?"

"Leave? I didn't think they ever would," he chortled.

CHAPTER EIGHTEEN
AERIAL BALLERINA

After the Madison Square Garden premier, Danny scanned morning newspapers looking for reviews. He placed a copy of the April 8, 1971 *Village Voice* on his empty pillow next to mine saying, "You've earned this unsolicited write up."

"What does that mean?" I asked rousing myself, rubbing sleep from my eyes, coming to life.

"The show sends generic press releases to newspapers. This article was written without the show's permission." I read the *Voice* article, laid it down, and dozed back off to sleep.

Reporter Edward Hoagland opinioned, "This year the most beautiful girl in the circus is Sarah Chapman. She appears in the aerial-ballet, then on an elephant, and on a trapeze. Although, as a star, her abilities are not much above mediocre, her hair is a feathery, jet-black brush set off by her white skin, her arms are round as a dancers, and her smile has a special symmetry."

* * *

I clipped and saved this article along with others I'd gathered and dismissed the word beautiful. The only person who ever said I was beautiful was Lucy who called me photogenic once, but more often, she said I was an ugly duckling, a brat, or a pigface. I paid special attention to the words "mediocre star abilities" and had to admit I wasn't a super nova, just a little twinkling in the vast spread of bodies held under mother circus's charms. *If I want to be a star, I'll have to hire a manager and press agent. That would take parenting time away from Ivy. No, I won't desert her. Maybe I should have another baby.*

Talking to Danny about my feelings wasn't going to happen so I simply told him, "The show doesn't have anything against kids, as you said. I want a baby."

"When do you want to start?"

"Tonight." That night and a few succeeding ones happened without a positive outcome. I went to a specialist for blood and urine tests checking my hormone levels. The real problem, one no doctor could fix, was the lack of sex and love. *I'm a trailer fixture, the mother, the teacher, the cook, the barber, the travel mate. I never was Danny's lover. My role of wife is long gone. I'm not sure who or what Danny loves.*

Sensing I was down he suggested a trip to visit Aunt Hazel and Uncle Robert. "Why don't we take a side trip and stay at the Red Lion Inn? I know your uncle would approve."

"Thanks for the idea," I said, it improved my outlook. We took a country drive into the Berkshires. Arriving late, Danny insisted we eat supper in the Red Lion Tavern. He knew century-old wooden booths and bees wax candles charmed me. Awakening the next morning, I noticed something grey and moldy hung on the wallpaper. "What's on the walls?" I asked, while he shaved at the sink.

"Its frost, formed where there's no insulation. It's cold outside, baby. Are you ready to go touring?"

I was stuck thinking, *Baby? That's what my mother called me. Why doesn't he use my name?* "Yes, Uncle Robert is meeting us for lunch in the dining room. Then he's taking us to the Jug Inn, where Aunt Hazel works in the gift shop."

We wandered in and out of Stockbridge venues. During lunch, Danny gave me a cookbook, *Country Inns and Back Roads.*

"Look inside. There's a recipe from the Tavern." Hugging the book to my chest and looking at Uncle Robert, not Danny, I thought, *I adore you Uncle Robert.*

* * *

The show played Boston after NYC then traveled to Philadelphia. I thought I put Danny not touching me far back in my mind yet, I harbored a grudge and went for days saying as little as possible to him. He never encouraged me to open up and acted no different from when I did talk with him. We were roommates, nothing more.

On the Sunday afternoon closing in Philadelphia, I hemorrhaged blood into a toilet of the women's dressing room. "Sarah," Judy McMurray tapped at the locked door, "Are you all right?"

"No, not really." Feeling fragile and physically drained was not as bad as telling Danny I was sick. That would break his rule for not seeing, smelling, or listening to anything having to do with blood. I didn't know what to do and it was time to perform. I cleaned up and dressed for my act.

I ambled to the backstage curtain grabbing it for support. My hand matched the white stripe. Performance Director Bob Dover planted his body in front of me. "Sarah...what is it?" he gently asked, peering into my weary eyes.

"I'm bleeding beyond control," I whispered into the ear of a man I'd had a crush on since I was fifteen. Mr. Dover was married and I guessed it was okay to tell him my problem, leaving out the part about Danny.

With authority, he gently, firmly said, "I'll tell Danny to take you to the hospital between shows."

"Mr. Dover?" I asked.

"Yes, Sarah. What is it?"

"I could kiss you." He smiled and tenderly patted my shoulder.

After my act, one of the women yelled into the dressing room, "Sarah, Danny's here."

I stepped outside the door in my robe, my arms limply wrapped around my belly. Danny barked, "I'm taking you to

Hahnemann." I kept my head downcast, his voice told me he was angry.

On the way to the hospital, blood spurted out at every lurch and bump. *It's useless to ask him to drive gently. All he cares about is the show.*

Wheelchair bound at admission, Danny left me, his departing words demonstrating a complete lack of concern. "The Felds are coming to the next town. I want you to work. These are your clothes for tomorrow."

Emotionally empty, I asked, "What are they going to do?"

"Stop the bleeding. Be ready to leave early for Hershey," he said. "It's a short hop and we're leaving early."

Me, the tough young aerialist, found the inner-city hospital strange compared to circus surroundings. My doctor, nurses, and maternity ward roommates were African Americans. Some had newborns. Others recuperated from tied Fallopian tubes. I had a D&C where I was dilated and vacuum cleaned of bleeding tissue. I woke up in bed with a nurse adjusting a pad between my legs and saying, "Yeaah, the doctor done fixed you. Yous not bleedin now. Ah, honey, you looks white as a sheep."

My mind registered, *not bleeding, white sheep. I want to stay in bed.* Another nurse rolled a wheel chair beside the bed. "Your hubby is here. Do you have clothes?" *Clothes, oh, it's Danny. I have to go.*

"Yes, in a paper bag. I want to walk."

"Sorry, honey, I can't let that happen. Yous need lots o'rest."

Ivy and Lacie enjoyed seeing me. I handed Danny a small package. "What's this?" he jibed.

"Pills. The doctor said I have to take birth control pills to control blood flow. I get regular periods whether I want them or not." I looked at the waiting truck. "Why did you bring Joey? Couldn't we be alone this trip?"

"No, I told him he was going with us."

"Then he can ride in the front. I'll lie down on the bed in the camper."

"Have it your way." That phrase of his made me feel guilty.

We dropped Joey at the trains in Hershey one-hundred miles down the road. "I'm taking you to an Amish restaurant. This part of Pennsylvania is America's breadbasket. My grandmother, Sarah Detweiler, was a Mennonite from here."

Finally settled into bed in the trailer later that afternoon, my hope to rest the following day went poof.

"Get up. You need a drive," Danny roared. "We're going to the Hershey Rose Garden."

"No. I don't want to go anywhere. Take Ivy with you." Car riding and rose viewing numbed me from head to toe.

"The Feld family is here for the opening. The show isn't the same without you."

"You mean I'm working?" I gasped shrilly.

"Yes, I talked to Dover. You're only doing your act."

"Just do your best," Danny's infamous words rang in my ears as he shoved me up my web in front of Gunther's tiger cages. When I descended three minutes later, I took my closing styles to front and back audiences thinking, *The Felds or the Queen of England can be in the audience. That doesn't make it important enough for me to work*. According to Danny's rules, losing copious amounts of fluids was no reason for time off.

Our photographer friend, Jerry Yulsman, said in a 1971 *Life Magazine* article on Ringling, "I am jealous of circus people. They live in a marvelous world of fantasy." I respected Jerry, but he didn't wear my shoes. To me, the circus was perilously realistic.

* * *

Traveling west, we worked Phoenix, Arizona, before the California dates. It was there the second of two whip mishaps happened to me on the elephants. Gunther and his assistant, Henry Schorer, both carried and cracked ten-foot whips making high-pitched thunderbolts, adding pizzazz to the act without touching any animal.

The first event happened backstage at Madison Square Garden. Tina and I sat neck-to-neck in the elephant line-up. Henry teased Tina and Tina rebuffed him. He drew back his whip arm striking a big lash in front of her elephant's head. The whip's popper seared the top of my left thigh. "YEOW," I yelled, and tears rushed down my face. Looking at Tina, I moaned, "I'm not riding," and slid off my elephant's neck. Strutting up to Henry, who conceitedly stood with his whip neatly coiled, I scolded him. "You tell Gunther why I'm not riding." The thick welt wasn't as bad as I expected and I performed my balancing trapeze without difficulty.

When I went to mount my elephant after my act in the next show, Henry approached. "I'm sorry I hit you. It was an accident."

"I forgive you. But keep your whip off me." Consequently he did.

Now, back to Phoenix, where Mr. Feld appraised the show. He probably scrutinized each production number including the theme and wardrobe. Tales of the Arabian Nights inspired the elephant ménage. Gunther and Henry wore tights and boleros. Dancing girls wore rose-colored midriff tops and long skirts flaring out from a hip-band. The riders, all girls, dressed in glittering purple, pink, red, yellow, green, blue, orange, and lilac costumes the colors of precious gems. My costume was my favorite color, yellow for topaz. The matching hats with many sharp points and tassels resembled a pagoda.

Sitting outside in the sunshine with Tina and I side-by-side, we rested our glistening hats on our elephant's heads before going into the arena. "Gunther asked you a question. He's trying to get your attention," she said.

"I don't care what he asks me," I said putting my hat on and fastening the hook under my chin. I looked up in time to see and hear a thunderous crack less than six-inches from my face. Glaring down, I saw Gunther smirking and gathering his whip. I unhooked my hat, took aim, and flung it at him. I, unlike Henry, missed by six feet. Gunther half grinned. I dismounted, swooped up my hat, and stormed off to Mr. Dover.

"I'm not riding until Gunther apologizes," I huffed, not caring who overheard, and headed to Women's Wardrobe where the mistress, Jean Carson, sympathized with me. "You're a doll, Miss Jeannie," I expressed endearingly to the wren-sized woman with the strength of ten elephants.

On the Red Unit, I dressed in a variety of backstage locations. My cubicle was dark-blue flame-retardant canvas supported by metal rods and poles. Inside were my trunk, wardrobe rack, and TV tray supporting my mirror, hairpins, brush, comb, and make-up case. The chair belonged to the building.

In this secure area, I calmly changed into my finale outfit, and then located Danny. "Before anyone tells you, Gunther got too close with his whip and could have blinded me. He can talk, but he can't use his whip to get my attention."

"I've heard all about it. Do you think he'll apologize?"

"I don't know. It's not his habit, is it?"

It was too hot to go to the trailer and I stayed in my cool, semi-lit cubicle between shows, embroidering a pillow. I grinned. *Gunther will have to hunt to find me.* "Zarah Shapman," his thick Germanic voice rang out.

"Yesss?" I responded, not moving an inch.

"Zarah Shapman, I want to talk to you," he pleaded pathetically. It wasn't proper for him to enter my dressing area, so I went out to him and noticed he was unaccompanied and in street clothes, possibly a nicety for me.

"Yes, Gunther," I said, as if nothing had happened between us.

"Today... I... sorry. I be more careful," he stammered, lowering his face.

"I forgive you, Gunther," I said, as I had rehearsed and then added, "My name is Sarah, not Zarah."

He shifted on his feet, took a breath, and offered, "Friends?"

"Yes, Gunther. Friends. Go back to your elephants," I said triumphantly, and turned into my cubicle, silently shouting, *Yes! The golden-haired one came apologizing. He's human after all. Tina won't believe it. No one will, because no one heard or saw us.*

I came so close to losing my eyesight that I decided not to jeopardize my life by riding Gunther's elephants any longer than necessary. I studied the dancing girls for months. *It won't matter where my feet go. No one sees them. All I have to learn are the arm movements. Anything is better than riding.*

California dates went as intended. Gunther and I passed each other in hallways making eye contact and nothing more.

* * *

Between dates, we took side trips to Bryce Canyon, Yosemite, and Zion National Parks.

"Stand for a picture next to this baby redwood tree," I told Ivy. In fifty years, come back and see how much it's grown."

I looked forward to trips with the show's young people. Dolly Jacob joined us when we toured Yellowstone's geysers, bubbling pots, and deep blue pools. "I want you to see things you miss on the train," Danny told her.

"Let's give the circus children a Halloween party for Ivy's birthday," I suggested to Danny.

"Where do you want to have it?"

"Champaign, Illinois. That's where we'll be for Halloween. I'll make a poster inviting the children and their families." Danny cooperated with the party and monitored two games—apple dunking and pin the broom on the witch. Costumed children from many nations exchanged gifts, ate candied apples, and brought me a time of peace.

I began my independence campaign in California because I heard contract signing would be in Chicago at the Amphitheater. "Danny, you can be The Aerial Chapmans. I want a separate contract paying me what I'm worth, not the $175 I'm getting."

No response. I clammed up the same way, pretending he didn't exist. Nothing I did or said changed his shrewd control over my career. Our contract stayed the same for the coming season meeting expenses and then some. I stopped collecting coins when the gold standard rose.

"I'm giving you coins for your birthday and our anniversary," Danny advised.

"Gladly accepted," I said, smiling back at him.

That fall a Hungarian acrobat from a teeterboard act came into my life. He was my age and I first noticed his attentions in Chicago when he walked from his adjacent train car and stopped at the Frolic after Danny left for the building. I looked forward to seeing him and convinced myself he came to learn how to speak better English.

In the buildings, we often chatted between acts in the hallways. Something about him made me want to handhold, kiss, and explore as much as I could of him. I'm sure we felt the same way about each other. In Quebec City, on the last night of the season, we had a plan.

"After the show I load trunks," he told me. "When Danny goes to sleep, you meet me at the back of the building where it's dark. Listen for my whistle."

I pretended I was asleep lying next to Danny. My heart raced with unfaithful thoughts. When his snoring started, I climbed out of the covers, pulled a muskrat coat over flannel pajamas, shoved feet into leather boots, and crept into the frost-chilled air. Our rendezvous was behind a loaded container.

"I won't ever see you again," I said. I spoke softly, near his face, letting his brown curls touch my cheek.

"That's right. My contract is done. I…must return…to Hungary. I will miss you."

"Me too," I answered, searching his face. Our passionate lips entwined, sharing the warmth of a first…and last parting kiss.

"Sarah, my friends are waiting. I have to go," he whispered, with his deep accent. Releasing our embrace, we kissed on opposite cheeks then turned our backs. In a euphoric daze, I plodded back across the empty lit-up back yard to my pink-and-white trailer, staring at my solo shadow. It lacked signs of infidelity.

The physical longing for my would-be lover ended when I roused Danny from slumber and forced myself on top of him extracting a gift he truly didn't want to give. It was a hopeless dream to think I would split up my family and take Ivy to a foreign land with a man I hardly knew. *No, Sarah, stay where you are*, was my last thought before finally falling asleep curled up next to the thin trailer wall.

* * *

Repeating the season on the Red Unit's alternate route gave us two months off and we moved back into the house. We returned to our familiar routines, attended church, and took Patrnella out for the day from her nursing home. We gave dinner parties to performers and attended funerals of aging circus friends. "You'll never guess whose obituary is in the paper," Danny told me.

"No, I won't. Who is it?"

"Mel Miller. He was only fifty-years-old and had a heart attack."

"I'm sorry to hear that," I said, backing away to the bedroom. Throwing myself on the bed, I wailed for losing people dear to me. On our last Savannah stop, Mel took us to lunch at Mrs. Wilke's Boarding House. Seated at the big round table along with other tourists, engaging Mel relaxed me as we passed food bowls back and forth. When my tears stopped, I admitted, *I had a thing for Mel.*

I cried often that winter. My chest hurt, my stomach hurt, and I was despondent. Not knowing what to do I made an appointment with Dr. Hoertz, my gynecologist. "I had a D&C eight months ago and take the pill."

"That won't help. You're pregnant," he smiled.

"No, I'm not!" I yelled in his face, burst into tears, and ran out of his office. "No, I'm not! I'm not," I shouted until the thought pushed me beyond sanity's edge. I didn't recognize any of my surroundings, including the mustard-yellow-truck where I sat sobbing over the steering wheel. "Pregnant, I can't be pregnant. I'm on the pill. Danny and I don't have sex." A small light went off in my mind. *I did have sex, with Danny—in Quebec.*

"I can't have a baby now. Ivy and my career are enough. Danny doesn't want a baby." My thoughts were chaotic. *I don't know what will make me happy. Dr. Hoertz can't be right. I've had three periods since Quebec. I'm taking my pills, cooking, and sewing costumes.*

"What did the doctor say? Danny asked.

"I'm pregnant. Due in September." I knew he wouldn't respond.

CHAPTER NINETEEN
BACKYARD

1972 RBB&B Red Unit

Heartburn and constipation, not heartache were my two problems during 1972 rehearsals. Gunther had a problem too. "Why aren't you riding?"

"I don't like small jerky elephants and hanging on for dear life. Give me a big elephant or put me in center ring. Then I'll ride."

"I can't do that. The others were here before you."

"Then I can't ride. I'll dance," I said dismissively, staring into his mystical aquamarine eyes, keeping my head even with his.

That season, even if I wanted to ride Gunther's elephants, I wouldn't have done so pregnant and I doubted that I was. I felt sick and my face looked funny.

Jeanette Williams' mother, Mrs. Williams spoke to me in Venice. "Sarah, I think you're going to have a boy. You have a mask."

We stood facing a mirror and she said, "See this?" gently touching the freckled area running across my cheeks below my eyes, "That comes when you have a baby and goes away afterward. Be happy."

"Thank you, Mrs. Williams. I'll try, even though I don't feel well."

"You will, in time, my dear," she said as we parted. *Jeanette's lucky having a nice mother.* (Mrs. Williams oversaw the Williams animal herd leased to Ringling.) I got the baby I asked for, but was unhappy because it wasn't an ideal situation with opposing parenting styles. I was thankful my body conceived and knew I would make the most of my gift.

Pregnancy for circus women is the same as for non-athletic women. My costumes were tight and I told myself, *This can't be happening. I won't believe it until I feel movement.* In April, a tiny tug happened in Washington, DC during Easter week. *I have to accept I'm pregnant. Besides, I can't bend forward to pick up my handkerchief.*

Burt Fagan, one of the Somerton Gang, drove from his home in Arlington, Virginia. "What can I do to help?" he asked brightly.

"Please take us to Easter service," I answered, realizing no request was too big or small for him.

"How about the Washington Cathedral?" Burt suggested looking at Danny.

"No, you go without me. I'll be putting on my make-up," Danny answered, sipping coffee. Danny's policy of getting me escorts agreed with me and I glowed from Burt's courtesies. The weather, spring greenery, and blossoms made a picturesque Easter day.

* * *

I used my time off during pregnancy to continue my education from The American School in Chicago. They specialized in certified correspondence classes. I rarely went to the building due to my course on Human Growth and Development. I preferred to read, type, and study in solitude. Danny came to the Frolic between shows, and approached me one afternoon. Out of nowhere, he laid down a new rule. "When I'm gone, I want you to go to a university town. Don't take the kids to your grandparents in frigid Minnesota." I glanced up in time to see his extended index finger retracting.

"It's my home away from home," I dreamily responded, bringing a time of reflection for Minnesota.

* * *

When I was in elementary school, the night before leaving for our summer-long trips, Mama unfurled a clean tablecloth with a snap, and then held on as it lightly glided over uncapped containers of oleo, guava jelly, and salt and peppershakers, covering them. We abandoned our unlocked house making no effort to tidy up. I always felt as if time stood still in the house waiting for our return.

Mama loaded Lucy, Merritt, and me into the packed Kaiser and left before sunup and drove long past sunset. When it was pitch-black, she parked on the edge of the road where other people also pulled off to sleep in their cars for the night. We vagabonds arrived five-to-seven days later in Remer, Minnesota, 1900 miles north of Sarasota. On the way, Merritt and I endured many clubbings from Mama's forceful arm for not sitting still or staying quiet. Lucy shared the front seat with Mama and knew how to distance herself. Lucy never defended us nor told us to behave.

Once in Minnesota, our peltings ceased. We freely ran with cousins, aunts, and uncles of similar age, and played outside all day and into the night. We shot marbles, picked wild berries, swam in lakes and rivers, caught lightning bugs, and danced with the locals at Friday night powwows. On rainy days we found corners and nooks inside, and read comic books.

Soft-spoken and diminutive, Grandma contrasted with Grandpa, a gruff giant usually swearing and pounding his fists on tables. They gave each child a chore and we kids knew to get it done. We cut hay, gathered eggs, milked cows, separated cream, weeded gardens, fed pigs and chickens, and overdid hugging the dog.

On warm evenings after supper and before bedtime, we kids gathered outdoors to play hide and seek or tag. About ten o'clock, someone usually called us dirty sweating ragamuffins to come inside. They had no electricity, running water, or indoor toilet. We washed up before bed with a washcloth and a pan of cold soapy water.

Balancing Act

When I first discovered butterflies in Remer, I caught, killed, and mounted them for display. That changed when Grandma made a comment one afternoon, "I like them flying about the garden, don't you?" Afterward I enjoyed their beauty as they augmented the garden with their varying display of color.

Once, when Mama took me along to Remer Pharmacy, she handed me a small roll of colored candy pills saying, "Here, these will make your hurts go away." What an odd statement from Mama. I didn't need the pills in Minnesota.

Mama hunted deer out of season with Grandpa and her brothers. Dressed in a red-and-black wool checked shirt, woolen trousers, and hunting cap, she carried a bag of meat sandwiches for the hunting party, a big thermos of black coffee, and a borrowed shotgun. Heading out before dawn to a tree stand, none of them returned until they ran out of shells or coffee. When the hunting stories started, us kids listened. If they got a white tail deer, I stayed away from the sheds because the carcass scared me. However I was thankful for the platefuls of delicious venison tenderloin fried for breakfast.

Memories of mealtimes at my grandparents stayed with me. Young and old, we ate in two shifts for breakfast and lunch. After the first setting, the women washed and dried the plates, glasses, and silverware for the next seating. Aunts and uncles passed steaming bowls of fresh vegetables, venison, beef or pork roasts, potatoes, home baked bread, and dessert around the table. Mama often took picnics to the men and boys working in the fields.

If someone got hurt, the nearest hospital was in Grand Rapids. Mama hoped Dr. Morton's tetanus shots given to us in Sarasota worked. Despite the shots and even wearing shoes, rusty nails often pierced our feet. Mama made nightly Epsom saltwater soaks a ritual to combat the red streak of infection running up our legs.

One day I was climbing on hayloft rafters and heard the boys playing hide and seek in the barn. I wondered how it felt jumping into loose hay. Grandly, I leaped for the middle of the pile and ran a pitchfork tine completely through my foot. "Stop it!" Merritt yelled in my face, shutting up my screams. "Grab my jeans and bite hard while I yank it out." Grimly he jerked the tine out and then removed my leather sandal. "Put your shoe back on and don't tell Mama." We both knew she would thrash me, even if we were in Minnesota, because she forbade the hayloft. I tried not to limp and wore the sandals with the t-strap to hide the puncture hole on top of my foot.

The annual Raines family July 4th picnic, complete with fireworks we Wheeler's bought in Georgia, took place at Mable Lake, one mile east of the Boy River. After a cleansing evening swim in the lake, when the sky was full of color and before dark, Mama told us, "Minnesota has the most beautiful sunsets. Be quiet and listen to the loon calling his mate and babies." Wrinkle-free water made an upside-down reflection of the sky.

Merritt and I wanted to stay in Minnesota forever. Pure-black nights seemed so different. The stars shone brighter and bigger, no sticky spider webs to meet, and we never needed to go outside shooting critters because there—wild animals stayed in the forest. We had no idea of the delicate spring, colorful fall, or unbearable winters, only the magical summers.

Mama gathered us youngsters in for the return trip to Sarasota where we went to school for another year.

"Don't you wish we lived here?" Merritt asked sadly, hunched down in the back seat.

"Yes. I do, but I think we should see Daddy. I miss him."

Less baggage went on the trip south. No amount of weight in our heavy hearts made the car stop moving. Merritt and I wept as soon as we half-heartedly waved goodbye and kept it up for the better part of the morning. Torn away from kindnesses, saturated tears of loss freely flowed, unlike the bitter tears we wept from Mama's vindictive pummeling.

* * *

My Minnesota reflection ended peacefully. I changed my thought to being pregnant on a big circus and in 1966 on the King Show—my salary stopping for five and a-half months stayed the same. My Ringling surprise baby shower happened in Memphis when a friend had me meet her in the building. On the slow stroll there I reflected, *Three years ago Judy McMurray said I was a butterfly morphing from the backyard to the arena. That won't happen again until my shape comes back.* The shower was a time of sharing for all the women on the show.

* * *

"I want a birth announcement using Henry," Danny told me when I was seven-months along. Henry, Danny's marionette in matching clown suit and make-up lived in a small trashcan. The showgirls used look-alike marionettes for a dance number on the front track during spec and Danny added himself and Henry at the end of the chorus line.

"Oh, what if it's a girl? She wouldn't wear tramp make-up."

"That won't matter will it? Wrap Henry in a blanket." We posed for a black and white photograph. The birth announcement was a fun project for Danny. It was the first time he enjoyed the incoming baby.

Deborah and Stephanie wanted to stay with us until the baby's birth. The due date came and went. "Sorry, girls," I said. "Your education is more important. We'll be home in three months and you can see your new sibling then." They flew to Sarasota from Las Vegas. With them gone, I slept in the truck camper to avoid clumsily crawling over Danny each night. I was excess baggage to him as I had been on the Moscow Circus in 1967. Lying with my dog, Lacie, at my side, I confided to her, "This pregnancy made me feel ugly. I don't want more children with Danny. I love you Lacie Faire."

Impatient with the baby coming late, Danny took me to a Las Vegas nursing home. "Stay here until the baby comes."

"No! I won't stay in a nursing home," I said, flat-out shaking my head, balling my hands into fists in the foyer of the home. "I'm not leaving the show. If you don't want to drive me across the desert, then I'll fly over it." *Danny's not going to red light me and make me travel with a newborn to God knows where.*

The flight went well as I expected. He met me with the trailer in Sacramento where we continued north to Seattle. Once there we turned on our TV for coverage of the 1972 Summer Olympic

Games broadcast from Germany. Danny and I watched the male and female gymnastic routines. Watching their litheness, I made a decision.

"Danny," I resolved, "I'm ten days overdue. I want the baby induced."

"Make the arrangements," he answered eyes glued on the TV.

On September 7, alone, orderlies transported me from the labor area through wide double-doors to the delivery room on a narrow hospital cot. I spied a crucifix on the doorframe and softly prayed, "God, I know it's late to ask. May I please have a son?"

When the doctor nestled Winston in my arms minutes later, I looked up at the shiny ceiling. "Thank you," I said aloud.

After I settled into a private room, Danny called. "Are you excited? You have a son." I exclaimed.

"I do, don't I. I wanted another girl," he said sounding peevish.

"I don't think God's going to change him back," I answered, not caring if he knew what I meant. I stayed in my private room for four days taking time for my second child and myself. Winston's head, badly bruised by forceps, had rested upside down in the birth canal. I loved him past the bruises, seeing his dark blue eyes and long-black hair, adoring everything about him.

* * *

From Seattle we drove to Vancouver, B.C., and back south to Portland, Oregon. From there we drove to Boy River. Ivy, comparable to me two decades earlier, anticipated scampering in my grandparents' yard. I proudly presented Winston. "Grandpa, he missed your birthday by one day. I'll help clean fish with you."

"That's good, I'll show you how I want them done," he said handing me a filet knife. I transferred Winston to my grandmother's arms.

Time spent with my grandparents was precious. Nevertheless, we had to move on to Duluth. The show hired Reverend Wells Newell Graham from St. Wilifred's Episcopal Church in Sarasota part time to see to the needs of the performers. Wells, as we called him, was on the lot when we parked at the DECC. He greeted us at our trailer. "Let me see your little one. How shall I baptize him?" he asked.

"Ives Winston Wheeler Chapman. He's had a cold since birth and I don't want to wait until we go to Sarasota. Danny named him Winston after Churchill and Ives Wheeler was my father's name. He's your new member of Christ's church," I easily told Wells. "Joey Matheson is his Godfather. The Godmother's not here."

"That's fine, Sarah. I'll contact a church and get back to you."

The next morning, we posed for photographs in front of an ivy-clad wall at St. Paul's Episcopal Church. Posing with my family for Winston's baptism trumped show publicity because the images were irreplaceable.

Photo shoot over and time to nurse, we returned to the DECC. Danny told me, "Dummy wants to see you."

Dummy was deaf rather than dumb. "What do you want Dummy?" I asked curiously.

"Danny said you need a new camera and I traded him my Konica for your movie camera. He said it was okay with you," Dummy told me in his sharp raspy voice, while hanging his camera on my shoulder.

"Gee, Dummy, he didn't tell me anything. This is nice of you. I'll take lots of pictures."

"That's right. We're swapping so I can take moving pictures."

I turned back to the trailer, stopped and asked, "Wait, is there film in the camera?" He nodded. "Let's have our picture taken."

* * *

Danny finagled something bigger than the camera switch after Winston was born and even asked my approval, a rarity. "The Frolic is due for a replacement. What do you think?" Living space and conveniences were almost non-existent.

"I've always liked the trailer. I won't miss the icebox, the broken oven, waking up to steamy windows, and no hot water. What have you found?"

"A 1973, twenty-four-foot Concord motorhome with air-conditioning and a generator. We can get it before the end of the season in Cleveland, if you agree. It costs $10,000 with payments for seven years."

"We can do that. What will happen to the trailer and truck?"

"We're trading them. I made arrangements to buy back the trailer and have it driven to Sarasota."

* * *

I pulled on fishnets and climbed my web three weeks after Winston's birth. We negotiated our 1973 contract in October 1972. My pay raise was $10/week, because showgirl salaries increased.

We returned to the Bayou in December and had a month long break until rehearsals started. "Let's stay in the motorhome," Danny said, "That way we can give a young-retired-military couple a two-year-lease on the house. They told me they won't bother anything left in the front bedroom."

"Smart idea, Danny. It saves me boxing up for storage downtown."

Our traditional Chapman/Wheeler Christmas day was notable. My brother and his second wife, Connie, had a baby girl, Jennifer Mae, born the same day. Merritt moved to Arcadia, Florida, where he bought a mobile home on five acres of scrubland. He dug a pond, and planted numerous live oak trees so one day it would resemble Oakairs.

* * *

For the upcoming season, I tried not to take everything so serious. "Danny, you said you were lengthening my cables two feet, giving me a longer swing. I have an idea now that I'm in Ring One with no tiger cages below me. Let's be pirates and sword fight for our entrance. You throw the web at me. I catch it and start climbing while it's swinging."

"Do I get to wear a hat with skull and crossbones?" he asked immaturely.

"You bet! I'll even make you a raggedy pirate costume. Mine is red stretch satin shorts and boots with a red-lace puffy-sleeved shirt tied at my midriff. I'll get my bar gold plated to match the wardrobe."

"Your handkerchief can be a pirate flag pulled out of your boot."

"That's a great idea. It reminds me, I have to make a head scarf."

I practiced with the new cables. "I work harder pushing the bar back and forth. The swings are slower, more graceful. The twist has the same tempo. I do feel safer being a littler closer to the ground," I said. "Thanks for making longer cables."

He asked about my pirate costume, "Where are the sequins and jewels?"

"I have a huge gold loop earring, gold trim on my forearms, and a gold buckle on the belt. I'm a poor pirate and prefer my talent shines more than rhinestones."

"The show might give you trouble."

"I'm wearing the pirate costume as long as I nurse Winston," I insisted. Then I asked him about something that troubled me. "Why do you hold him under your arm as if he's a football?"

"I do? The Super Bowl's next week." That wasn't an answer and didn't explain why he didn't hold Winston upright and in front of him as he held Ivy. I ended up watching Danny who was supposed to be watching Winston.

CHAPTER TWENTY
TOUGH SEASON

1973 RBB&B Red Unit

When rehearsals started in Venice, Vince Dillmann found me sorting through my trunk contents under the bleachers. Vince was the catcher for Wayne Gill's Australian flying act, The Flying Waynes, along with Wayne's wife, Mary, and another leaper who did a triple somersault. "Sarah, will you be the AGVA alternate steward this year? I think there will be contract issues later in the season. I can represent the performers better with your help." Vince asked and informed me.

"Yes. Anything to help the performers," I told Vince, who always looked a little displaced due to wearing trousers, a belt, and buttoned shirts. "I hear you're from Tallahassee."

"Yes, that's where I went to school. I joined the Flying High Circus and have been with it ever since."

"What did you really want?" I asked, looking into blue eyes framed by a well-shaped face and sandy colored hair.

"I studied law."

"That says it all. Good luck getting circus performers in agreement. Most of us have fixed minds."

* * *

The 1973 Red Unit opening number placed three women performers, including me, on the three largest elephants. Our outstanding wardrobe, designed by Don Foote, was a sequined mini dress, ostrich plumed hat, matching gloves, and long-sleeved sequined cape stretching back to the pachyderm's tail. I waved and smiled warmly in that flame red costume.

* * *

Circus life didn't stop me from working on my education. "Sarah, this came for you from Chicago," said Mac, the show's mail carrier.

"Thanks," I said, ripping open the package.

"Hitting the books again?" Danny quizzed upon seeing a notebook shoved into the tote.

"I got a high grade in the first class. This is Western Civilization. One day I'll graduate from college." He exhaled and slightly rolled his eyes.

* * *

Mothering Winston was easier than Ivy. I think it was my infant's calm nature and my maturity. *This baby is yours,* came from nowhere at his birth. The message told me Danny wouldn't nurture our son. When it was time for spoon feedings, diaper changes, baths, any event connected to child rearing, Winston had me and not his dad. Maybe that was why he carried him oddly, so they wouldn't bond. Danny rarely voiced any opinion on his last child and when he did, it was odd, like the time he said he didn't like him dressed in a matching knitted outfit when he was seven months old. He didn't go on to say how he wanted him dressed so I dressed him how I pleased.

Ivy turned six and I taught her first-grade lessons each morning. She was one of twenty-five circus children of the staff, performers, clowns, showgirls, and concessionaires.

Infant Winston adapted to circus life. His Sarasota pediatrician ordered a brace for his feet for a leg condition called internal tibia rotation. Left untreated, his legs would bow inward. Initially he wore the brace on his feet under his long gowns during the day. "Put Winston on skim milk to lighten the load on his legs. Keep the brace on twenty-four-hours a day until he's one-year-old," the doctor said, at his six-month wellness check in New York City.

"Poor, baby," I consoled Winston. "Wearing a brace day-and-night. First you lost Mama's milk at five months because you bit me raw. Now it's sleeping with your brace. I'll do a better job feeding you real food." With help from a blender, Winston ate the same food as us.

True to the care shown for me at my baby shower many of the circus women doted on Winston. The Bulgarians passed him in his playpen calling out, "Chou Chou," meaning cute little one.

Our family life separated us from Danny. After the night show, the children and I went to bed. Danny stayed outside, repairing light plugs or water hose fittings, or so he said. I didn't miss my nightly peck on his cheek. Years later fellow performers told me he nursed a bottle of whiskey in the wooden box at the back of the motorhome.

Weekly shopping trips with Danny disturbed me. I did drive the truck, but not the motorhome, so I depended upon him for grocery shopping and laundry. The option was taking a taxi or asking to go along with my neighbors living on the lot. I did neither and went with Danny in the motorhome. Limited time and extra responsibility complicated the short trips.

"Do we have to take extra people with us? Can't we go by ourselves?" I whined before anyone joined us, uncomfortable with his loyalty to Clown Alley.

"The clowns have a hard time getting to the market and laundromat," Danny answered, pulling off the lot heading for the nearest shopping center. Once there, he pressured me to hurry so he could go back to the lot. He needed forty-five-minutes for his intricate make-up. He also left early for the building to prepare for come in—twenty minutes before showtime. Finding me folding baby clothes, Danny griped, "Why can't you throw all the clothes in a bag like everyone else?"

"I fold them, so our clothes don't have wrinkles, and it gives me a chance to talk with town people," I answered quietly, compensating for his loudness. "I'm doing the best I can. Help me and we'll get done faster." When we hauled the last of the clothes and both kids to the motorhome, we left for the lot with or without all the clowns. "How will they get back?" I asked, not understanding how he could leave them stranded.

"They'll catch a ride. Don't worry about them." Petty laundry arguments escalated for years with neither of us giving in.

* * *

My dog, Lacie, was eight when she disappeared during rehearsals in Venice. I left her with Stephanie and she never returned after she went outside. Lacie's absence created a huge void in my life, and I longed for her throughout the day and night. I felt similar longing for my father even though he was gone for seven years. Each time in my act I focused on an older man in the audience, I thought, *Maybe this man has a New England accent. Maybe he has brown eyes. Maybe this man could be Daddy watching me.* My grief grew into a mild obsession. Often I woke in a frantic state from dreadful dreams, where I closed in on fine details of a stranger's face, the same face I saw earlier in the audience…always hoping, but never seeing Daddy.

* * *

The publicity department featured me as a show biz mom. Rereading an article from when Winston was five-months-old makes it sound simply like I wore many hats. Press stories included photos, sometimes a recipe, and always comments about the Ringling show.

Dear to my heart is a reading unit in the 1980 Macmillan fourth grade textbook *Rhymes and Reasons*. Featured are interviews and photographs from Ringmaster Bob Welz, the Gaonas, Gunther Gebel Williams, Rudy Lenz Chimpanzees, clowns Peggy Williams and Bobby Kay, and me. "People want to see people doing things they would like to do themselves." Quoted in a schoolbook! It goes on with my bio. "Sarah does a balancing act on a swinging trapeze high above the circus floor. Standing on the trapeze as it swings back and forth to the music, she looks like a ballet dancer in mid-air."

* * *

Deborah Chapman arrived unexpectedly in New York just prior to Easter carrying only a small backpack. She looked different. She'd gained weight, wore baggy clothes, and she'd quit school.

"How did you stop school?" I asked.

"My mom signed for me. I'm fifteen and want to be on the show," she freely announced bouncing Winston on her knee.

"Do you want correspondence courses?"

"I guess so," she answered. I left her in the motorhome with the children and went outside to find Danny chatting with a neighbor.

I motioned that I needed to talk to him. He glared at me, nodded to the neighbor, and approached. "Did you know Deborah was coming?"

"No. She can sleep in the front of the motorhome. We'll figure something out."

"I think she needs professional help for problems we can't fix. Can she get counseling?"

"No! Leave her alone. Can't you see she's depressed?" he fumed, ending the discussion.

* * *

Stephanie joined the show for the summer and it was like old times. She slept in the high bed in the motorhome. I noticed Stephanie, now thirteen, wincing whenever Danny raised his voice or swore at her. "Danny, please tone down your language around Stephanie. Talk respectfully to her or she won't come on the show again." I think he heard me because I seldom saw them together.

"You're doing well in school aren't you?" I asked.

"Yes, art class is best. Look at me, Sarah, I ride the unicycle now." She demonstrated riding forward in a circle.

"I see that. Come with me to bottle feed the newborn tiger cubs."

"Do I have to?"

"No, keep practicing." Assured and jolly, Stephanie cycled towards other children her age. I supplied drawing paper and pencils, encouraging her frank cartoons. Stephanie captured on paper our family's dominant male/submissive female format. Her sketches journaled outcomes to domestic issues like the time she and other youth sprayed graffiti on an exterior wall to an arena and Danny made her scrub it off. She expressed her thoughts on paper. I didn't have enough nerve to ask Danny if he cared for her cartoons. I framed several of them and put others in the scrapbook. Her sensitivities inspired me to lighten her load.

I encouraged her to learn the basics of the web routine. "It's nice having you here this summer, Stephanie. I want you kids to pose for a photograph to match the one we took when Ivy was a year old," I told her while slowly rotating her as she hung upside down in the web's foot loop.

Finally I wanted to give Stephanie something when she was not with us. "Would you consider taking after-school art classes in Sarasota? I'm thinking about the Chase School of Art on Bay Road."

"Well, maybe," she answered not totally understanding my offer. She did go to art class and benefited enough to thank me more than once.

* * *

One of the privileges of being a circus performer in the Los Angeles area was meeting the Hollywood celebrities who came backstage. Walter Matthau came and sat in a front row seat. I flipped him a note in the web intro. It went something like—"Hi Walter. You have a cool guy name. Your friend, Sarah. P.S. Look above you." When I saw him read the note and gaze upwards, I blew him a pixie kiss.

* * *

The elephant number went out of control with Gunther's antics towards the dancing girls of which I was one. He held us captive by his ever-present whip. It was hard for me because he stood at my shoulder on a ring curb saying, "You and I could make a beautiful act."

"Go away Gunther. Tell your elephants what to do," I growled, through smiling teeth. *I could probably have any man on the circus and you're so not on my list.* One day he extracted a coarse black hair from Congo's tail placing it on his open palm in front of me. I reached for the hair and thanked him with my eyes. Later, in the hallway, we just smiled at each other and said nothing. I put the hair in a scrapbook for good luck.

* * *

I took the photo of the three sisters with their baby brother wearing his first pair of shoes, although not yet walking. He did, however crawl backwards with the precision of a crustacean. Stephanie flew back to Sarasota with other summer circus children. Estranged Deborah stayed on the show with friends on the train.

* * *

Two days later, I was hemorrhaging. I went looking for Deborah in the building before the show started. I found her at a concession stand blowing up plastic animals. "Deborah, I'm sick and going to a hospital. Will you pack my trunk and help your dad with Ivy and Winston?"

"Sure, I'll do it."

I didn't need Bob Dover's aid. I told Danny flat out, "After finale take me to the closest hospital. I'm doing my act and Deborah's packing my trunk." His mouth dropped open and no words followed.

Corresponding to Philly, it was Sunday and closing night. Profuse hemorrhaging forced me to pace myself hoping for enough strength to make it through the second show.

It seemed hours passed before Danny stomped in to the back of the motorhome. I lay on the double bed in darkness, a paper sack holding my necessities beside the bed. His sagging jaw showed his disgust. "I'm taking you to a hospital on the way to the next town. It's about thirty miles."

I blinked my eyes, exhausted, unable to complain. "I want a hysterectomy, not a D&C. Pills aren't the answer. I want the bleeding stopped."

I wobbled into the vacant emergency room, where they helped me into dry garments, and assisted me to a waiting bed. I told the attendant, "I want a hysterectomy." I dozed off and awoke to a doctor in surgical gear leaning over me.

"I understand you had a D&C," he said.

"Yes, two years ago. Now I want a hysterectomy."

"We're giving you a pregnancy test."

"That won't be necessary," I whispered. *Why isn't he listening?* "It's the law," he answered. I fell into the deep sleep of exhaustion.

I woke the next morning and grabbed my chart at the end of the bed. "Why another D&C?" I demanded when the doctor finally arrived.

"Because you're still young. You may want another child. You have a rather large fibroid that I left in place. You will heal with rest."

When Danny walked into my room, I wasn't dressed. "Why aren't you out front?" he shouted far too loud for a hospital.

"I'm not ready. I'm still bleeding."

He tossed clean clothes on the bed and put my soiled ones in the sack. "The doctor said to keep taking pills."

Two weeks later and still bleeding I confronted Danny, "I'm not getting better. Can Deborah work in my place?"

"She can try. Single trap?"

"Yes, she's willing. I'm making her an audition costume."

Deborah performed a better than average single trapeze routine. The show turned her down as my substitute. "You're free to leave but we can't contract Deborah."

I knew Danny wouldn't budge. He wouldn't allow me to stop work and he wasn't ready to leave the Ringling show. "Deborah wants to work in concessions and live on the train."

"I know." I didn't see her much for the remainder of the season. I listened to Danny's accounts of her experiences.

* * *

Tragedy struck the 1973 Red Unit season in Ottawa, Canada. Towards the end of the show's second half, the clowns cavorted and performed to provide ample time to set the flying act nets and tighten all guy wires meant to hold the Flying Waynes' four-foot-long wooden pedestal board in place. Reliable and lovely, Mary Gill climbed the pedestal ladder first. At the top, she expected a sturdy platform and released one hand and then the other from the support wire to step aside for the next person.

The pedestal wobbled and she plummeted outside the net to the arena, hitting her head on the ring curb. She lay motionless. Wayne descended the same rickety ladder Mary scaled moments earlier and knelt at her side. From the catcher's trap, Vince had helplessly watched Mary's plummet, grabbed his web, and slid down it. The Farfans, the flying act in Ring One, also dashed to Mary.

Clowns returned to the arena to distract the audience, which rose up in shock and dismay. This was the most confused scene I ever saw at a circus and I witnessed many accidents. The cast was crying, stunned, or consoling each other in groups. When Mr. Dover felt we were ready for finale, he blew his whistle. The sullen shrill and equally sad musical chords guided us robot-like performers in a simple parade criss-crossing the track partially hiding emergency crews working on Mary's lifeless form.

Despite the deep-rooted ingrained desire to entertain and amuse the masses we were unable to smile. Our thoughts were for Mary. It could have been any one of us in her place. A doctor from the audience rushed to her and stayed with her on the hospital trip. A brain injury specialist relieved him. She was in a coma for most of her thirty-second year. Another year passed before she relearned how to walk and how to speak. I sent her biography to *Circus Report* in California, and Don Marcks published it in his weekly news magazine.

The Flying Waynes were never the same without Mary's beauty and broad smile, not to mention her smooth double somersault.

The accident deeply affected the show a month later during the two Thanksgiving Day performances in Springfield, Massachusetts. Usually performers are in an upbeat mood at the end of the season. A rumor circulated from someone irritated enough to say, "Have you heard? We're doing two shows on Christmas." It wasn't true, but it could have been.

I prepared our family's Thanksgiving dinner a week ahead of time in Hartford, Connecticut. "What shall I add to the menu,

Deborah? Your dad asked for stuffed Cornish game hens."

"Pumpkin pie," she said, handing the menu back to me. "Why don't you write a cookbook?"

"I might. If I do, I'll call it, *A Circus Girl's Cookbook*."

CHAPTER TWENTY ONE
DOWN THE ROAD

1974 RBB&B Red Unit

New season preparations occurred during our break in Sarasota. The rehearsals were in Venice as usual. My second ten-dollar pay raise yielded me $195/week. Danny's $275/week stayed the same.

I don't know the politics how Deborah joined our contract. Just sixteen, Deborah was the youngest Aerial Chapman. Her beginning salary of $185/week was fifty dollars more than mine was five years earlier. She was worth it and I had no hard feelings.

Deborah resembled Danny the most of his four daughters. Honey-blonde, hazel-eyed Deborah stood five-foot-two with a powerful upper body suited for aerial work. Her temperament blended well on the show. Unlike me, she didn't bog down with the showgirl-plus-act syndrome. I accepted that she considered herself an adult.

Besides doing five production numbers Deborah performed with me on the revolving ladder. The show carried the ladder on the train and for shows, hung it on the track using Ringling mainfalls (long lengths of rope attached to the rigging and the building ceiling).

Deborah and I did a quick trapeze routine on the ladder and finished with a fast revolve. Our pink costumes didn't match and the act was my career low point. Cut to less than three minutes, mediocrity honestly describes this former feature presentation.

The additional aerial act took me out of the aerial-ballet and ménage leaving me in five numbers.

* * *

Two accidents happened during rehearsals. The first one potentially fatal to sixteen-month-old Winston.

Danny lugged him into the arena in his usual football carry dressed only in a diaper.

"Where are Winston's clothes?" I asked.

"Don't worry." he announced to everyone within hearing. "The hospital just finished x-raying him and there are no broken bones."

"Broken bones? What happened?" I shouted trying to stay calm. Then I saw scratches all over Winston's face and arms, none of them deep.

"I turned right off the Trail and didn't see Winston by the motorhome door. He hit the handle and rolled out into the ditch. I saw the door swing open and he was gone," Danny said, half laughing.

"Oh my, poor baby," I wept tearfully into his chubby face, then hugged him tightly. "We'll put a lock on the door."

"See if you can get a harness for him and attach a rope so he doesn't wander off or get in front of the show trucks."

"I'll shop for one today."

The second accident left me heartbroken. We left daily rehearsals, our motorhome packed with young people to drop off in town. As Danny started to pull out I heard a single yelp from my new puppy. I knew instantly and instinctively it died. Rivers of tears and wailing released a backlog of hurts. The ridealongs stepped out of the motorhome leaving kids, Danny, and me. He stepped out of the motorhome and returned to a fresh new burst of tears.

"I buried the pup at the edge of the lot. Father Connie's in the building. He's waiting for you at the back door."

Sobbing somewhat less, I entered the darkened arena to meet with Father Connie.

"So, you're the one who lost your dog. Tell me what happened."

"We were leaving the lot, when someone let my puppy out. It got under the tires. I adopted two other dogs last season and gave them both away. This puppy was special."

"You were with your family in the motorhome?"

"Yes. And the extra people who wanted a ride to town."

"You need to realize your priorities. The welfare of your family comes first."

Father Cornelius Docherty, pastor at Incarnation Church, had a fondness for circus nomads. After a while I saw the remedy. "We're not giving rides anymore," I insisted when I returned to the motorhome.

I thought I needed a dog to give and receive love, the love I was missing from Danny. When my Sarasota vet called saying he had a puppy he thought I would like, I went to see it. Brown and black fur covered the chubby six-week old pup and it wasn't hard to pick it up and cuddle it in my arms. "I'll take it and thank you for thinking of me." I paid for puppy shots.

Deborah liked the puppy too and came up with a boy's name for it that I can't recall. Puppy licks on my ears smell like perfume. I knew this puppy would grow into a faithful obedient companion. Running over the puppy made me wake up to my family and accept I couldn't tackle more responsibility.

* * *

Starting the season physically worn out, I failed to decide whether I was going to do or had finished doing my balancing trapeze. One show blended into the other until performing was scarcely perceptible. Unawareness is an ill state of affairs for an athlete. No longer in prime condition, my body remained partially numb, barren as tundra. I taught Ivy in the morning, cooked our meals, cleaned the motorhome, did the shows, and longed for Sunday night and travel day.

* * *

Bernie Gersen offered a brief respite from my overwhelming depression. The Somerton Gang's only remaining bachelor seemed like a visiting angel when we hit Washington DC. "I'm on my way to Israel to set up a scholarship in my name at the University," he told me.

"Good for you Bernie. You're such a sweetheart helping someone's education."

I was exhausted. I watched as some showgirls jetted to Puerto Rico on their days off. I admired their tans. Others went to Broadway shows. My days filled with dull laundry, grocery shopping, and other chores. I found no joy to lighten my days.

* * *

In Boston, Jeanette Williams helped the circus children perform a mini-show for their parents. Winston, now nineteen-months-old, matched his father's tramp clown make-up and wore a red-and-black clown suit. Together, they stole the show, posing for an Associated Press photograph bearing the caption, "Like father, like son." Ivy tumbled in the kid circus, something I'd taught her between shows.

I didn't feel well during the first week of the Boston date. Precisely ten days after Winston's measles shot, I woke up with a fever too high to work. "I'm going to a clinic. See you later," I told Danny. It was an effort walking there and returning to the motorhome.

"Well, what did the doc say?" Danny sounded absent minded, distant.

"I've got the flu. Stay in bed and drink fluids. Please shut the curtains." I laid down tugging blankets around me and closing my eyes.

Sometime later, I heard Danny open the motorhome door and say, "She's back there."

I couldn't focus on the young man in street clothes who raised a thermometer trying to read it in the dim light.

"Who are you?" I mumbled.

"I'm the doctor from the building. How long have you been here?"

"I don't know (it was three days). What's my temperature?"

"It's 104°. Stick out your tongue please."

I obliged. "Can you roll on your side? Good. Just what I thought. The rash indicates you have German measles and need darkness for several days. Stay in bed and drink fluids. When the fever breaks, you'll feel better. If your eyes get discolored, go to a doctor."

"Thank you for coming," I whispered.

Between shows, Danny looked at me with his sad face. "Work is out of the question. Don't even ask," I croaked. "The show will go on. Besides, I'm in quarantine." I felt better knowing I had measles, it provided the appropriate answer, giving me time to recover.

Deborah fussed over me and cared for Ivy and Winston. Many of the showgirls signed her homemade get-well card to me. She asked the circus vet, Doc Henderson, to pull Ivy's loose tooth. Then she set it under a glass and the tooth fairy, aka big sister, exchanged it for a quarter.

When the whites of my eyes turned bright yellow, I saw another doctor who believed the discoloration came from the intensity of the virus. I squeezed antibiotics into my eyes for a month and gladly went without eye make-up.

* * *

My showgirl friends Judy Bottler, Tina Torres, and a new one, Pamela Nelson Strongman, comforted me. Pamela, a buxom blonde from California, had a novel way of curving her fingers backwards when she styled. Dummy, a light-hearted person like Pamela, took a picture of me sitting outside the building in Fresno in partial sun waiting for my act cue. Lithe anemic limbs contrasted sharply with shining raven hair, full red lips and an odd expression I know inside was, "Is this all there is to life?"

I still yearned for a dog. In Kansas City in a mall I saw a cute wire-haired fox terrier. "Let's buy him," I said without weighing the matter. We left the store with a three-month-old pup. Danny named it Hogan after a caretaker of a Kansas City burlesque house. Hogan wasn't my favorite dog. He was a good family pet and worked in Danny's clown numbers.

***

The second half of the season came and went. The show closed in Cleveland. Only a select group had contracts for the upcoming year. Of the American clowns and showgirls, ninety-five-percent were let go. Deborah stayed close to us after we learned we weren't coming back. "There are other circuses and other ways to earn a living," I told my family during an evening meal.

The vigor I once had for performing was lost. I wanted to return to a routine warm-up followed by a precise performance. I yearned for a fresh start. I didn't know how to make my marriage better. Ten years with a much older man had prematurely aged me and I felt lost—a child with two children and two stepchildren. I nurtured others, but never myself.

1975 Sarasota

After six grueling years on the Ringling Circus, my family looked forward to having home life in Sarasota. We accomplished many things from January to September: I earned an Associate in Art degree, Ivy attended my old elementary school, and our circus acts found new energy, coming alive.

"I want to break in the revolving ladder," Danny excitedly told me. "The place to do that is the Circus Hall of Fame. Deborah wants to do single trapeze and she started juggling. Curtis is joining us as your new partner." He wants to live in the Frolic.

In 1973, twenty-year-old Curtis Kidd Cainan joined Ringling as a groom, the least dignified and lowest paying job in a circus. Platinum blonde, blue-eyed, Curtis juggled and rode a unicycle. Danny envisioned him doing the revolving ladder one day with Deborah and me and told him to wait until the opportunity arose.

Danny tossed a paper sack on the kitchen counter top making a clinking noise.

"What are these big nails?" I asked fingering one.

"They're spikes. I've always wanted a screened-in patio."

"I hope you don't need my help. I want a vegetable garden by the bayou and Rhode Island Red laying hens for eggs."

"You sound like a farm girl," Danny laughed.

"Sort of," I said softly in return, liking my queen bee position, where not all work needed my participation. My hands were full caring for the children, now ages eight and two, cooking, setting up the house, learning the head balance, and sewing new wardrobe. Sunday, our day off, allowed me the luxury of attending church.

After Mass we picked up Patrnella and brought her home for Sunday dinner. When the table cleared, I settled Patrnella into her padded rocking chair where she napped or peeked out watching the activities. Grandchildren combed her white bobbed curls, the same ones Danny had in brown. Patrnella held the copyright to the Chapman blue eyes.

Monticello Subdivision welcomed us home. Joan lived in and managed apartments where Montclair Drive meets the Trail. Willie and Annie Edelston were active in Sailor Circus, he coached hand balancing and flying, and she volunteered in wardrobe.

Emerich Moroski made daily stops at our side door as if it was an extension to his room next door with his parents, Gena and Charlie. Lolita and Frank Perez added a German shepherd to their existing pets: noisy, aggressive society finches that dove at doe-like Negrita, Lolita's dainty Chihuahua. Frank built a concrete wall on the property line adding an iron gate to access our practice yard.

* * *

"Do you think you can teach Hogan to be a pad dog?" Danny asked me.

"I can try. Give me used rope for a handle and I'll make Curtis quick-release dog catcher pants."

I sat at the sewing machine for a half hour, then gathered the project. Finding Curtis wasn't hard. I went outside carrying my liberally sweetened iced tea and ducked under the large water oak at the side of the house. I took a couple of deep breaths of tree-cooled air and watched Curtis practice bouncing five rubber lacrosse balls off a sheet of plywood laying flat on the ground. Thump-thump-thump-thump-thump hummed the white balls.

"That's good juggling, Curtis." I told him. "Here's something new. You're playing the part of a dogcatcher. Please try on these pants I made for you. Lightly tack the outside seams and hold the tie at your waist."

"Okay, Sarah. What's the rope at the back?"

"That's what Hogan grabs a hold of after you say, "Hogan! Hit!" When you feel him tugging, hold tight on the tie. Turn around twice, release the tie, and run out of the pants."

"Okay, Sarah." That's all he ever said to me.

* * *

Each night our family gathered for dinner at an antique oak table bought in Plum Tree, Indiana. A steal at $100, it amply spread its leaves feeding up to twelve. Open discussion followed three-course-meals. Topics ranged from rigging, garden construction, and schoolwork, to contract progress for the Hall of Fame.

I enrolled in the spring semester at Manatee Junior College. "Danny, I'm studying in the front room and need help with the children. Can you do that?"

"Do what? Help?" he said pouring boiling water on instant coffee mixed with three spoonfuls of sugar in his mug. He added a generous amount of milk and returned to the table. "Oh, I suppose." Danny's hearing was fine, yet he appeared far away in thought. Instead of asking what help I needed, he changed the subject. "I'm growing tomatoes with hydroponics on the patio."

"I'm off to bathe Winston, read bedtime stories, and study," I said, carrying a stack of dirty plates to the kitchen where Curtis did his part, washing dishes and tidying counters.

When the children bedded, I sat for hours studying until I was satisfied with homework assignments. Campus life exposed me to current trends and youthful ideas. I pictured myself with short hair, despite breaking Danny's hair rule.

He rebuffed me when I got the courage to cut it. "You should have left it long. You don't know what you're doing."

"It's too hot for long hair," I declared, meekly and then I fibbed. "I mainly kept it long for the Ringling Show hats."

I dreaded my graduation. I wanted the kids to see me graduate but didn't want Danny to go. He was getting unpredictable. *Sarah, you can do this.*

"Big crowd today, kids. Stay with Dad. Mom's walking across the stage for her diploma," I told them, when I slipped into line with the other graduates. After the brief ceremony, I opened a leather folder for Ivy and Winston. "Associate in Arts, Home Economics Education. One day, I'll have a Bachelor Degree. You will too."

"Come on, let's get out of here," Danny voiced sharply, pulling Winston towards the parking lot.

* * *

I was in bed reading a magazine when Danny excitedly returned from the Showfolks of Sarasota Clubhouse. "We've got work!" he declared, pacing the floor. "George Hubler from Dayton, Ohio, gave us most of the show at the Hall of Fame. He wants the ladder, your trap, swinging ladder, the juggling act, and me for clowning. You can work Ivy into the juggling on her unicycle and she's old enough to do swinging ladder. Alfredo Langdon also clowns. You'll like him."

"That's wonderful. Our renewed professionalism is paying out." I paused a moment to consider what needed doing. "I hadn't planned to make wardrobe for Ivy…hmm... When does the Hall open?"

"Memorial Day weekend."

Morning practice became mandatory due to the head balance trick I started learning the previous year. I tipped upside-down for an eternity on chairs in buildings. For the trick, the top of my head nested on a cork grommet. My back held straight, legs out, toes pointed, and arms spread, I gained competency on my bar and practiced it swinging. At age twenty-nine, a late learner for that skill, I posed upside-down for photos.

Each afternoon Deborah, Curtis, and I practiced the revolving ladder. Then Deborah and I passed juggling clubs and fire torches. Deborah and Curtis were the real jugglers.

"You guys are getting good at passing. Why don't you put Ivy in the middle?" Danny hinted, during a practice.

"I don't think she'll stand for that," Deborah said, smiling at the thought of her kid sister holding still with clubs whizzing past both ears.

"She'll have to. It's part of the act. What's the wardrobe theme for juggling?"

"Curtis suggested western wear," I answered. "For the ladder act, I'm recycling old wardrobe and making new, white costumes. Since next year is the Bi-centennial, I picked red, white, and blue trim on white-coque-feathered hats."

"Sounds classy," Danny said, returning with me to the house.

* * *

I wandered to the porch to continue sorting papers from the cherry wood dresser that Mother gave me. When I was a child, the serpentine front dresser held her clothes and an assortment of make-up and cologne on top. The dresser came filled with boxes of handwritten letters to Daddy from Grandmother Wheeler from 1914 until her death in 1933. It also included fragile silverware, Daddy's WWI military records, and lovely photographs I had never seen before. *Daddy's been gone nine years. This is an odd way to re-enter my life.*

"Danny, I'm emptying the dresser and sending it to Jura Studios on Worrington Street for restoration," I said.

"Curtis can help you load it in the luggage trailer," my helpful husband replied.

"Thanks," I said distracted by what I'd just read. *Grandmother Wheeler listened to classical music. I wonder about her personality. Her letters share a portion of Great Barrington's history. I'll keep a few and toss the rest.*

That was a bad archival decision, but good for making Daddy tangible and helping me stop yearning for him.

"Look at the new pictures in the hallway. Your names come from this man, Grandfather Wheeler. His war medals are different from American Legion convention medallions. He would take you to ball games if he were here," I told the children at the supper table.

Accepting my father's death, I vowed to grieve openly, let tears flow, and talk about my pain to anyone who listened.

PART THREE

CHAPTER TWENTY TWO
INTERLUDE

Once the circus Hall of Fame show got underway, all aspects of our performance improved. "Tourist attendance could be better," Danny told Deborah, Curtis, and me at a pep talk. "But don't worry about that. We're here to practice."

For my featured act, I twisted a metal plate holding the cork grommet in the center of my bar. Next, I pulled upside-down, positioning my head in the grommet keeping the bar under my body, the same as when I stood on it. This trick completed what I wanted as a teenager—head and foot balancing trapeze. Between shows, I practiced the same position swinging. I had rocks in my head!

Another act in the show included Hugo Schmitt's son, Roman, presenting a rhinoceros act.

"Winston loves your baby rhino," I said, watching Roman give the rhino free exercise. "Can he have a ride? I want to take pictures."

"Sure. I'll give him my bull hook so he looks professional."

I took pictures of Winston with the camera Dummy gave me. Winston giggled with glee—a rhino cowboy. "Thanks for Winston's ride."

Cheerful Winston did two age-appropriate clown walk-arounds. Often grinning, his comical eyebrows arched, framing his dark-blue eyes and red-greasepaint nose.

Nine-year-old Ivy's performance included riding a unicycle in the juggling act, staying still during juggling club passes, and swinging back-and-forth on a white ladder resembling a frilly-pink-petunia in the breeze. She was the show's busy beaver, full of energy, always upbeat.

* * *

I gained fifteen pounds, and slept at least that many hours a day. After each number, I told anyone nearby, "Wake me up for my next act." Our family physician, Dr. George Scherer, drew blood.

"Your lab test showed you have an under active thyroid. You need medication, which I'll prescribe to you. Come back in two months for labs." Dr. Scherer's calm voice informed me. Bespectacled George Scherer, about my age, was fair-haired and thin with a knowledgeable disposition.

"I feel fine, lost weight, and sleep only at night. Now my arms ache. Its hard holding them out." I said when I returned to Dr. Scherer.

"Hmm," he paused, writing a diagnosis on my insurance receipt. It said myalgia.

"What's that?"

"It's something in your muscles we don't know how to explain. Your thyroid's okay. I want you to continue taking the pills and get tested annually." He closed my folder and left the exam room.

* * *

Labor Day ended the circus show at Sarasota's remarkable tourist attraction. We moved our rigging, props, wardrobe, make-up, and the Frolic back to Phillippi Bayou.

Deborah and Stephanie lived with their mother only two houses away from us on Montclair Drive. I grew accustomed married to a man with two wives on one street. Joan was a mystery. At one time I wanted her off the show. I knew we parented differently. Still, I lacked antagonism towards this extremely quiet person who faithfully performed yard duties keeping the apartment complex's lush shrubbery green and growing. So many things were off kilter, one more thing didn't matter. I infrequently saw Michele Chapman. Unmarried, she shared a house in Sarasota with a friend.

* * *

"I think Ivy needs some type of lessons. Can you check what's available?" Danny asked before school started.

"I'm ahead of you. There's ballet at Mrs. Swope's studio on Osprey Avenue or gymnastics at Culbertson's Gymnastique in Bradenton."

"How about both?"

"Let's ask Ivy."

In addition to ballet and gymnastics, I enrolled Ivy in fourth grade at Phillippi Shores. I mulled over some of the Danny Rules I'd heard for years. "Girls don't need school past tenth grade." I wanted Ivy to receive a far better education. Deborah quit when she was only fifteen. Stephanie switched from high school to vocational classes. Michele earned a GED. I wondered if he would let Winston go to college.

That fall, I took a correspondence course (Middle Year Child Development) from the University of Florida. It was difficult and fun at the same time. When I sent in the first lesson, I wrote to my mailbox teacher, "Why do I study myself in child psychology?

"Understanding yourself is a beginning tool. As you ponder your childhood, find constructive thoughts," she replied. This gentle tip helped. I put my heart into the class and gained from her wisdom. I favor their middle years when working with children. Oh, to be ten again—half of twenty and half-grown up. My continuing education allowed me to escape to logical and rhythmic textbook assignments, no conflict, no disdain heaped upon me while I studied.

* * *

Hard questions about birth order, parents, social skills, education, hobbies, and religion made me think deeply about my childhood. I felt loved by Daddy. He named me Sarah, a family name, and Kate, from Kate McComb, first lady of American radio. I think he liked my turquoise eyes, different from my family's dark brown and hazel. Mama wanted another boy after Merritt, not a girl. Then she had a hysterectomy and couldn't have more children.

Mattie, our African-American domestic, probably loved me too. Daddy paid her to care for me from birth to age two. "Some days," Mother wrote years later, "Mattie appeared out of nowhere to take the burden of you children away from me."

I knew Mother was different, though never pinned down why. It was hard to tell if she used force because she was angry and unhappy with us or just angry at life in general. She seemed happy when she drove Merritt and me to Crescent Beach taking the north route with the humpback bridge where she sped up the car making it fly over the hump. Wind gushed through open windows and vents, we lifted off the back seat squealing delightedly. Maybe she couldn't hear the difference between that and our terrified screams.

Cleaning opposite sides of windows when I was fourteen, she nonplussed me, "You're too big to hit." Verbal abuse replaced fists from that day forward, punishing me as much or maybe even more than her brute strength. My periods started after a ninth grade school day and I searched for pads hidden in my closet. Mama drove me to circus practice and stopped at Off Shore blatantly announcing to Daddy in the parking lot, "Sarah commenced her menstruation. I'm taking her to show off in front of the boys."

Daddy's downcast head reflected my mood as I sank lower in the back seat. Mama rattled on. "I suppose we'll have another Lucy on our hands." Daddy gazed into nothing, turned, and trudged inside. *Poor Daddy.*

When Merritt and I were little, Daddy took us dime store shopping and let us pick out small toys. Mama pampered us when sick and brought a bell to ding when we needed her. She gave alcohol rubs, took temperatures, and had Daddy call Dr. Morton if we didn't get better. We knew we would be out of bed soon when the food tray had a bowl of poached-egg-on-toast with yellow butter dots dancing in warm milk.

I preferred singing hymns with Daddy at St. Boniface on Siesta Key better than going to High Mass with Mama at the stodgy

Church of the Redeemer downtown. She squeezed my wrist and whispered, "Don't make a noise. Put your hands at your sides and keep them there. You daren't dangle your feet." Released from her grip and afraid to move this way or that, I sat rigid.

Daddy listened well and never put me down. Unconstrained, I chattered after church, "I have a favorite song now. It's *I Sing A Song of the Saints of God*. I want to be an acolyte...girls aren't allowed."

* * *

Danny jolted me back from my thoughts to Montclair Drive when he covered my textbook with a form. "Here, sign this. It says you're my wife. You won't get a check, but three of the kids will. I'm taking my Social Security at age sixty-two."

When he opened his first check, he gloated. "I get a fat check. It doesn't matter what I'm paid for clowning."

Many times Danny boasted, "Winston was born on Social Security." I understood better when $1,000 regularly came our way. Women my age didn't have husbands drawing Social Security. I felt old at age thirty because I looked forward to both the serene photography in AARP's *Modern Maturity* magazine and listening to the Lawrence Welk Show on TV, typical activities for retirees.

Our three waterfront acres sold for luxury condominiums to a Tennessee contractor. His vision for Phillippi Creek profited us $55,000 plus interest, all invested in CDs.

The guaranteed income didn't keep us from going on the road.

Sweating at the Circus Hall of Fame paid off. Danny came home excited one afternoon. "We got a one-show contract at the Tampa Dog Track. It's the Greater Tampa Showmen's Association annual circus night. I want everything first class. Is the new wardrobe ready?"

"Yes, sir. The wardrobe's striking. Hat feathers flutter as expected."

For the second time in a year, the revolving ladder twirled seventy-feet above the banks of the Phillippi Bayou. Deborah and I sped upward on ladder rungs without stopping until we reached the top. I studied the wardrobe: our white skirts floated to the ground, and our skimpy rhinestone-studded leotards flashed like body diamonds.

I felt safe with Deborah balancing her end of the ladder. She kept us level while I did trapeze tricks. When the trap routine ended, I stepped off the ladder to an upright and Curtis stepped on in my place. He twirled, slid, peeled off his hat and jacket, tried standing up, and then whirled around in the opposite direction before taking his style.

"You did well," Danny shouted up to us. After the finish trick, all three of us scattered off the ladder and styled before a rapid descent to the ground.

"You both did a great job. Regardless of where you perform, each time you work treat it like a practice." I said to my partners. *This act has potential.* "Thanks for finishing your wardrobe. Let's meet at the same time tomorrow."

Our team effort paid off in Tampa and continued for the Showfolks of Sarasota benefit circus. During a set-up break at Robarts Arena, Danny coached us, The New Aerial Chapmans, "Lots of producers looking for acts come to this show. Knock 'em dead."

"We'll try," Curtis answered. Deborah nodded. We thrilled agent George Hubler, who signed us for a family package. He contracted us to perform three aerial acts, clowning, and juggling for several '76-spring Shrine dates, starting with the Hubert Castle International 3-Ring Circus.

Danny seemed proud and somewhat pleased. "I'll work on filling in the route. We need mainfalls. I'll order rope and tackle."

* * *

Even though I stood on my head, and Danny powdered his face, sometimes we behaved like an ordinary mom and dad.

"Danny," I reminded him, "It's your turn to pick up Ivy at Culbertson's Gym. I took her there after school."

We celebrated the November and December holidays as in the past ten years. Lucy, single again and relocated to Sarasota from New Mexico, joined us with her son, David.

"Uncle Merritt's here!" I called, watching my children and stepchildren rush outside greeting my tall, dark, and handsome sibling. He had a way with kids, grabbing them and cradling them to his chest. Holding his arms out straight, he let multiple kids hang from his biceps and forearms, all clamoring for his attention. He stayed busy providing turns on the rope swing in the yard, while I finished trimming the table. I chatted with my sister-in-law, Connie, holding my new eight-month-old nephew, Charles. Stuffed with turkey and dessert, we posed for an annual family picture. Those big all-day dinners were my happiest memories living on the bayou.

CHAPTER TWENTY THREE
CURSED TRIP

Spring dates for George Hubler, Hubert Castle, and Sam Polack circuses started March 18 in Dayton, Ohio, and ended June 27 in Wheaton, Illinois. We spent one month of that time in Canada. Chapman family performers completed indoor riggings, practiced, and drove to the Dayton encampment.

"You bought 3,000 feet of rope?" I asked, incredulous.

"Yes, for six 100-foot main falls. They create a storage problem. Curtis will have to get a travel unit and carry rigging."

"What do you suggest?" I asked, foreboding where he was leading.

"We'll help get something. A converted school bus might work because it can hold the ladder on top and the uprights and tackle inside. Everything else goes on the motorhome floor."

They found a bus and I drove Curtis to the bank where I signed for a personal loan using CDs for collateral. When we returned home, the phone rang. Danny answered it and a moment later hung up.

With a long, disbelieving face, he recounted, "Deborah's in the hospital with hepatitis."

"She got hepatitis? How?"

"Her doctor is running tests. She's in quarantine," Danny mumbled.

"We'll go see her," I said, thinking her condition short-lived.

I knew she was gravely ill when I saw Deborah's discolored skin.

"A doctor stuck a needle way inside my liver and it hurt so much," she whispered softly. "I can't go on the road. I'm so sorry. All of you need hepatitis inoculations. Even Winston, and he's so young." She wept as though her illness were her fault.

"Don't worry about us," I answered. "You're the one with needs. The act won't be the same without you. When we come home I want you well and strong."

"I'll try," she whispered, resting her head on a pillow.

* * *

With only six weeks remaining, before we hit the road Danny placed a newspaper ad asking for a female circus partner for aerial work. It brought us a tall, slim food server.

"Hello, I'm Edith Bickford. You can call me Edie," she said as I walked her to the house. She continued, "I performed in the Wenatchee Youth Circus during high school in Washington State. I'm in Sarasota looking for a job on the road." I motioned for her to sit at the table where I placed photos of our acts. Danny joined us.

"Then you've come to the right place. Our partner is ill and we have spring dates," I told Edie. "Look at these photos and see if you're interested in what we do."

"You want me to do single trap," Edie smiled. "I can show that to you today. I brought practice clothes."

"Yes, we would like to see your routine. The ladder isn't hard. It's rigged at ground level for practice," I said and told her where to change. I knew the extra practice needed to break in Edie added strain to my skimpy 108-pound body—down from a stable 115.

While she showed us her tricks, I hoped Edith Bickford was reliable. I thought her pleasant looking face and Cheshire cat smile appealing. I pictured her in makeup and a curled light-brown hairpiece pinned on over her ponytail.

"Edie, become familiar with the setting under the trees. The show expects you to do two or three swinging tricks, nothing spectacular because you're in a display with several other women." That said I conferred with Danny. "She knows the basics. What do you think?"

"We're short on time and have to take her. Her weight and height make the ladder easy for her to balance. I think you're going to have trouble with the handstand when Curtis sways the ladder," Danny cautioned.

"Tell me why."

"Her legs are longer than yours and it will throw the balance off. Go slow and let her take a foot position she feels comfortable with during the lay back and arabesque."

Danny, Curtis, and I told Edith what we expected, explaining we carried our rigging, set it up, and tore it down. We weren't on the Ringling show where riggers did it for us in exchange for a weekly tip. Our salary for the combined acts: two men and two women doing clowning, three aerial acts, and one ground act (juggling) was split four ways compensating my partners for the extra work. Empowering them further, I requested they buy their share of the group wardrobe at cost and keep it clean and repaired.

Edie did have trouble with the handstand. My pride prevented me from pulling the trick. The result of that decision hurt our image more, than if we had done the act without it. "Edie needs to feel comfortable in the lay back position. Stand in front of her and give her your hands for support," I suggested to Curtis during practice. We repeated the up-side-down lay back to arabesque many times.

I was pooped when Edie finally said, "I can do it now. Thanks."

"Thank you. Your effort paid off." I clapped my hands. "That's it for practice. Tomorrow's Sunday, take the day off. We rest one day a week and you should too," I said watching her nod in agreement. "Thanks for helping alter your costumes. Oh! You can move into Curtis' bus when you're ready. Don't mind the critter running around. It's his guinea pig."

Balancing Act

On Monday, in pain I gripped at my left hip, unaware I tore many ligaments during Saturday's practice. I drove to Sarasota Memorial Hospital Emergency Room.

"Doctor, I'm a circus performer. It hurts badly but I need to work soon." What I failed to tell him was my powerful legs propelled me upward on my web or the uprights to the ladder act. Leg extensions from torso to pointed toe gracefully framed my balancing bar tricks through each part of the act whether I was kneeling for the silken handkerchief, or beginning my routine with an arabesque on the web. The best balance in the world isn't possible without functional legs.

"How soon?"

"Six days."

"I'm treating you for torn muscles. This will help with the pain," he said handing me a prescription. Soft-tissue imaging wasn't available in 1976.

I'll rest on the trip, I believed at the time.

Danny, Ivy, Winston, Hogan, and I (using a cane, limping badly, and favoring my left leg) left Sarasota in an excessively loaded motorhome. Lagging behind in a beige school bus were Curtis and the First of May partner.

* * *

"Do the best you can," Danny called out as he pushed me up the web for my balancing act. There wasn't much I could do besides politely stand on the bar until the other acts ended. Wrapped from thigh to waist in elastic bandages, I felt guilty and insisted doing my share. Pain or not, we fulfilled the contract.

The show jumped to Columbus, Ohio where a stranger, whose name I can't recall, planted himself in front of my chair outside the women's dressing room. "I watched you perform and walk. I think I can help."

"Really?" I said, sourly adding, "I'm getting clever with my cane."

"I see that. Look, I'm a circus fan and a doctor, Director of Rehabilitative Sports Medicine at the University of Ohio. If you come for morning therapy, I promise you'll feel better."

"Maybe I'll be there. What time in the morning?"

"Eight o'clock," he answered, knowing show people sleep late.

For ten days, Danny took me to therapy for the benefit of the show. My pain didn't involve blood, so he understood it better, but he didn't help me heal. In the motorhome, I lay in bed swathed by many pillows. Ivy humored Winston and prepared our simple meals. I thought I would bounce back to work quickly.

At physical therapy, ultrasound calmed torn tissue. Isometric exercises started strengthening adjoining muscles and ligaments supporting my severely injured hip, thigh, and leg.

My circus-fan doctor emphasized at my last treatment, "I think ultra-sound helps. Pills won't heal you, only time and exercise. Your pain is from tissue swelling and inflammation." He also told me healing comes from the mind. "Your body heals naturally. Painkillers take away the sensation of healing."

"Thanks for the pep talk," I said, limping away with my cane. I knew I wouldn't stop taking pain pills as they removed the stresses from a broken body, a sick marriage, and more responsibility than I could bear.

* * *

Curtis was living with us in the motorhome. He l-o-v-e-d juggling. When he should have done routine and seasonal maintenance on his bus, he juggled instead. Danny cautioned him in Sarasota, "Curtis, make sure there's antifreeze in your radiator because it's going to get cold as we go north."

"I will Danny," he said, not missing a bouncing ball on the plywood base. In Columbus, water froze in his engine, cracked the block, and burst the radiator forcing him to leave his bus for repairs in a gas station. Danny invited Curtis and Edie into the motorhome. What was he thinking? More wasn't merrier. Curtis went with us and Edie flew to a friend in Sarasota between the next two dates.

Within a week, another peril, acute bronchitis, pierced my weakened body. "Danny (cough)," I said, believing in strength in numbers, "tell the performance director (cough) that I am taking the (cough, cough) ambulance along with the working men with the same (cough) symptoms to the hospital."

"Oh, all right," he sighed, after the Saturday morning show. At the hospital, I got my chest x-rayed and codeine pills. When I remembered, I did what I could of the isometric exercises for my hip.

Danny's behavior changed from energetic to distracted and lifeless. Of the six or more cups of coffee he made daily, I found four of them untouched and poured them out. I asked him several times, "Help me with the downward exercise. I can do the right, left, and up ones." Not getting a response, I left that one out unless Curtis was around.

* * *

Throughout the Canadian dates, Curtis slept in the men's dressing room, Edie was hard to pin down. Danny told me as long as people did the act and helped set up and tear down, it didn't matter what happened in their private lives. He was right and wrong about that.

"Edie, where are you staying nights?" I asked her anyhow.

"An act guy and I share a motel room," she said, applying mascara. "I'm not going to Sarasota anymore. I had a fight with my boyfriend."

"You'll get more rest now," I answered, speaking too soon. That same afternoon, she slid off the ladder rungs into the arms of spotters. From the audience view, the act ended shorter than others did and without a style. It could have been a serious accident. Luckily, we rigged the ladder at practice height, due to an odd ceiling in the Canadian building. The usual dressing room chatter doubled after the accident, and after much needed sleep, Edie performed in the ladder act and on her single trapeze. She willingly slept nights in the women's dressing room after her slip.

Circus performers work at their own risk and there's minimal liability from the show and less, if any, from the building. I believed Edith Bickford had private health insurance as we did.

* * *

Danny gave instructions to Curtis at the last Canadian date. "I want you to take the Greyhound bus to Ohio, pick up your rig, and meet us at the lot in Mt. Clemens, Michigan. Here's some money to help out."

"Thanks, Danny. I'll see you there," Curtis waved goodbye from the Calgary bus station. We proceeded south to Minnesota Raines country.

"You survived, and you're walking better," Aunt Tootie observed.

"Yes, it's been rough. We have some Shrine dates left and then a circus in Lima, Peru. That may be interesting."

"Lucy went to South America, didn't she?"

"Yes, Lucy was a Ringling showgirl in 1960,"

"Grandma and Grandpa asked about you," Aunt Tootie let me know.

"We stopped in Boy River before coming to Remer. I love it here in Minnesota," I said, eyeing several children including my two playing together in the yard. What I didn't tell her was I'd wanted the serenity of my aunts and a normal family life since my teenage years. Their eyes glistened when they laughed. They looked blessed and vigorous, as if they didn't have a care in the world.

* * *

We arrived in Mt. Clemens and found Curtis juggling at a gas station across the street from the tented circus lot. Danny parked the motorhome and I bounded out, "Where's your bus?"

"I picked it up without checking the antifreeze. It froze that night and the radiator broke again. I called the garage and they fixed it."

"That's too bad. I was ready to have you move out."

"I will. Someone is driving it here today," Curtis expressed with the optimism of a rainbow.

In Canada, Winston often held his hands on his forehead. After two trips to emergency rooms and two nasal decongestants, I concurred with the doctor, "Winston is allergic to changing climatic conditions and needs stability." *How does a circus family grant stability? Traveling is what we do for a living!*

I'd had it managing inept people to maintain their health and well-being in a dangerous lifestyle. Danny was no help except for driving. Since Indianapolis, a slack guy wire on my trap act forced me to check my own rigging before I worked.

Nevertheless, I dutifully applied for passports and took everyone for small pox immunizations for our impending trip to Lima, Peru. The contract called for fifty consecutive days with Circus Togni. Frazzled nerves and intense nonstop pain demanded pain relief and my pill supply dwindled.

When I thought clearly, I knew our excellent salary came from the high caliber of our acts. Danny allowed me to represent us. I signed contracts, the latest for $39,000 for the 1977 season with the Hubert Castle Circus was an all time high. It included four acts with four people totaling $6,000 more than the 1974 Ringling season. Our financial success contrasted sharply with our lack of harmony. Debt free with $30,000 invested in CDs, we had money, yet were remiss in some of the most important aspects of life.

Health for starters. My pain and Danny's nastiness increased in tandem. As his impatience grew, I alienated myself. And I took more pills.

One clear day the fragile Midwest springtime seeped into my aching bones. "When it gets warmer, we'll all feel better," I cheerfully announced.

Delicate blooms that sweetened the air accompanied deciduous trees aglitter with fresh green sprouts. Lively beds of tulips, lilies, and daffodils burst from the ground, wiping away the cold and gloom of winter blahs. Jackets replaced heavy coats.

Ivy and Winston explored inside the big top while I stepped on top of it along the ridgeline and saw working men affix an American flag to a center pole. "Please take a picture of me with Lake Huron in the background," I asked handing one of them my camera.

* * *

In Mt. Clemmons, talented performers presented skills to audiences traditionally starting summer fun with a trip to the circus. Not everyone was excited about that starting with Curtis, who'd reacted poorly to his inoculation. I removed my apron and went next door to his bus. Edie came to the door when I knocked. "How's Curtis?"

"He vomited all night and has a fever," she said. "I'm better."

"I'll send Danny over with soup. You need nourishment," I said, and closed the door feeling sad because while their health was improving mine wasn't.

* * *

These tented circuses had wood shavings and sawdust on the track and in the rings. High from drugs, I pretended the sawdust magically crept through the soles of my feet and upward renewing my strength. Nothing dampened my spirits, not even a tornado in Wheaton.

As usual, fearing the worst, Danny herded us into the designated shelter at the county fairgrounds. "Go, all of you, and take Hogan. I'm dropping the rigging in the big top," he said, ordering us down the basement stairs. A party-like atmosphere greeted us as the townspeople offered us and other performers sloppy joes, chips, brownies, coffee, and soft drinks. Drenched from the rain, my disheveled husband joined the refuge just before the worst of the tornado's violent fury blasted overhead. Wind gusts slashed sheets of rain on one side of the building and then the other before the storm moved on to destroy its next victim. Everyone piled outside to view the scene of destruction. This time Danny's fears had come true.

The tornado had chugged along adjoining commuter train rails, sidestepping a bit to yank up the big top—center poles, quarter poles, canvas, and stakes. It didn't touch the show trucks and most of the trailers yet it deposited several hundred square yards of faded worn canvas on top of Billy Barton's Airstream.

"Have you seen my home? Well! Of course, you can't see it!" Billy screeched half crying and half laughing at the beige canvas draped, sand-dune-style in curving mounds over his trailer. "I need the big top crew to drag the canvas off."

"Billy has a humorous story for his column in *Circus Report*," I chuckled to the children. In my mind I compared the contrasting stormy-weather views, Danny's fear mongering versus Billy's flippant attitude. Billy's views endangered him, he actually defied the storm to hurt him.

Edie and I joined the other circus women and children cleaning up the lot (cherry pie duty) and picked up sidewall poles, stakes, ropes, and wooden seats blown helter-skelter in the tornado. Men, including Danny and Curtis, drew the canvas taunt and started stitching rips and tears. Together they erected the tent and the show went on.

* * *

Something else happened while we performed in Wheaton. "I can't feel the bar under my feet. What should I do?" I told Danny after the opening show.

"I'll find the nearest clinic," he said, knowing from experience my legs were in paralytic shock. Within hours, I lay on a cot in an examination room with a team of doctors poking needles up and down my legs.

"Do you feel this? Do you feel this? This?" they repeated.

"No. I don't. What's going on in my legs?" I asked perplexed, and impatient with their prodding.

"You can get dressed now. I'll see you in my office," one of the white-coated doctors replied.

"Mrs. Chapman, you've been examined by a neurosurgeon, an orthopedic surgeon, and an MD. You have excellent range of motion, yet lack motor control. We all concur. Your torn left hip ligaments caused permanent damage, resulting in the limp you exhibit when walking. In order to regain movement in your lower torso, withdraw from all medications except your thyroid and vitamin pills."

"That's a tough prescription. I'll see what I can do," I said, weakly pushing myself out of the chair in front of his desk. I conceded the pain pills had to stop, but I didn't believe I'd be limping for the rest of my life. *I can do better! Starting by kissing pain pills bye-bye.*

All night, I swore loudly, threw pillows, and even punched at Danny. Hallucinating was proof that addiction had possessed my mind and body. Throughout the next day, I felt sensation returning in both legs. I apologized for my bad behavior. "Danny, my hip doesn't hurt. I thought it would."

"We're just glad you're back," was all he said, sipping coffee and reading *The Chicago Tribune*. "The kids are going to the zoo today. You can relax."

"I'll sit outside. What's the plan for South America?"

"We drive to Sarasota, store the motorhome, repack the rigging in Curtis's bus, and head to Miami International Airport. Togni doesn't want me clowning, because they use local clowns."

"What about Curtis and Edie?"

"Edie's visiting her parents in Oregon. She'll join us in Miami. After Curtis drives his bus to Sarasota, he's flying to Colorado."

CHAPTER TWENTY FOUR
RUNNING AWAY

Before we left Sarasota for Miami I mulled, "I'm worried about Curtis. He doesn't have his passport." Danny drove Curtis' bus, I followed with the kids in our VW bug.

We unloaded the rigging in Miami at the airfreight hangar, stored the bus, and took a motel room across the street. "We leave in two days. When did Curtis say he was coming?" I asked Danny for the hundredth time.

"He's coming today by bus."

Carrying only a small suitcase, Curtis calmly greeted us in his usual demeanor and appearance—jeans, T-shirt, and canvas shoes.

"Hello…" I anxiously said, "Did you get your passport?"

"Not yet. I came anyhow and hope that's all right with you." I grew frantic.

"You don't have your passport?" I yelled, now angry. "Get on the phone and see where it is. Pronto!"

If we weren't in a public place, I swear I would have strangled him. My behavior was worse than bad and I knew it. *Danny's* deliberately annoying me at the motel by playing with frogs. Its unthinkable putting Curtis on a separate flight. Our contract is doomed, all of our hard work this year, doomed.

Curtis' voice jolted me out of my misery and rage. "I guess I forgot to give them an address in Miami," he apologized.

"That won't help, Curtis. We're disbanding. While we waited for you, Danny, Edie, and I discussed breaking our Lima contract. Edie is going back to college and you can do whatever. Please drive your bus to Sarasota." We had no way knowing his passport rested in the Montclair Drive mailbox.

* * *

"Load up everyone, we're going back to Sarasota," I said at the beginning of our return trip. Later, on a whim I suggested, "It's July 4th, let's go air boating in the Everglades." Danny didn't object.

Three adults and two children uncoiled from the light-blue bug, unprepared for the wild windswept cruise across a portion of Florida's sawgrass sea. We covered our ears from the deafening prop and held onto seats and each other on pinpoint turns. My ruminating thoughts about the Lima contract all blew away. I accepted The Aerial Chapmans second retirement. Disbanding came guilelessly; we had no work.

"Look at us," I said at the landing and tugging facial skin in place. "airboat riding on our nation's 200th birthday instead of a jet flight to the Southern Hemisphere. Que sera, sera."

* * *

In Sarasota again, Danny and I consulted our attorney and personal representative, Robert Henshaw, to cancel the 1977 season with Hubert Castle Circus. He assured us we were in no financial danger. "Independent contractors have liability advantages over union contracts. Don't worry about it," he said, setting the Togni contract on his desk and picking up the Castle contract. "This one's the same. Without partners, you can't fill your contract. It's rough when things go awry. I'll send Castle a letter explaining your predicament. It's early enough and he probably won't hold anything against you."

"Except our reputation," I said, miffed. "Thanks for your help, Mr. Henshaw."

Our young Sarasota attorney specializing in real estate transfers represented us amid the Phillippi Creek cut-through. We retained him afterwards for legal scrapes. I admired his cowboy boots, head of brown curls, and friendly business manner. Henshaw's community work as a youth advocate was a plus. In 1969, he recommended joint trusts and guardians for Ivy and Winston. We complied, left him our wills and safety box key, and gave our fate to God.

* * *

Not long after the Peru fiasco, I asked Danny, "Are there show agents in Sarasota?" Danny was happy with his monthly check. I still wanted to do circus work. Inside I cringed, *It isn't easy being the head of an uncooperative family.*

"I don't know. I'll check it out," he said before leaving for the Showfolks Club. Later he announced, "Jerry Swartz is new in the business. He's a pharmacist who books a few dates. I checked with Deborah and she's back in shape. Jerry thinks he can get us some local work."

"Ask him to supper." Jerry was the first agent we called a friend. He lacked a pompous attitude and didn't leer at me. Always casual, this densely freckled man shaved his head of what looked to be red hair. He worked hard getting us dates at a variety of Sarasota events.

My hip finally healed well enough for me to perform and I didn't need my cane. However, I limped noticeably, lagging my left leg. During stretching exercises to regain flexibility, I felt tearing from the same hip I injured months before.

"I'm going to the orthopedic surgeon, Dr. Michael DiCosola instead of the hospital," I told Danny. Dr. Mike, as circus people called him, confirmed stretched and torn ligaments. He sent me to physical therapy.

"Sarah Chapman. I have you scheduled for several ultra sound treatments," Chuck, my new physical therapist barked at me.

"Right—isometric exercises. And, I'll do all four of them." I demonstrated pressing my knee into my palm. *He's probably a military medic who forgot he left the Marines.*

"Yes, that's the ones." He marched away to badger another patient.

* * *

We took advantage of the quiet time the rest of the year. Danny was a regular at the Showfolks Club. Ivy was in ballet and gymnastic classes and attended fifth grade at nearby Phillippi Shores. Winston, ever the intellectual, played chess with Jerry Swartz and toted encyclopedias to his bed. I played 'kooky' mom, and hung his bed frame with block and tackle from the ceiling. I returned the books to the living room shelves in the morning, never asking him what he saw or read.

My reading material, *Circus Report*, inspired me. *Danny loved the simple life on the King Show. Small shows are a tonic to some people.*

My clown husband broke his Sarasota boredom by going on the road with Hoxie Bros. Circus as a promotion clown. He performed well at senior centers, discreetly omitting his tramp make-up and wardrobe for that of a nondescript character clown. Most people didn't notice the subtle less-active changes in his routines. His multi-colored two-piece clown suit remained baggy and contained his magic props and balloons. This new clown persona was closer to the real Danny out of makeup. Shrewd. Vindictive. Argumentative. The greasepaint and baby powder smell that gave me a feeling of mystique within breathing distance of him was gone.

I improved the vegetable garden with a raised irrigation system, still enjoying my country girl beginnings. At thirty-one, I adjusted to staying home with the children. "Why doesn't Deborah come any more?" Ivy forlornly asked.

"Families spread out, Ivy. Uncle Merritt and Aunt Lucy don't live with us. Our family got smaller when Deborah and Stephanie grew up to live their own lives. You have me, your father, and Winston."

* * *

The day after Thanksgiving Danny snuck up on me sitting in the kitchen, "You've always wanted a vacation. There's a job at a disco on Long Island for your solo web and the comedy whip cracking."

"Now? It's cold up there."

"It's a vacation," he pursued.

"What's the date?"

"A holiday—your birthday," he got closer to the facts.

"You got me work on New Year's Eve?"

"It's an expense paid trip."

"Are we stopping in Philadelphia?"

Danny raised his chin and eyebrows at the same time. "Sure."

"I'll do it," I agreed.

"Sign here," he said putting a contract and pen in front of me. "A vacation has to pay for itself. Look how lucky we are to have a pleasure trip."

We motored to Long Island and hung my web from girders at the On Stage, a vintage movie theater turned nightclub. "You're not getting an act announcement or any music," Danny hollered during web practice. I pre-determined I would work theatrically to operatic music in my head. My motions wouldn't match the canned rock everyone else heard. I didn't care. "The audience may not watch you."

"Right-o," I said, and slid up-side-down twenty-five-feet to the middle of the dance floor. "Can we do the whip cracking?" I asked, standing gracefully. "I want to review the cues." Danny complied, shuffling several feet away to the stage while I picked up a five-foot whip and folded a newspaper page.

"You'll get a polite announcement when we walk on stage from opposite sides," Danny said. "Motion me to stay in place." I did that and waited. "Walk away in the opposite direction, I'll be pantomiming to the audience. When you turn facing me, I won't be there. Come get me and haul me back in place by the neck of my coat. We repeat that twice, except the third time, you stay put, impatiently tapping your foot, then crack the whip. I haul myself back. That'll get a laugh."

I nodded. "Then I hand you the sheet of unfolded paper and do continuous popping. You tear the sheet in bits long after I've stopped. Then I chase you off the stage."

"You're wearing an evening gown?"

"Yes, it's my birthday. Remember?"

"How could I forget?" Clowning with Danny was fun. He said I matched his timing and he depended on consistency. *Yeah, consistently dumb.*

* * *

The ersatz vacation ended and Southern warmth thawed my chilled bones with each passing mile. As if it were New Year's Day, I spent time cleaning my room and organizing my thoughts. I believed if I started a New Year with productivity, it would continue for twelve months. With little interest in home or property improvement projects, I focused on our family. The children seemed well, though Danny acted as Winston's playmate, not his father.

I was troubled and imbalanced, clueless for answers to too many questions. Not coping, I turned inward, isolated myself, and functioned in a haze—never quite fully waking up, nor fully sleeping. I needed a spark, a light in the deep, dark pit where my spirit dwelled to guide me. I hid, silently aching for the tools to fix my broken parts. Hope for improvement dimmed in 1977.

Curtis asked to winter at our house and we said yes. We lived on Danny's Social Security check and what little money he made performing on local shows. We lacked contracts so practicing was optional.

"Danny, my hip is healed," I said, when I found a smidgen of energy. "Do you think I can do a whip-cracking act? I twirl a serpentine, juggle clubs, and can learn to throw knives like Pietro Canestrelli on the King Show."

"Ask Frankie Perez. He'll tell you what you need to know."

I went next door asking Lolita if Frank could come see me. He found me outside after his workday.

"Show me what you can do," Frank said, resting his thumbs in worn belt loops. I swung the eight-foot bullwhip around my head, paused slightly, and flicked my wrist forward. The whip uncoiled the tip and popper its full length—CRACK. Frank clenched his teeth.

He put the handle of one of my five-foot whips in his hand and smiled. "Sarah, use your eyes. Put one foot in front of the other, pick your mark, and keep you eyes on it. Follow through with your arm and you'll hit your mark. Nail a board on a tree and stick folded newspaper from the sides." After three cracks in perfect form, he handed me the whip.

"Thanks, Frank."

"Any time." He sauntered back through his iron gate.

Pop! Pop! Pop! Cracked the whips. I found Danny. "How do I use two whips?"

"Put one in each hand and alternate cracking them over your head," he replied. "Rex Rossi cracked whips on the Tom Mix Circus. He used both arms for long whips. That makes it look harder than it really is." Danny wandered away looking like a homeless person.

I intensified my whip practice, aiming each strike with the same deftness a rookie pitcher throws for the plate. I took my stance, pinpointed where I wanted the popper, and followed through with my arm and wrist. Bingo. *Why do I try to make things right? What am I practicing? Maybe things would be okay again if we went out on a small show. Danny's life is in the ring. I'll ask him about Franzen Circus.*

Danny hadn't complained about leg pain in years and he'd gained weight all over, including his paralyzed left leg. Bellicose, Danny often contradicted the littlest things with friends and neighbors. His combative voice quickly led to swearing. Asking him to fix anything around the house was out of the question. It started a rampage. I wanted our bedroom painted a light green. He scoffed, "Don't spend money on the house."

I didn't have the nerve to tell the person I married in 1965 that I didn't like him anymore.

A parade of young, male, Clown College students found their way to our house and hung around Guru Chapman, hoping to glean savvy circus-know-how. Exploited by Danny without any compensation, he put clippers and shovels in their hands for clearing brush on the remaining strip of Creek property. When the project ended, Danny's philosophical lectures ceased. It was hard watching Danny use these young men almost the same way he took advantage of me. I made a conscious decision to never take from people, only give.

Danny's existentialism alienated him from society. He condoned drug use. People opposed to drugs were villains to him. The chasm between us widened. When I should have walked out, I didn't.

"Look!" I said. "Franzen Bros. Circus is hiring. The show goes out before Easter." Optimistically I thought, a small circus might soothe him.

"How big is the show?" he asked.

"It's their third season. They have a tent, an elephant, and a few trucks. They want all our acts and they'll hire someone to clown with you. The coloring book pitch is part of our salary." My last comment perked him up because program sales were good at the Circus Hall of Fame. "It's a short fun season."

Kathy Franzen sent a contract for clowning, juggling, and balancing trapeze. We co-signed committing to Franzen. The opening was set for East Prairie, Missouri, the Saturday before Easter.

* * *

Practicing juggling for Franzen outside in yard, Danny happened by asking, "What's your wardrobe?"

"I'm leaning towards a comedy jungle theme with me dressed in a long wig, bare midriff, fake-fur, and boots. I train a monkey, an orangutan, and a gorilla."

"Ha, ha! Have you asked Curtis if he'll wear a gorilla costume?"

"No, I know he will." Curtis winced when I told him about his hairy jumpsuit.

Curtis and the kids joined me for practice. "I'm an animal trainer and you are my pets. You enter the ring with me cracking the little whip behind you. Ivy does flip-flops and cartwheels and I twirl the serpentine. Curtis juggles three balls, then five. Winston just sits on the ring curb eating a banana. Curtis passes clubs with me. Then I juggle three knives and throw them at a board on the ground. For the finale Curtis and I pass fire torches. The ape, orangutan, and monkey run out of the ring. I crack the big whip and take a bow. Any questions?"

"Yes," Danny spoke up behind us. "How do you think Midwesterners will react?"

"We'll find out."

"What's my costume?" Ivy wanted to know.

"You're the monkey in a roomy-brown-knit jump suit." She seemed pleased. "Thank you, kids. You're free to play."

I turned to Curtis. "Danny and I want you to come with us on the show. Can you leave your bus in Sarasota and live in a show truck?"

"Sure, I can do that. Thanks for taking me along."

"You're welcome. You're in the juggling/whip-cracking act. Kathy is giving you a separate contract and the show's paying you to set up the tent."

"Okay, Sarah."

* * *

The loaded motorhome pulled out of Sarasota leaving our troubles behind. Or did it? North of Tampa Danny pulled into Weeki Wachee. "First stop! Mermaids," he announced. We and other enthralled tourists watched an underwater theater production performed in crystal clarity. Ivy and Winston watched entranced as the handsome hero slewed the horrible villain, rescued the forlorn princess, and then swam off with her to live happily ever after.

After crossing the churning, muddy Mississippi we headed for our first stop in Missouri.

We were the solitary rig on the East Prairie lot for two days. "Are you sure the show meets us here?" Danny asked countless times between scouring antique shops.

"Yes, the posters around town say so too." Kathy Franzen and her two small sons pulled onto the lot in their fifth wheel rig. Next two beleaguered working men in a semi-truck pulled up and collapsed in the cab.

I stepped up to the truck and asked the unshaven driver, "Where's the rest of the show?"

"You're looking at it. The elephant's in this semi along with the horses, goats, snake, and pigeons. The seats, poles, and canvas are in the cat-semi that Wayne drives. He works the lion act. He'll be pulling in soon."

In 1977, Wayne Franzen operated an unkempt and haphazard show. Well-worn show trucks broke down often delaying the show's start-time. More than once the show generator ran out of gas during the performance, shutting down the light and sound systems. Personnel failed to show, and both attendance and weather could have been better. The saddest part for me was the elephant, Okha, who was too small and too young to pull stakes. They had a stake driver at the back of a Bobcat. I didn't get to listen to the casual process of a pachyderm and handler working in unison pulling stakes when all else was quiet on the lot.

Ivy was a big help in the concession department and assisted Wayne with his goat act. Curtis, an asset to the show, learned to set up and tear down the big top. Another blessing was the fifty-mile-a-day jumps. I baby-sat the youngest Franzen and gave everyone haircuts. Danny ran show errands.

Things still didn't turn out as expected. Program sales didn't equal the intended twenty-five-percent of the cash value of our salary.

Teaching Ivy school lessons also had drawbacks. My rebellious ten-year-old announced, "I hate math and I'm not doing it anymore."

"Oh, yes you are," I commanded.

"No, I'm not! And Dad won't make me!"

"What's the fuss about in there?" Danny called from outside the motorhome. When I explained it, he looked at Ivy's recalcitrant face. "Math! Girls don't need math."

A distant memory rose up. *He doesn't care if girls go past tenth grade.* Prior to going on the road, I'd checked out Incarnation Catholic School. They placed an emphasis on the basics, and religion. I believed my daughter would thrive if she stayed a full school year.

When my composure finally returned, I calmly explained to Danny that lessons did matter. "I don't want to teach her anymore.

I don't mind staying home while the children go to school." After hearing the alternative, Ivy recanted and resumed math assignments.

Danny left the lot each day to make phone calls. He returned and sat down at the dinette. "Jerry Swartz can get us the summer season at the Hall of Fame for the same money we're getting here. He's booked the Berosini Circus. They need filler acts." He sat staring at me, maybe waiting for an argument. But I never argued. "Curtis wants to stay with Franzen."

It didn't take long to persuade me to leave Franzen, a mere sixty-days after we started. As the circus saying goes, we headed for sunny skies and grassy lots.

CHAPTER TWENTY FIVE
FEELINGS

We moved back to the bayou and parked the motorhome at the Hall of Fame. Otto and Cookie Berosini supplied the tent, a few acts, and all the animals. We settled into our new routine doing the four brief daily shows. Our acts were my balancing trapeze and his clowning.

"Compared to the Midwest, the heat is awful, both day and night," I pouted to Danny between shows.

"Just hang in there and do your best," he answered, taking a sip of coffee. *He's making an effort not to drink. I'm glad he drinks at home and not in bars. Right, hang in there...*

Unfortunately, my best wasn't present when I twisted my left ankle in the ring. "We don't like you limping," The Berosinis told me.

"I'm wearing a beige ankle support," I apologized without feeling guilty.

Three days later their Great Dane attacked me, throwing me to the ground. An orthopedic surgeon examined my left ankle, now painfully swollen black and purple with a torn Achilles tendon.

"Thank you, Annie, for taking me to the doctor. The exam hurt...that's why I cried out in the doctor's office."

"Don't worry about it, Sarah. You'll heal and everything will get better."

"I hope so," I waved as she dropped me off at the Hall of Fame and I hobbled inside on crutches. *Annie Edelston must be an angel to help others they way she does.*

I reported to Cookie and Otto, "The doctor put me in a cast. It's a bad sprain. The dog did this too." I raised my skirt exposing a black bruise wrapping around my thigh. "I'll be out for the rest of the summer." Silence. I adjusted my crutches. "Ivy can do single trapeze in my place. She has wardrobe." Otto and Cookie hooked eyes and nodded in unison. Ivy rescued me the same as Deborah on King Bros. in 1966. I didn't have to offer Ivy in my place. I did it for the good of the show like any circus family.

A sprained ankle provided the opportunity to spend time at home with Winston. His impish, yet studious almost-five-year-old ways were refreshing and relaxing. We learned phonics together and he read books to me.

Danny and Ivy tolerated the Berosini Circus quirks and the Florida humidity up to the Labor Day closing. We had no way of knowing that little Franzen Bros. would flourish with increased crowds, improved weather, and a successful season.

* * *

Ivy started sixth grade at Incarnation School and fell in line with the other uniformed students. *My daughter. I'm proud of her already.*

* * *

Sick again, I hemorrhaged worse than ever before and was a regular at Dr. Hoertz's office where I got injections to stop the bleeding. There was no pattern, it just happened.

Danny didn't know what was going on in our family anymore. He lived a separate life, sometimes staying away nights. I suspected he was down the street. He told people he invited to the house, "I've only made two mistakes in my life—my two marriages."

Put-down statements about me were normal. His need for pity worked on strangers.

To me he said, "You're not my intellectual equal." At first that hurt because I guessed he was smarter than I was. He was great at manipulation, he was an officer, and he worked in Europe more than once. *All that doesn't make him smarter, I'm on to his reverse psychology.*

"I'm working on my bachelor degree," I reminded him knowing it wouldn't change his tainted view. If I could put my finger on one thing that caused his disillusionment with me it would be alcohol, a predisposition from his father. Alcohol ruined his taste and kept him away from our dinner table. Our thirty-plus year age difference probably played a part along with my stubbornness to accept the facts. Running off with Franzen wasn't wise. Our family was a rudderless ship on a tempestuous sea.

* * *

I faithfully took the children to church and read the bulletin each week. I watched one ad in particular, Marriage Encounter Weekend. I blamed my marriage for my dysfunctional life and unhappiness. *Maybe Marriage Encounter will jolt us back together.* It was worth a try. The small circus didn't work.

"Danny, you're right about me not being your equal," I said standing next to him where he sat on a lawn chair in the patio. (He loved to hear 'you're right.') "I do think differently. I want a better marriage. I want to renew our relationship. If that can't happen, I want a divorce." He finally turned his head to look at me.

"Here's an ad for Marriage Encounter. It's held weekends and should be fun because the motel has a pool."

"You want me to go to this?"

"Sure. Either that or a divorce. It's your choice." I don't recall what got in my head to go that far with him. Three long years and thousands of dollars later our divorce was finalized.

Marriage Encounter was inapt for Danny. It fit me closer than a kidskin glove. At the opening get-together, three friendly couples introduced our weekend theme—communication through feelings. We sat in the back row and I let the concept soothe my mind, an antidote against the years of Danny's poisonous words. The idea was so magnanimous, I wanted to stand up and scream, *Feelings are okay. They're beneficial, mine, and only mine.* Good manners forbid me.

Containing those relishing thoughts, I smiled radiantly all evening. In our room I eagerly rattled on. "Wow, Danny. Marriage takes time, thought, and energy. I want a Marriage Encounter marriage. Don't you? I like touching. I definitely want to express feelings. Danny...Danny?"

He fidgeted with the television remote for the evening news. "You didn't hear me, did you?" I said, a peaceful expression on my face.

"No, what were you saying?"

"It doesn't matter. Good night."

Danny didn't follow the Marriage Encounter weekend plan. I spent twelve years vainly wishing for the impossible. *Marriage Encounter is the jolt we needed. Thank you for enriching all the wholesome couples passing through your doors. We are leaving as we came—apart.* Aware of the awakening, I watched as my wedding vow taking Danny for better or worse ruptured and my vision of death parting us vanished. Not being his wife felt right. *Underneath my tarnished surface is a shiny new penny.*

* * *

Instead of following through with the divorce after Marriage Encounter, I postponed it thinking it would hurt Winston. I wanted to wait until he was older. I hadn't hit bottom.

I aimed the energy I'd found for marriage improvement to my health, faithfully stretching my left ankle. "My cane's going in the closet the day I wear pretty shoes," I told Ivy.

"Dr. Hoertz says my hemorrhaging is out of control and he recommends a hysterectomy. Can I get one?" I asked Danny.

"No, your voice will deepen or you'll grow a beard." At night, sporadic bleeding often woke me up to find myself lying in a pool of blood. Other times when out in public blood slid down my legs. It annoyed me that his signature was necessary for surgery. I wanted legal responsibility for my body.

The fear of Danny getting into bed with me caused sleeplessness. He sporadically showered or shaved and reeked of filth and alcohol. When I complained about Danny to Dr. Scherer, he listened. "Attend Al Anon meetings," he advised.

"What for?"

"It will make you feel better."

"Me feel better? I'll go to one meeting. It's not going to help. I'm not the one who drinks."

Dear Annie dropped me off at my first of many rewarding Al Anon meetings. Al Anon's twelve steps opened the door to improving my life beginning with eliminating control tactics.

I stopped marking bottles. Pouring out jars of vodka stored in tree crotches wasted my time. When Danny ran over Ivy's bicycle, showing anger didn't help me or fix the bicycle. Trying to figure out where he was at nights wasn't my business. Taking care of me was.

My thoughts and behavior changed when I gave myself to a higher power. I asked Danny to go to Alcoholics Anonymous. He did. "You can stop meetings," he told me when he returned. "My mother's doctor was at my meeting and he said the alcohol I drink is medicinal. You're wasting your time."

"Fine, then I'll waste it how I choose, one week at a time in Al Anon."

* * *

A not so joyous Christmas came and went. I stood on a ladder reaching above my head removing ornaments. Off balance, the ladder and I crashed to the floor with me hitting my tailbone. I tore my left ischial, a ligament connected to my pelvis.

At physical therapy, I was a regular patient. "Chuck, it hurts to sit down."

"Here's an ischial ring. Take it wherever you go," Chuck said, prepping me for Dr. DiCosola, who injected cortisone.

"Owie, ouch. YEOW!" I bellowed so loud I'm sure it scared other patients.

"If you stop doing circus work, you won't need to come here. How about learning something new?" Chuck suggested.

"I don't need another person telling me what to do, and I don't want to do anything else," I snarled grabbing my purse and the foam donut from the leather examination table audaciously hissing, "I am an aerial…ist."

Despite the unnecessary wit, I felt horrible. Something guided me back to Dr. Scherer. "What seems to be the problem?" he said, entering the room carrying my expanding medical chart.

"I have bad headaches, lasting days. I stay in my room where it's quiet and dark. I don't sleep."

"Who watches your children?"

"Ivy's eleven, she watches Winston. He's five."

"Hmmm," he murmured. "Don't go away." I sat in a chair blankly staring at an empty wall. He returned. "I've scheduled four days for you in the hospital. We'll run tests and see what's going on."

The hospital improved my spirits giving me the opportunity to stay in bed and sleep. Dr. Scherer reviewed my labs. "You have reactive hypoglycemia."

I left the hospital with a new lease on life and a new sugar-free diet.

"Do you want work at the Hall of Fame next summer?" Danny asked. He wasn't concerned with my health or frequent physical therapy appointments. He worked parades, malls, and benefits around Sarasota. He was financially secure and content.

"Yes if I'm well. I have marketing and publicity ideas." Hypoglycemia didn't change my performance. With more than a decade of circus experience, my polished foot and head-balancing trapeze was as much a part of me as the air I breathed—inhale, exhale, smile.

* * *

The tuition for my current University of Florida correspondence course dwarfed the values learned. Traditions do count, families that pray together last, and Danny's rules don't exist in a healthy marriage. The Wheelers and Chapmans had few traditions, no courtesies, and even less loyalty. Danny and I grew apart, not together. I knew other families who loved each other and stayed together through the worst and best of times.

CHAPTER TWENTY SIX
DELICATE WINGS

The chaos I felt at eighteen was nothing to the agitation I faced at thirty-three. In 1965, I established a professional identity on a trapeze. Poor health in 1978 kept me away from my rigging, possibly providing the opportunity to establish my true persona.

The epiphany I gained at Marriage Encounter ebbed away as days turned into weeks then into months. Anxiety crept in and took control of my life. Lying quietly in bed, I felt a hammer's steady rhythm in my chest. If Danny returned from the club, my heart pounded louder. I lay in my bed, afraid of the night. *Think, Sarah...*

I came up with a minor solution and asked Ivy to help me put her twin beds in my room, trading them for the double bed. Danny said nothing. I slept better, and my thumping heart subsided for a time.

The flat roofed house leaked badly. Every day the afternoon thunderstorms released their deluge. Rainwater gushed down Ivy's bedroom walls, the buckets placed under the copious drips overflowed making her room a shallow lake. During nighttime rainstorms, if thunder and lightning didn't wake me, my five-year-old's crying did.

"The house is flooding, it's flooding! Whaaa," Winston whimpered, pulling me to Ivy's bedroom lake and pointing to the water with his little index finger. His blue eyes welled up and tears ran down his cheeks.

"Its not flooding, Winston," I explained. "Sit on the bed and watch Mama open the doors and sweep the water out to the patio." When most of the water drained, I carried him to his dry room and tucked him in bed.

For Winston's sake, I promised to mention the leaky roof to Danny.

"The roof needs fixing. Winston cries when it rains."

"What do you care? It gets the floor clean, doesn't it?" he said sarcastically, flashing his angry eyes. I bit my tongue not wanting to become embroiled in yet another fruitless argument.

* * *

With the time off from performing, I rested in bed as much as possible the early months of '78 to heal my inflamed ischial joint. That done, I wanted to increase my activity, yet still couldn't get out of bed. A round itchy spot aggravated my mid-back.

Danny came to the bedroom door. I greeted him with a cheery "Hello," wanting to hear his friendly, "Top of the morning," or "Fair to middling."

Instead, he narrowed his eyes, "You know, there's nothing wrong with you. You can walk," he said in a threatening tone.

"I'll try." I swung my legs to the side of the bed and stood up straight. I swiveled my feet and we stood face to face, six feet apart. I leaned forward to take a step and crumpled in a heap on the tiled floor. My legs, once agile, were akimbo. Raising my head, I studied him as he ambled away down the hall, leaving me on the floor. I wasn't hurt emotionally or otherwise, having long ago given up longing for his love and approval.

* * *

Flat on my back in bed, I stared at the white ceiling. Weak in body, not mind, or spirit, I passed the time listening to baseball games on the radio and memorizing prayers, an evening prayer, the Lord's Prayer, and the Hail Mary.

On Annie's visits I thanked her for sending me *Daily Word*. I dreamed as I read. *I want to go to Unity, Missouri, and smell the rose garden... I want to see the window where the light continually shines.*

Lastly, I read and reread the Al Anon book, *One Day at a Time*. It was an effort to "Let Go and Let God." That spring I watched the oak tree outside my bedroom window shed its leaves, tassel, and then grow new delicate leaves while I lay trapped in bed.

* * *

"Come on in," I called to Winston when he peeked in toting his books and toy truck. "It's the second inning and the Braves have one out." He played quietly or catnapped on my bed as the game progressed.

Ivy called out from the kitchen, "Mom, supper's ready." It took me ten minutes to join her, carefully lurching forward between walls and doors. The food was cold by the time I arrived. After that Ivy called me sooner.

"Thanks for the tasty supper, Ivy. I'm going back now." My bed was a jerky thirty feet away. I knew it was unhealthy for Ivy to take responsibility for me. Still, it was better than having my mother come and dispense her unwanted innuendos about how I ran my household. Her cold-eye stares were almost as bad as Danny's angry ones.

Two wooden canes helped my stability on rare public outings. Spasmodic torso movements jerked me forward in a series of rickety leaps.

"I think you should go to a rheumatologist," Danny suggested. "You might have arthritis." I made an appointment from my bedside phone.

In an exam room I softly told this new doctor about my symptoms, including the spot on my back. He studied my face. "May I lift your shirt?" I nodded.

"I believe I know what's going on. You're describing shingles, a viral nerve inflammation linked to your spine. Most people get shingle sores on their face or neck, occasionally it goes lower in the body and may have little or no manifestation on the skin. The sores are still there," he explained.

"I'm putting you on prednisone to calm down the nerves."

I improved rapidly after the visit, but too late to work the 1978 summer season at the Circus Hall of Fame. "It's ironic," I opinioned to my children during an evening meal I prepared, "that I finally get my own contract and can't fulfill it." They looked up. I smiled. "Sewing your wardrobe and making props for Hogan is plenty. The important thing is getting better."

"That's right, Mom," Ivy said, walking me back to my room. "Listen to your ball game. I'll wash the dishes."

"Come back when you're done and I'll fit the waist of your skirt. Confinement with a weakened body isn't the worst thing that could have happened to me, Ivy. There are those with less."

"I know, Mom," she said helping me into bed.

* * *

Ivy presented a pony act as part of our family package at the Circus Hall of Fame. Earlier that year, Danny brought Ivy to me. "I checked around and Ivy can get pony lessons from a lady who trains and rents show horses."

"We do a pony act?"

"Ivy can, if she's interested."

"I'm interested, Dad. When do I start?"

"When we meet Barbra Dudgeon in Fruitville."

Barbra knew horses, except she didn't perform in circuses. "How old are you?" she asked Ivy.

"Eleven and I love horses."

"Super. I've got a Shetland pony named Barnum available Saturday mornings. Can you come?"

"Yes, oh yes!" she declared to Barbra, then looked at us to verify.

"Horses kick at one end, bite at the other, and are uncomfortable in the middle," Danny mused on the way home.

"Amen to that," I agreed.

"Horses are great," Ivy yelled from the back seat.

Her weekly lessons included basic horse care; grooming, feeding, exercise, and equitation. Barbra trotted the pony in circles holding on to a lunge line. Ivy bounced up and down in Barnum's western saddle. Advancing, Barbra had Ivy hold the lunge line while Barnum jumped low hurdles placed around the ring.

"Can you teach Barnum a comedy routine?" asked Danny.

"Yes, he's ready to learn that," said Barbra, utilizing great people skills to two dubious parents.

"Ivy, Barnum will do what you want if you signal with arm motions. Start by having him nod his head," Barbra patiently told Ivy who was always eager to learn.

Ivy and Barnum polished their routine. She got her bangs cut; he shed his winter coat. I finished her red satin cowgirl duds, she slicked his palomino mane and tail. "Daddy we need a horse trailer to haul Barnum."

"I know, we're buying one. Barbra is renting Barnum to us and you're taking care of him."

"I want to take care of him!"

"We have a horse woman in the family," Danny said sourly. He clowned that summer. Poised and youthful, Deborah did single trapeze with ample strength, despite my trembling over her twisting heel catches.

Our terrier walked around the ring with a dolly sitting in a saddle on his back. When Winston said, "Hogan—UP," Hogan pranced on his hind legs out of the arena. No one escapes work in show biz families.

At the end of the thirteen-week season, Barnum returned to Barbra, Danny sold the horse trailer, and everyone involved with Ivy's pony act benefited from the experience.

* * *

I learned to live one day at a time. Prior to Winston starting first grade, I briefly enrolled him in kindergarten classes to familiarize him with group activities. In silence, I drove Winston and Ivy to Incarnation. Ivy joined her friends and left us standing on the sidewalk. I looked at him, smartly dressed in homemade blue slacks and a white knit shirt, and handed him his book bag. "You're a first-grader now. Ivy is here if you need her." He walked to class and I softly shed tears watching him grow—he turned six in a week.

* * *

Over the summer, the shingles receded. I resumed cooking and prepared hearty evening meals for my performing family. I drove again and attended weekly Al Anon meetings and church, nothing strenuous. When school started, new symptoms plagued me. Most afternoons, monumental headaches forced me to my room again, shutting away all noise and light. I'm sure I told myself *I hate being married to Danny*, repeatedly until I dozed off. Whatever was going on in my mind, it wasn't healthy.

I went to Dr. Scherer and told him how my forty-pound bar hit my left temple back in 1973. "Check with the nurse. I made an appointment for a brain scan."

It was negative. All the same, the headaches accelerated in strength and duration and I grimly returned to Dr. Scherer. "My heart pounds at night."

"It does? All night?" he asked.

"Uh huh, all night. I hear it, and feel it," I nodded clutching my left chest.

"I have a friend who can help you. Here's his number. His name is Dr. Kenneth Piotrowski."

Ready for any type of salvation and seeking rest from exhaustion and relief from the constant pain, I considered checking myself into an institution in Arcadia. On the way to Dr. Piotrowski's office, I wondered if seeing a psychiatrist meant I really was crazy.

"Sarah," Dr. P said, with a grin. "You said my name correctly. Most people can't do that. So, tell me what's going on in your life." Two hours and many soaked tissues later he officially ended the visit. "Our time is up. I'm prescribing Darvon for pain and placing you with one of my therapists."

"Thank you," I reached for my purse and rose to leave.

"Julie can see you Tuesdays and Thursdays," the receptionist said. "Is that okay?"

"Fine," I answered. *What am I getting myself into?* A few days later, I met my new thought coach.

"Hi Sarah, my name is Julie. I'm going to help you learn to control how you feel." She might have said it a little bit differently. Together we worked through Rational Emotive Therapy, RET. I reviewed homework assignments, read books by Dr. Albert Ellis, and listened to relaxation tapes. I started a notebook, saving material for future reference.

Learning that thoughts control actions took months. At a dreadfully slow pace, I changed my thinking and improved. I spent years afraid of myself and harbored real and irrational fears. I discovered my unhealthy marital/family situation contributed to my physical pain. It all connected directly to my mental health.

Writing my thoughts nearly became an obsession. I jotted down pent-up feelings, feelings and thoughts I'd bottled up for over a decade. Julie patiently and painstakingly led me to sane thinking, decision making, and positive actions. Learning a new way to think intrigued me as much as watching a ball game to see who wins. I put my all into RET.

Therapy, Al Anon, and *Daily Word* worked because I believed God made me a whole and happy being at birth. When Julie asked what type of relationship I had with my father and brother, I quickly replied, "I love them and believe they love me." After thinking I added, "Daddy was good. I wish I'd listened to him back in high school when he protested me leaving the house. I disobeyed his simple request, and felt bad afterwards. I didn't apologize. Our family didn't do that.

"Merritt and I were pals. I got angry when he hit me. At twelve, I knocked him down and pummeled his back with my fists yelling, 'Stop hitting me.' He got up and never hurt me again."

"You behaved the way you knew—striking. Is that right?" Julie questioned.

"Yes, we understood violence."

RET dealt with the present, not my dreaded past. Not my mother beating Merritt and me. Not Charles using my body. Not Danny avoiding my body, taking my salary. The deep hurt of my teenage affair lay dormant because I didn't hold Charles responsible for the headaches. I'm sure my life needed more straightening out than I let on. I was only willing to go so far. I was satisfied to absorb the RET formula nearing the end of therapy. "Is the idea of RET living in an irrational world and controlling emotions as each situation arises?" I asked Julie

"That's it. Continue using the situation forms, writing the action followed by your reaction, and then rewrite your reaction positively. This helps you choose future behavior."

"And get rid of could, would, and should?"

"Yes, they tend to cause problems."

Logical thought started when I replaced those three words with four—'it would be nice.'

* * *

Self-improvement began with clearer thinking, then muscle toning, and better walking. After six-years of hemorrhaging I finally had a hysterectomy. Dr. Hoertz sounded annoyed the morning of surgery. "Sarah, where's your husband? He hasn't signed for you."

"He doesn't want to sign. Call him," I confessed dressed in a gown and lying on my back in the pre-op cot. I checked in the night before and requested no visitors because I didn't want Danny around.

Thirty minutes later, a nurse told me, "He signed, you're next."

"Thank you. I owe whoever made the call that got him to the hospital."

Drugged from post-operative anesthesia, a heard a voice call out, "Sarah. Sarah, I'm your nurse. Someone is here to see you." I covered my face with my hands.

"I don't want my husband here. Send him away," I wailed.

I peeked and relaxed when I saw the white coat belonging to zippy Dr. Hoertz. Cupping his hands together he gave me a detailed report, "Sarah, I took out a fibroid the size of a grapefruit." He circled his thumbs and index fingers. "And there were several smaller ones."

He looked at my busy hands. "What are you making?"

"I'm crocheting a shawl."

"Come and see me in two weeks."

"Thanks for coming."

I luxuriated in the hospital. Danny traded our VW bug for a different one. "You did what?" I asked when he picked me up.

"I think you can drive this; it has a partial automatic transmission," he answered, closing my passenger side door.

Due to my weak left hip, I couldn't work the shift pedal as he'd thought. I drove the car to the Volkswagen dealer and traded it for a used VW wagon with an automatic transmission. I pulled into the driveway at home. "Now what did you do?" Danny mouthed off.

"I bought a car. I've never owned one," I hummed as I took the manual inside without feeling guilty, wrong, or bad. Al Anon meetings and RET fed my growing positive outlook.

Danny's cohorts stopped coming by at all hours after I nicely required notice. "Please call before you come." He continued drinking a fifth of vodka everyday. As long as his behavior didn't directly affect me, it didn't matter how he looked, smelled, or dressed. I sidestepped him when he lay passed out on the living room floor. It mattered not to me if he missed meals and family activities including birthday parties.

American women liberated themselves in the seventies. They burned bras, stopped wearing dresses, stockings, hats, white gloves; and they demanded equal partnership in the sexual revolution. Before counseling, I resented pumping gas, and felt guilty sitting at a movie without my husband, but not after. Liberation meant accepting responsibility for my children's security and eventually, household maintenance.

***

Besides beginning to think during psychotherapy, I learned who my friends were. Not Danny for sure. Nor my mother, who I didn't tell I was getting help until I stopped going. I wanted therapy to be for me and with me—except for one other person. For fifteen months, Annie listened in her home to a review of each appointment. Her gentle support helped me during other experiences as well, especially this one.

I picked up my Amway soap at a distributor's home. "Go on inside," the sales woman directed. "My husband's there. I'll get the soap." An open Bible lay on the kitchen table. Christian plaques adorned the walls.

Before sitting down, I studied each one. "These are nice. I don't understand that one."

"Give thanks for tragedies, heartbreaks, accidents, or any adversity," the woman read the plaque.

"Why? How can that be?" I asked wide-eyed in disbelief. "My roof leaks and I'm supposed to give thanks?"

"Do you have money to fix the roof?"

"Yes, we do." I nodded, wondering how praising problems helped.

"Give thanks that you do. We wish we had money to fix our house." I sat pensive for a time and struggled with the idea of keeping money versus putting it to good use.

"I've never heard of this and don't understand giving thanks for problems…" I considered the possibilities. "Do you know a contractor?" I blurted out to the couple.

"We do." The woman handed me the information, her husband placed his arm around her shoulders. "You're welcome back anytime to learn how God takes much better care of us than we do ourselves." I wanted what they had.

I couldn't wait to tell Annie what happened. "Sure, Sarah, that's old. Give thanks for your problems, it helps you move on." I was stunned.

The next day I hired the contractor to put a new pitched roof over that flat leaking one. I repaired the solar water heater myself and hired a plumber to install a backup electric water heater. The kids and I stopped showering at the YMCA and were finally able to bathe at home. *Thank you, God, for my problems.* My sour attitude against change seeped slowly towards the sweetness of gratitude. When rainwater covered the floor, we were fortunate enough to get a new roof and hot water.

* * *

I didn't improve all at once. When my body hurt, my mind got fuzzy, I neglected completing my RET response sheets, and negative behaviors crept back in. Each obstacle towered enormous, unreachable. From Al Anon I learned to practice loving detachment from Danny and found it worked for my relationship with Mother as well. I was whole without the love or approval of a parent or child and vice versa. I was also free to choose my own friends.

Getting rid of some, not all, of my weighty baggage, lightened my load. The first bag I unpacked was the feeling of utter loss when Daddy died. Next, my stepdaughters breaking away, leaving me behind. Before RET, I hung onto fragments of a relationship, hoping for improvement. After RET I accepted that the only heart I need to concentrate on is my own. God loves me. I love God.

The trap door of my self-confinement inched open. I participated in Ringling Museum's third annual Medieval Fair. I opted to be a barbarian, choosing a dark brown fur costume, including a long, unkempt wig, and slinging three leather whips about my neck and shoulders. Casually circulating the grounds as one of the village idiots, I felt truly in character for the medieval times. Sunshine and peacefulness warmed me as I strolled the area randomly cracking whips, to add authenticity to my role.

CHAPTER TWENTY SEVEN
SERENITY

"Welcome to 1979. A New Year of Mind, Spirit, Body," my scrapbook logo, became my mantra all that year. Small entertainment jobs contracted from Jerry Swartz were fun. My health care cost me more than I was earning doing circus work. There was nothing left to do but get out of the business. The voluntary demise of my fourteen-year circus career loomed large in my mind. Circus performers don't have employment pension funds or retirement celebrations. Still, I wanted my exit to be special.

Circus Report printed ads by an older man named Freddie Daw, circus paraphernalia pitchman. "Dear Freddie," I wrote, "Will you please sell my wardrobe to circus fans?"

"Sure, doll. Send me a list of what you have and I'll run an ad. You handle the postage and I'll let you know who wants what. My charge is a seventy/thirty split. I get thirty because I have all the mailing lists with lots of customers. You'll see."

That's exactly what Freddie and I did—we sold my leotards, jewelry, shoes, feather boas, make-up boxes, capes, gowns, tiaras, and photographs. I kept four outfits and gave away the rest to friends. Oddly, no one bought my collection of colored silk handkerchiefs. After picking them up off my trapeze bar with my lips, those colorful squares lazily floated to arena floors in a myriad of buildings and locations throughout North America. My handkerchief was the same thing to me as a baseball player's bat—a trade tool.

Danny saw me emptying the walk-in closet for inventory. "Going on a show?"

"No, I'm selling my wardrobe for ballroom dance lessons."

"Dancing? Geez, you can't even walk." He shook his head.

"That's right, watch me."

"Women!" Danny sauntered away.

I haven't picked the easy way. I wonder if dancing stays inside like balance.

Ballroom dancing coordinated my feet. Richard Barstow would have fainted. It mattered not to my instructor that I used dancing as a form of therapy. "I heard you're an injured performer. I think I can help."

"Good, I'm tired of limping. My legs once earned my living," I told him, with a hopeful smile.

"We'll learn things slowly and you tell me when it's time to stop. Wear leather dancing shoes. I am here to help you." I straggled into the studio with two canes. A year later I envisioned the world in my hands. Freely moving again, wearing pretty clothes, I lived. Greetings and smiles bubbled forth, I was a goodwill fountain.

* * *

My unruly family life hadn't changed. In fact, Danny approached me. "I can put the property in trust to all the children and let you live here on a life estate."

What kind of a deal is that? It puts the children in charge and only two are mine. It makes me feel unwanted. I felt I deserved more from a marriage partner than a tentative roof over my head.

I consulted Julie. She advised making an asset and debt list about why I stayed on the bayou. I had a bad marriage to an old alcoholic, a dysfunctional home life, and an estranged extended family. I was grateful for my children, my individuality, and being Sarah Chapman, retired aerialist. At that time I couldn't zero in on the finer points of my marriage. I wasn't ready to create waves when I still felt guilty about everything connected to Danny.

God's miraculous love was a gift continually guiding me onward. That omnipresent love met me at every corner even when I tried hiding. It encouraged me to raise my head and greet the world. It said, "Come out, Sarah," the same way Zacharius was told to come down from his tree. I felt God's love most when I was quietly reading *Daily Word* or saying my evening prayer.

Al Anon observations taught me some people love their alcoholic. Deep in thought at a meeting, I posed a question, *Do I love Danny? No, I don't. I don't love Danny Chapman as my partner, husband, lover, or friend. I love his tramp clown persona.* Releasing the guilt I'd harbored when I admitted I no longer loved him was a "gift."

Granting myself permission to terminate my marriage happened after that inspiring meeting. I went home and phoned an attorney I picked from the yellow pages. He summoned Danny, who was on the road. Daily life changed little during the next month. Danny returned home and politely went about his business. I smiled. He was glum.

"You can't be serious about this divorce," he said friendly-like, a mere forty-eight hours before default.

"I am," I replied with confidence. "Who's your attorney?"

Switching to his hateful viper face, he snapped, "You might have won the battle, but you haven't won the war." He scurried off. My mind blanked out. I was unprepared for his ferocity.

The war began.

He stuck by me in the house, yelling obscenities, following my every step. Tears washed down my face. I went outside, he followed. "Stop belittling me," I blubbered, dropping my hurting head to my chest.

Ivy and Winston witnessed the nightmare from a distance. I think it was as horrifying to them, as the scene I'd witnessed when Mother whipped Merritt. They never saw Danny on this type of rampage. I'd never taught them how to protect Mom from Dad. If I didn't understand what he wanted or why, how could they?

Danny lifted my chin repeatedly, "You have no right destroying this family. The kids will hate you for tearing us apart."

"I have rights. Leave me alone," I screamed. "Leave me alone." My eyes shut tight.

Darkness came eventually and fully dressed I crawled on top of my bed. He turned on the ceiling light. I pulled a pillow over my head. He yanked it off. "You shouldn't have started dancing lessons. Your mind is poisoned. I heard you've been running around." That's when he got trashy. "I hear you're a nice number. A cunt. That's all you are." He dramatically stood up and pulled at his hair. "Why didn't I see it coming?"

"Don't say those things about me. You know it's not true. Leave me alone." I sobbed wrapping my arms around my face. I relaxed and appeared to sleep, he droned on. He pulled a chair next to my bed, sat down, and continued his negative tirade. *He sounds evil.* No one slept.

I tried escaping in the morning. He followed me outside to the oak trees. Little by little, I weakened. I couldn't think. It was too late to leave. Driving a car wasn't safe and I wouldn't go without the children. I barely knew myself.

There I sat, crumpled in a ball in the yard and whittled to a puddle of tears, comforted by dried brown leaves next to my legs and long dark oak arms above. Between the trees and me loomed an enraged Danny, taunting the very air with venom. The lost child in me cried. *I must be as bad as he says. Maybe I should agree with him. Maybe he'll stop yelling.* From deep within me, a rasping devil-voice crackled. "What do you want? What do you want?"

"I want you to go to your attorney's office and tell him the deal's off. Cancel the hearing. Cancel the hearing. Tell your attorney the deal's off."

"I'll do it. Stop yelling at me," I screamed up into his bestial face.

"Go. I'll call him and say you're on your way." He pulled my car key from his shorts pocket and grabbed my hand forcing the key on my palm. Hand and keys dropped onto the leaves. He picked up the key and my arm and wrapped my fingers around the key. Straightening up, he triumphantly strode to the house.

What a blurry ride up the Trail to Main Street. I parked the car outside my attorney's modest office, went inside, and stood wavering back and forth in front of his desk with swollen face, red eyes, messy hair, dirty clothes, and tear-stained skin.

"Please have a seat," he offered. "You're aware today is default?"

I nodded, making every effort to stay standing and breathing.

"You're lucky, no one responded. You needn't go to court."

"I want it canceled," I whimpered.

"What? Are you aware what you're doing?"

I nodded again.

"I'm not so sure you are," he shook his head in disbelief. "If you cancel this hearing, you'll have to start over in the event you want to file again." *No legal jargon, it's too much. I said what I came to say.* I felt faint. My attorney was unable to help me. So was I.

I drove home in a black out. I hardly recognized my swollen face. Small distant eyes reflected nothing. My body gently urged eat, sleep, don't think. I didn't want to ever see Julie or tell her I failed, how I let Danny take charge. Had I thrown away all the RET training? A deep thought shook me to my core. *If I'm not divorced, then I'm still married. I'm still a parent.*

* * *

Victorious, Danny left the house for several days. Caving in to him left me with a tremendous guilt for staying in a bitter, loveless marriage. My life was as mixed up as before RET, maybe worse.

Daily routines absorbed my sorrow. I had psychotherapy, dance lessons, Al Anon, and Avon sales; Ivy had ballet, gymnastics, and 4-H club meetings; and Winston had piano lessons. They were in eighth and second grades at Catholic school. Waiting for them in the parking lot each afternoon, an idea came—confession.

Doggedly I walked into the rectory and asked to see a priest. Aged Father Gordon compassionately met me in a sun-lit room with a desk and two chairs. I heard children's voices from the playground. He went to the window. "Excuse me while I pull the shade. It's too bright."

Darkness softened my words. I breathed deeply, and found my voice. "Father, I want to confess something horrible. I married a much older man and it hasn't worked out. I'm terribly upset and want to leave him. I tried to leave and ran out of strength."

"Do you feel you're carrying a cross?"

"Oh, yes! I do—a big heavy one holding me down."

He waited. "That's no good. A cross is the heaviest object on earth. Let Jesus carry the cross. That's what he does. Give your problems to Jesus and be forgiven."

"You mean I'm not a bad person?"

"No, you're not bad, my child. Your sins are forgiven. Jesus takes every problem. Say five Our Father's and five Hail Marys. I pray you have the strength and courage to face your situation." Father Gordon left and I prayed. I stood up and felt or imagined crosses beside me, in front of me and behind me, no longer pushing on my shoulders. I stepped forward. The crosses moved with me, only to the doorway. I left the rectory uplifted, stretched tall. No longer weighted with the cross of guilt, I knew what I wanted—strength and courage.

An Avon customer handed me a light-blue Gideons *New Testament*. "It has the Psalms and Proverbs"

"Thank you," I said, leaving her house. Scanning the little book, I looked for anything helping me to bear my burden and chose the first suggested reading for needing God's protection, Psalm 27:1"The Lord is my light and my salvation; whom shall I fear?"

There it was—a Bible verse reminding me to cling to God. I needed strength and courage for the daily mayhem. Danny knew my every move, checking my whereabouts unnecessarily. I repeated the Serenity Prayer often: God, grant me the serenity to accept the things I cannot change, the courage to change the things I can, and the wisdom to know the difference.

I tried to accept my marriage and I tried to change my marriage. Neither one worked, so now I wanted to run from it. How?

When? My thoughts turned inward, *Be patient. God will speak. Why didn't I ask Fr. Gordon for guidance to forgive Charles and Mother? Next time.*

One evening I left Ivy and Winston washing the supper dishes. "I'll be down at the dock watching colors after sunset." I often sat there alone waiting for the evening star.

Pale-blue sky lightened as it turned to grey. Evening dew accentuated nearby plants, colorful rounded seagrape leaves, and pointy cabbage palm fronds. Lengthy strands of Spanish moss whispered gently, "We see you." The live oaks knew they were special and watched over me studying the Australian pines across the bayou. I checked for herons, then noticed a reflection of clouds on unwrinkled water. *Peaceful bayou.*

Believing no one was watching, I closed my eyes, tilted my head to the sky, raised my arms and palms up high to heaven, and silently prayed. *Dear God, Jesus, Mary. Help me. I need strength and courage to make my life better.* My arms strangely lifted higher, like cords pulled them closer to the sky.

Opening my eyes and looking west, I saw behind one-white-fluffy cloud, highlighted with yellow rays. An angel dressed in a white-billowy garment descended in a flash. She placed her fingertips on mine. She lightly touched me and clearly said, "You have strength and courage." *That was an angel. She talked...*

It happened so fast. I looked for the angel's face and saw a second flash disappear behind the cloud, now smaller. Still holding my arms up high, unusual warmth in my fingertips seeped down to my hands, arms, chest, midsection, and my legs folded beneath me.

I have strength now. I have courage. No more tears. Was it real? *Oh, yes! An angel touched me.* The evening breeze silently slid through the oak trees rippling long curly strands of moss. The tips of the branches shook lightly as if asking, "Aren't you going to tell anyone?"

Tell someone. My arms felt transparent. Patting them convinced me they were part of my body. *Oh, angel, no one will believe me. It doesn't matter. I know you're real. You're my angel come to give me strength.* Glancing one more time at the sky, all I saw was a lone, bright-shining star. The evening air chilled. *Time to go inside.*

Tucking my children into bed with a kiss, I told each of them, "An angel touched me on the dock. We're going to be okay."

Heavenly angels have an enduring quality. Their substance lasts forever. That night, I promised myself, I would hold my head up, leave there, and never look back.

CHAPTER TWENTY EIGHT
AFTER THE SHOW

I became a grownup in my thirty-fourth year. I was encumbered with baggage, yet confident about the future. My ability to walk improved, providing me freedom of movement. My psychotherapy appointments decreased to every other week. "Julie," I said optimistically, "RET saved my life. It wouldn't matter how strong my body got, if my thinking wasn't healthy."

"I'm glad you feel that way. You've grown and now you have inner resources for when things get tough."

"I don't want to make mistakes."

"No one does. But you will. You're human. It's how you look at them that helps. You're a survivor."

Dr. Piotrowski looked at my chart, then peered over his glasses at me. "You've recovered. Your clinical depression probably began six years ago."

"That's interesting, Dr. P. Why didn't you tell me earlier?" I wondered.

He continued without answering my question, "I see you

stopped taking the Darvon. You learned productive life skills with RET. However, your sex life was never addressed...I can, err, help in that area."

I'd heard this overt suggestion from lawyers, doctors, both men and women professionals. Dr. P and the others all received the same polite response. "I have a policy to deny your help in this personal issue, but thank you for offering."

"I do have one last question. Why do I bother with men?"

"Your father and brother were non-threatening in your early life." He nodded and closed my folder. "Good luck, Sarah Chapman."

* * *

"Kids, we're going on a mini-vacation. I'm taking you to see a passion play, Bok Tower, and Cypress Gardens. Plus, the azaleas are blooming."

"Will we like it?" they queried in unison, excitement raising their voices.

"I think so. Going away broadens your perspective." I wanted decision making ability, strength of mind, functioning joints and muscles, and a clean slate from my paralyzing habit—denial. My hip injury and inadequate marriage were facts. I decided to reckon with anything coming my way head on.

Involvement in community activities rewarded me with a sense of belonging. I pounced on the chance to teach the St. Boniface sixth-grade vacation bible-school class. With a bag of tricks and a borrowed white rabbit, I performed as the Court Jester for the fourth annual Medieval Fair at the Ringling Museum of Art. Years spent watching Danny do magic tricks, helped me perform with ease in front of crowds.

I decided presenting my head-and-foot balancing trapeze at the Sailor Circus Alumni Show would be my farewell gift after nineteen-years of performances. I wore a red-sequined-costume to express the radiance and warmth I felt within and knew the wafting descent of my final red-silk-handkerchief would be an eternal ember seared into my memory.

Accepting early retirement was logical. My tired,

myalgia-racked body harbored good and better days. People sometimes asked if I missed performing. "No, I had my turn. Besides, the law of averages might eventually catch up to me. I don't want a paralyzing or fatal fall."

I believe rigging failure is responsible for some circus accidents. Producers compete against each other, booking more shows per date and expecting multiple acts from each contractor adding additional stress to already frazzled overworked performers. Working men, also over-worked and under-paid, set our riggings and props hoping they get every detail, but often not quite sure. There's the possibility of alcohol abuse and illegal or even prescribed drug miss-use in circus life. These facts helped me in my decision to stop aerial work.

* * *

We Chapman's had CDs, owned property, and were debt free. However, we had no cash flow. Danny spent his monthly Social Security check on alcohol or gave it away in personal loans. I compensated by taking a series of part-time jobs and asked him to mind the children after school. I waited tables in the Old Heidelberg Castle some days and assembled aluminum patio furniture on others. Returning home after work, the kids were often ravenous.

"It's seven o'clock. Haven't you eaten supper and done your homework?"

"No, Dad wasn't here." The next day I found a job during school hours allowing me to care for my children. Danny left with Roberts Bros. Circus as promotion clown. Home life functioned better without the daily drama.

I contemplated joining Incarnation Church choir and dickered several weeks before attending a Wednesday practice. Director Nina Kor welcomed me. I knew her as the hostess from one of my numerous television interviews for Ringling Bros. "Choir members, Sarah Chapman is with us tonight. I'm putting her with the sopranos. Let's warm up your voices. Me me ma mo mu." Nina's talented choir, a mixed group of twenty, sang for love of God, vocal expression, and friendship.

The Catholic Church dubbed 1980 the Year of the Family, emphasizing values. The diocesan newspaper, *The Florida Catholic*, listed family events for parishioners at home, within the parish, and at the diocesan level.

Reflections on Life, a column on love and spiritual growth by Father Jerome LeDoux, zeroed into my heart. I clipped, saved, and memorized his articles dealing with love and spiritual growth. Pasting them into my counseling notebook, I knew I wanted to give and receive love.

* * *

Two and a-half years after I gave Danny a choice between Marriage Encounter and divorce and one horrendously failed divorce attempt, Danny summoned me for divorce in the spring of 1980. The terms split child custody, a sore spot with me. He claimed psychotherapy and dance lessons made me an unfit mother. My newfound philosophy encouraged me not to resist, get what I can, and fix what goes wrong later. I didn't understand court settlements are binding. The custody terms generated many problems for all of us. *Give thanks. Take a deep breath and be grateful that I have two wonderful healthy children. I have my freedom. I have my health, both mental and physical.*

I moved out of the marital home, complicating my life. The Worrington Street cypress house was for sale at a price I couldn't afford. I chose a moderately priced "handy man's special" and for mortgage collateral used CDs from the property that were solely in my name. The bank ignored a law saying a married woman couldn't purchase real estate.

I needed help with the down payment and went to Mother. She'd relocated closer to Merritt in Arcadia, fifty miles east of Sarasota. Merritt wasn't okay with this and kept his family apart from Mother as much as he could.

"Mother, I've never asked for anything since I went to Sullins. If you have money, may I borrow $20,000?"

"If you need it."

"I thank you. I'll keep you informed how the house purchase progresses." When she gave me the check, I asked, "Do you want a note with monthly payments?"

"No, I forget about money the day it leaves my hands." I pondered how she never saved for a rainy day and spent all the child support allotment from Daddy when I was young. The money she had in 1980 came from the sale of Oakairs.

* * *

The divorce began with the attorneys bickering about Danny's assets. He carried an air of superiority, stopped drinking, and started exercising. During a lull in the proceedings he announced another show date. "I'm going on the road with the Moscow Circus. Art Concello asked me to do advance." He gathered a few clothes and left. "You'll be fine."

A month later, he called on the phone. "The show's coming to Atlanta. I want you and the kids to come."

"And why would we come?" I was suspicious.

"This is your only chance at reconciliation."

We flew to Atlanta and took a room in his hotel. I insisted the four of us eat supper in the hotel restaurant and I picked a seat opposite him at a linen draped table. Half-civil, half-hostile, Danny campaigned. "I think you're crazy wanting a divorce. Look at me! I never did anything bad to you. You're tearing the family apart. I brought you here so we can reconcile and stop this divorce stuff."

Slowly, taking a bite of cheesecake, I steeled myself against his words. *Danny shaped up his body. His mind stayed the same. He's trying to make me feel guilty, but I refuse to be intimidated again.* Placing my fork down, I tactfully, calmly replied, "I don't want to be married."

The next morning, he barked at our door, "Where were you last night? Think what people are saying about you in a separate room."

"You're divorcing me."

"I am now, baby," he shouted. "You're breaking up the family, not me. You shouldn't have those kids." He tore down the hallway heading for the OMNI building. I took those kids home to Sarasota.

Our new haven was a three-bedroom, two-bath, concrete brick house on Suntan Avenue. It was within walking/biking distance of a Publix market, a drugstore, the YMCA, and a pay phone.

The emotional separation from Danny happened long before my physical detachment from the residence we shared for fifteen years. It seemed right moving away from the bayou and I left without regrets on July 4th, Independence Day. I had no idea what direction my future would take. One thing was obvious, supporting my family was up to me. Every dollar spent counted ten times what it had in the past. We no longer had a paid roof over our heads.

Ivy was a freshman at a Christian academy. She continued gymnastics on a less expensive team. I switched from ballroom lessons to YMCA aerobic classes. Winston continued at Incarnation School. I joined two carpools.

The no-fault divorce culminated in October, 1980. Each attorney read off our respective terms, prior to Danny and me signing our names in front of the judge. I wanted a celebration when the children joined me outside chambers. "Let's get ice cream," I suggested, driving to a convenience store. "Today's special and we're eating dessert before dinner." We munched ice cream and smacked our lips. *Getting divorced wasn't that hard. Life today is no different from yesterday and hopefully tomorrow will be better. We're safely on base.*

The terms and conditions of my settlement are public. I got the CDs—$35,000. The children got $50 each monthly support. Bob Henshaw wrote a clever paragraph deeding the restaurant property to Ivy and Winston. In the event Danny died, any income generated from that source went to their education. Danny gave me the copyright to a novel he wrote in 1960 because, "You believe in it more than I do."

Danny's attorney and mine fixed my monthly income at $800. My expenses were the house mortgage, car payment and insurance, tuition for two private schools, gymnastic and music lessons, food, electricity, water, sewer, and garbage. A phone was out of the question. I felt I owed the children a television and reluctantly bought a used black-and-white set. Gone were years of verbal battles, profanity, and ugliness. Cost of peaceful living? Priceless.

My cool Girl Friday job at a restaurant on Lido Beach stopped when the restaurant closed. More jobs followed. Being home after school took priority over work. *Time and love,* my inner voice reminded me.

* * *

"I don't understand the custody agreement. The court made a mistake," I strongly advised Danny when he picked up Ivy and Winston for the weekend. He insisted we abide by the court ordered guidelines. I balked, believing them unrealistic and harmful.

"Well, you'd better reread your divorce," he growled, pulling away from the curb.

I did reread it. Joint custody split their school-weeks in half. When Danny wasn't on the road, I shared them every other weekend. What I didn't do was send Winston to Danny in the mid-week because he adjusted poorly to change. Rearranging furniture bothered him and beds, toys, and clothes in two locations were beyond his eight-year-old comprehension. Ivy spent all weeknights with me to be closer to her school. Weekend trips continued until Winston cried often, wouldn't leave my side, and needed counseling. "Let's ask Ivy what happens at Dad's. Maybe she can help."

"Dad walks around naked, even when my friends come over. He has girlie magazines in his bedroom and makes Winston sleep there. He puts traps by the kitchen sink to catch rats."

"Rat traps?" I asked, sticking to the safest topic.

"No, bigger ones. The traps and the rats scare Winston."

"Thanks for telling me. You're not sleeping there again," I said warmly, wrapping them in my arms. "Now, who hasn't finished their homework?"

It was think time. *He didn't expose us to nakedness before, why now? Danny and magazines? That's odd. He had his girls sleep with him after Joan left, now Winston...hmm. The trap they're talking about could hurt them. No more overnights.*

* * *

Our first Christmas away from the bayou left me feeling isolated, but not lonely. I turned to the children. "You kids are gifts from God." They heard me say that many times. I was thankful my health allowed me to participate and actively play with them again.

Major repairs on the house happened as money allowed. I did a great deal of the work myself. My quest experiencing faith, hope, and love stayed with me. A statement from a catechism class, "Without hope, there's nothing," bolstered me through down periods.

Mother joined us for the 1981 Easter Sunday dinner and stayed overnight. I was up early Monday getting the kids off to school and washing breakfast dishes. I admired the soft lemon yellow paint job on the cupboards. The sunshiny kitchen always brought a smile to my heart. The neighborhood was quiet.

I heard Mother leave the bedroom and stop near the kitchen door opening to the garage. I glanced backwards and nothing seemed out of order. She stood with her nightgown crimped by a forearm and held an empty coffee mug in her other hand.

She announced across the room, "I want my money."

"You do?" I said, still washing dishes. *So this is why she came. She wants me to give back the money I borrowed.*

Pause. "I want it now."

"I'm not sure. I planned to give it back as the CDs mature over the next five-to-seven years."

"No! I want it now." The only sounds were the running water and clinking dishes as I continued washing. "Damn you." Her face grimaced in anger. "I never want to see you again. I never wanted you in the first place. You can go to hell." Her voice escalated as her breathing quickened.

I dried my hands and turned, facing her. "Mother, do you know what you're saying?"

"Damned if I don't. I knew you'd never amount to anything. I was right," she said, a wan expression growing on her face.

"What is this all about?" I asked, staying calm, and stalling to gather information.

"I wanted to give the money to Lucy and now I can't."

Carefully keeping distance between us, a childhood technique learned at Oakairs, I thought aloud, "If I did give you back the money by cashing in the CDs, I'd lose the house because they are collateral. We'd be living on the street."

Looking out the kitchen window again, I pictured the three of us in rags. Thankful for the clarity while gathering my thoughts, I continued looking outside. "No, I don't think Daddy wants us homeless."

Facing her again, I focused on her. "You disown me? Is that what you want?" I looked into her hazel eyes for any sign of emotion.

"Yes, that's right. I'm having my attorney take you out of my will."

"I'll ask you again. Are you sure you want to disown me?"

"Absolutely," she returned, tightening her broad shoulders and raising her head a bit for her next statement. "I want to see Ivy and Winston."

"No, it doesn't work that way. You can't get rid of me and keep them," I answered, shaking my head slightly side to side.

"Then…how will I see my grandchildren?" She sounded and looked forlorn gripping the mug until her knuckles whitened.

"Write letters. Send pictures. You have a telephone. They can call you." I stood firm, strong in my conviction.

"So, that's the way it's going to be?" she condescended somewhat shifting her weight.

"Yes, it is. It's your choice." I turned and gestured toward the door. "Do you see that door? That's where you go out."

Three years later, she returned clutching a card for Ivy's grad party.

Mother had never treated me with such rigid disregard…such abhorrence. After her scene, I changed her name from Mother to Dorothy, wishing we'd never had a parent/child relationship. The nastiness of her actions and words brought back memories of my childhood nightmares. I made an appointment with Bob Henshaw to check my reaction to Mother's ultimatum.

He summarized the predicament. "There's no legal action to take. The money Dorothy Wheeler gave you wasn't attached to a note. You made the right decision."

"Thank you." I shrugged. "Now I don't have a mother."

"You're resourceful, Sarah."

I prayed. *Please, dear Lord, give me strength and courage. Keep my thoughts straight. I feel bad not obeying Mother. I choose Mary for my mother. I will love her for the rest of my life and she'll never disown me.* Mary's love was special. It was better with a mother I venerated. My vespers usually ended repeating the last line of a prayer, "Grant us…peace at the last." Ah, peace. That is what I want—peace at the last.

* * *

Ivy bounced inside after returning from a Sunday outing with Danny and Winston. "Dad wants to see you at his car."

I went outside and Danny was sitting behind the wheel. "I want Ivy and Winston for the summer."

"No!" I shouted, stepping backwards. "No way!"

"You'll be sorry," he threatened me between clenched aged teeth. Danny subpoenaed me for a June hearing on contempt of court. I dreaded the outcome having lost faith in attorneys with the exception of Henshaw. "Gratis," he coached me on speaking to the judge, court procedure, facts, and a plea. There were no guesses about probable verdicts.

The children went with me to the 4:30 PM hearing. The judge, the same one I saw eight months earlier for the divorce, moved swiftly, as predicted by Henshaw. He left court promptly at five for his golf game.

Representing myself, I stated what I knew of Danny's drinking habits, the condition of the house, and Winston's need for counseling. I asked the court to restrict Danny's custody to public places, nothing after dark, and no sleepovers anywhere.

The withered old judge, flipped papers in front of him, squinted at his wristwatch, and pointed the handle of the gavel in my direction, "You are to abide by the custody agreement. I rule in favor of the plaintiff." He tapped the gavel, pushed back his oak chair, stood up, and stripped off his black robe exposing Bermuda shorts and a colored polo shirt. He placed a hand on the doorknob behind him, extended his other arm to Danny and his attorney and said, "You boys can figure this mess out."

"Nooooo!" I howled, outrageously loud and long. My hands grasped the wooden arms of my chair. "Nooooo!" I howled louder and then savagely, "TAKE ME TO JAIL. I WON'T LET HIM HAVE THEM." Danny and the stenographer stared. Danny's counsel glared at him and said, "Get her out of here."

My hands gripped tighter and my spine and head froze. My eyes, the only moveable part aside from ears, heart, and lungs, saw motion. A door opened. Bailiffs grunted as they pried my fingers away from the chair one at a time and lifted my forearms. My body stayed in a sitting position. Danny looked shrunken and bewildered. His attorney spoke impatiently, "Can't you do something with her?" To the bailiffs he ordered, "Turn her loose." I plopped down in the padded chair, flexed slightly, but remained rigid.

The door at my back opened. Ivy and Winston rushed in. I relaxed somewhat, yet couldn't feel her hand on my arm. Ivy said close to my ear, "Mom, we can go downstairs." She shifted in front of my face. "Its okay, Mom. We can leave now." With the children at my sides, we rode the elevator to street level.

Danny and I sat in wire-backed chairs at a tiny round table in the jail's empty waiting area. It resembled an ice cream parlor. Ordinary sobbing replaced shock paralysis. Me going to jail wouldn't solve anything. Ivy supplied ample tissues. She and Winston patted my shoulders soothingly. "We won't go with Dad. We won't leave you. We love you, Mom."

I never figured out my bizarre behavior in chambers. Once my breathing stabilized, Danny left me at the table with the kids.

Deep in my heart, I knew I had to let them go for the summer, despite my sense of foreboding. On the short ride home, the children rejoiced. "You were great Mom! You're our mother bear."

* * *

I turned to friends in hope they could help me think straight. I met them buying used boards for my house refurbishing projects.

"You look troubled," John said, as we loaded planks together.

"I am. May I talk with you and Beulah about what's bothering me?"

Seated in their kitchen, I began. "I have a problem. I lost a contempt case on child custody. I don't want my kids going to their dad for the summer. Can you pray for me?"

"Oh honey, that's too bad. Sometimes when we want something so much, we try too hard," comely Beulah, told me.

"What would you do?" I asked my friends.

"I'd pack their suitcases and trust in the Lord. You have enough to do with your house. Summer will go fast."

"You mean I should willingly send them?"

"Oh, yes. Jesus takes care of us all. Letting go strengthens our faith."

"Thank you, both, for your help."

That night, I told my children they were spending the summer on Montclair Drive.

The next day I met Danny in the YMCA parking lot. "Come pick them up. I'll have their clothes packed."

"I thought you knew. I can't take the children, not with my job. I'm still working dates. They have to stay with you," he theatrically stated.

"What? You don't want them?" I stuttered trying to understand what just happened. I considered asking, *Why bother with the hearing?* but didn't. I answered my own question—he wanted to win in court, not in possession. We'd all wasted energy and emotion over nothing.

Before leaving he said something I didn't expect. "I wish you were the mother of all my children." He wedged into his car and pulled off the lot. His last statement left me open-mouthed and dry-eyed.

Danny never questioned me about the ground rules I dictated in court. He arranged by mail to pick the children up early Sunday mornings when he was in town. When they returned one evening, I asked Ivy, "What do you do with your dad?"

"We go out for breakfast, then church and lunch. Then he takes us to the mall, a flea market, or a circus."

"Does he ever take you to his house?"

"Nope. We don't go there," she said, pulling Nike shoes from a shopping bag. It was nice Danny bought them anything they needed.

I breathed in deeply. *Trust in the Lord and the Lord listens. Gradually, I'm getting stronger.*

CHAPTER TWENTY NINE
FINDING BALANCE

Rationally thinking for myself felt right. Rereading my therapy journal helped me cope with some things effectively, a broken vase, a distressed child, or just the blahs. Emotional hurts took a little more time.

Not one to be idle, several ideas circulated in my mind. One project had economic promise, Danny's manuscript. A local literary agency edited *Circus Buffoon* and solicited thirty publishers, who sent back thirty rejection letters. Plan B was self-publishing 5,000 paperback copies at one dollar each. While the book was printing, I set book marketing, publicity, and distribution wheels in motion.

"Kids, I'm quitting my job and working full-time on the novel. I'm calling bookstores, newspapers, anywhere I need in order to get *Circus Buffoon* into readers' hands. Sarasota's a circus town and I'll do book signings, craft shows, yard sales, church picnics, and flea markets."

"Let the Book Sales Begin" was my motto in December 1982. The house consumed four huge pallets filled with boxes and boxes of books. We hastily made a box sofa, a box room-divider, box beds, and Winston even built a book-box maze. When researching self-publishing, the information omitted mentioning obtaining storage and the back strain that followed from lifting, pushing, and shoving heavy boxes of books under beds, tables, and into closets.

Adrenaline flowed into 1983, I jumped into the hype of instant success with a determination to sell, sell, and sell. Danny did his share, taking the novel on circus dates. Book proceeds funded a cedar deck at the back of the house, nothing more. The initial sales splash waned to a skimpy stream.

Unlike personal relationships, the challenges I faced self-publishing didn't flinch my nerves. I totally believed in the book establishing it as a reliable mail order business. Self-publishing was a positive learning experience.

Ivy's sussie was a slip of paper. "Here's our telephone number." Throwing down her book bag, she ran to a newly installed phone making several short calls to friends.

Semi-retirement offered many advantages, namely spending time with my youngsters. "Let's go see the space shuttle take off!" I announced. "We'll leave at 2 AM for Cape Canaveral." Waiting before dawn with other shuttle watchers along a strip of mangroves next to a highway, we saw a gigantic burst of billowing clouds and covered our ears from massive rumbles.

"Wow! That's bigger than any fireworks display. Imagine the energy it takes for liftoff," Winston exclaimed.

"The astronauts are heading to outer space, how about us returning to our launch pad?" I asked, handing Ivy the car keys.

* * *

During quiet moments I gave thanks for little things. Robins, mockingbirds, and whippoorwills entertained me daily with birdcalls near our home. Shrubbery produced vivid hibiscus for year-round table decorations. Rainbow-colored prism splotches shone on kitchen cabinets. One therapy technique stayed with me—closing my eyes and concentrating on a field of wild flowers for one minute. Sixty seconds meditating went a long way when there were eight to ten active hours left in a day.

Danny and I eventually struck a peace of sorts, meeting monthly for lunches at different Sarasota restaurants. We enjoyed the meals, discussed mutual circus friends, and shared the tab. He gave me the child support check.

As we ate, I wondered his response to my thoughts. *Did you scheme to incorporate me into your life? I think so. With Daddy a generation older than Mama, you didn't get objections from them. Maybe it's true when you said, "My chronological age doesn't matter. Age is purely a state of mind." What about with age comes grace, understanding, patience, and compassion? Did those states pass you by?*

You, a man broken in limb, finances, and spirit, had everything to gain marrying me, a youthful, energetic nineteen-year-old. My sine qua non enabled your retirement plan. My introverted personality allowed you to separate me from the 1965 herd of circus girls. I was entitled to marriage without rules. Could he comment without raising his voice? Would he apologize? I think not.

The important thing was I figured it out and could express it to myself. Keeping it simple for Danny, I confided, "My back hurts. What's the name of the physical therapist that helps showfolks?"

"Cosimo Pedicini. He works from home, his number is in the book." We ended lunch peacefully, the worst of our relationship behind us.

Cosimo intensely stretched my aching upper back until it relaxed. "You can sit up," he said, wiping lotion from his hands on a towel. "You have to exercise for the rest of your life. You abused your rib girdle and need to maintain strength and flexibility to support your spine. I'm giving you a few simple exercises."

"Thanks, Coz. I'll exercise. I promise."

* * *

On a quiet evening in October 1983, just before Ivy's seventeenth birthday, she snatched up a ringing phone as usual. "Mom, it's someone asking for you." She handed me the phone, miffed it wasn't for her.

"Do you know a Henry Chapman, ma'am?" a male voice asked.

"Yes, I'm his ex-wife. Why do you ask?"

"I'm an officer with the Florida Highway Patrol. Your number was on a card in his wallet. It's my job to tell you that Henry Chapman died in Ocala. Can you tell me whom to contact?"

"Yes, his daughter, Michele Chapman. I don't know her number." I hung up and sat still, stunned with the news.

"What was it Mom?" Ivy asked.

"Please call Winston. I have something to tell you both."

Danny Chapman died as he wanted, still working circus dates. Driving south on Interstate 75, he pulled into a truck stop, told the cashier he didn't feel well, please call 911. He died there of a coronary attack.

During the six days waiting for his funeral, I led the children in countless Hail Mary's and Our Fathers. My minor role included adding a poem in the funeral flyer and ordering marigolds, a flower he admired. At his service every nerve in my body tingled for each note of the solo, *Oh, Danny Boy*, a song I played for him on the piano. The chasm between his first and second families was evident with us sitting at opposite sides of the auditorium. Willie Edelston's eulogy of Danny calmed me down.

At the burial site, I commented to Ivy, "Your dad's grave is close to Grandma Chapman's and Grandfather Wheeler's." Sitting passively behind my children under the graveside tent, my mind wandered into numbness. *The world lost a great clown. My kids don't have a father.* Of the three of us, I was visibly upset. I'm not sure about Ivy and Winston. They didn't cry. Perhaps they felt differently about their dad, than I did about Daddy.

Mournful military taps snapped my attention back to the ceremony. I dreaded the flag presentation. Two uniformed VFW members removed the American flag draped on Danny's casket and neatly folded it. I nudged eleven-year-old Winston to stand. He accepted the flag, sat down, and cradled his last memento from his dad as if it was breakable. I grasped his shoulders in my palms.

As we meandered across the lush sod of Sarasota Memorial Park, a positive thought formed, *Ivy and Winston can go to college.*

* * *

Danny's passing morally terminated our marriage. With school-aged children, I felt every bit a bereaved widow. I never craved Danny when he was living and the finality of his death didn't change that.

My ex-husband's death jolted the kids and me out of poverty. His Social Security check that I contributed to from my salary re-routed to Ivy, Winston, and me. After drinking powdered milk for seven years, I boycotted it forever more.

All I wanted with Danny gone was the freedom to mother my children with love. If it looked like a good sunset coming on we three jumped in the car driving west to Lido Beach. Dreamy pastels to stark black and white clouds framed the white sands and warm Gulf water. After the colors dissipated and the evening stars peeked out, crisp white thunderheads billowed in a slowly darkening sky often illuminated by lightning bolts out of our reach. Huddled together on one towel, I'd say, "Look, God is at work."

"I think it's cool, look in back of us," Winston would point to a mirror reflection in the eastern sky.

Always afraid of storms, Ivy whimpered, "Can we go now?"

I developed my vocal talent and learned a children's program on feelings. I knew if I taught youngsters that feelings are natural, they would grow up better, relate well with others, and protect their identity. Children in control of their emotions don't need to keep secrets. My program taught healthy age-appropriate self-expression. The goal was to have children know its okay to open up making one less child with problems like mine.

* * *

Burt Fagan stopped by after Danny's funeral to say hello and see how I was doing.

"We're fine, Burt. Thanks for looking in on us," I said trying to sound composed.

Burt knew me better than I thought. "I'm sending you a book that changed my life. It's by Sammy Davis Jr."

"I met Sammy in San Diego. He was cool chatting backstage with the clowns and showgirls." I remembered happily. "I'll read his book and send you my comments. Thanks, Burt."

Davis' *Yes, I Can* meant to me, "I know I can." Learning that phrase replaced part of my rigidity with a more flexible outlook allowing room for growth and exploration. Davis didn't let an automobile accident and partial blindness end his life. Setbacks weren't my end either. I was ready for new jobs, roaming, or a companion. But best of all—I had the desire to grow and change.

* * *

Ivy's graduation took center stage. "Please write invitations to Grandmother Wheeler, Emerich Moroski, and your God-mother," I said. "Would you like a strawberry cake?"

"No, please don't make my cake. Please get one from the bakery," Ivy begged. I felt snubbed with the store bought cake request. "Will you be coming to the senior assembly today? I get a perfect attendance award."

"Yes, I'll be there. The *Florida Catholic* says one-percent of teenagers haven't had sex, drugs, or cigarettes before graduation. That describes you. How do you feel?"

"I don't know. Do you have my plane ticket?" Ivy's protected life was the complete opposite of how I grew up. She either turned down the opportunities to stray or respected my authority and her Catholic vows, or both. She looked safe and secure each time I saw her in bed cuddled with her stuffed animals.

Within a week, she was gone to Cedar Rapids, Iowa majoring in Equine Science. Accompanied to the airport by a friend, he asked, "Sarah, what is it? Why are you crying?"

"Ivy's never coming home to live again," I lamented watching the disappearing jet.

Ivy deserved her own path—aspiring horsewoman. She wasn't a bear cub anymore. Part of her strong spirit lingered at Suntan Avenue. Her remaining possessions went into the attic for her removal when she wanted them. I took Winston to school and played increasingly hard racquetball games with him at the Y.

"Hi Mom, what are you're plans?" Ivy asked, on one of her numerous calls home. She held me accountable for words borrowed from Thoreau, "Know who you are, what you want, and where you are going." Ivy knew I avoided unpleasantness and insisted on a positive home environment. She knew I didn't sell out or kiss butt. And I knew I trusted people.

"I'm spending the next six years taking care of and enjoying Winston. He listens to music for older kids and most of it's neat. We both watch Dr. Who on TV. You know you kids are first. Guess what? I'm reading books and liking it."

"That's good to know. Be careful whom you meet. I hope it's someone nice."

"Will do, Ivy. I love you."

* * *

It was a year since Danny's funeral and I commemorated by driving to Monticello Subdivision to Annie and Willie's home. We chatted, caught up on family, and shared photographs. When the time came to leave, I looked into Annie's tender face. "Annie, it's been nice visiting. I know you and Willie didn't endorse me leaving Danny, but I'm glad we're still friends."

"Sure, Sarah. What's past is past. You haven't had an easy time and you've done well. Winston will keep you busy."

The coach in Willie couldn't help speaking. "You know the saying 'Go for it' when your act got under way. It means we can't stop once we start. That's what happens in our lives. We go for it and do the best we can. If things don't work out, then we make it better."

"That's a good simile, Willie. Thanks. I'll come when I can to visit. Your family made a difference in my life. Take care."

Driving across town, I reflected on how my life changed over the nineteen years since I married Danny. It was a mixture of things I liked, disliked, and disregarded. Challenges appealed to me, and I'd picked hard goals, beginning with my circus career.

What made me choose an intensive trapeze? And what kept me safely on that unstationary bar through thousands of shows? Jesus. Jesus gave me the gift of balance. He knew I was different, and my trap bar made life bearable during my teens.

My aerial career turned out better than I anticipated. Kaleidoscopic is how I describe the circus. Its music, tents, animals, faces, rigging, food, and applause are a palette of sensations here one day, gone the next for most people, staying with me for life.

When I gained weight in college, I turned to my trapeze. A two-inch moveable bar forced me to focus, trust my feet, and know two thin cables were my safety net. If Judy McMurray thought I morphed into a butterfly prior to performing, I believed I was a radiant butterfly fluttering in the air, bringing joy to the audience. The sequins, rhinestones, bugle beads, feathers, and fabrics were wrapping paper to my precious interior gift—balance. My bar was my refuge, my favorite flower with the sweetest nectar.

Town-life was much harder for me than show business. Most town people I knew stayed put with marriage, child rearing, and jobs. The thought came to mind that maybe I didn't belong on a circus because I enjoyed staying in town. Believing in education, health care, and law enforcement helped me adapt. It didn't matter because I wasn't in the circus anymore and my mission was what I made it. A balanced life was my new act.

When I retired, I willingly let my wardrobe disburse among circus fans, hoping it contained enough unadorned radiance for them to imagine my vision in motion.

When the contracts, costumes, make-up, hairdos, music, and lights stopped, new focal points appeared. I still flitted, not as graceful or quite as glamorous, maybe a little loopy, but a living butterfly, not flattened under glass. I was—Sarah Chapman, retired aerialist, mother, woman, earth child.

I know beauty comes from within. I saw some of my physical beauty; full lips reflecting on the odometer when I drove home from dance class, hair pulled off my cheeks exposing short dark curls in front of my ears. Slicked backwards they reminded me of Merritt's sideburns.

Correspondence courses inspired me to continue learning how the mind works. Collecting pets ended for the most part. I wanted to stay well, cheerful, and loving.

I pondered love. Tears easily flowed when reminiscing my love for Daddy. Rereading Father LeDoux's wonderful articles helped my search for answers on love. Love was time spent with and equal treatment from rational people. It wasn't giving away power to people in authority: a husband, parent, or employer. Love accepts me as I am and doesn't pour me into an envisioned mold.

Did Mama love me? I don't think so. Her indulgences weighed far less in balance than her pounding ill will. For each teacher that built up my esteem, Mama had a way of removing it. When I attracted attention by asking a five-year-old's questions, Mama told others, "I threw away her mold when she was born." I thought she complimented me because she didn't say that for Merritt or Lucy. Had Mama shown she wanted me, or said I was doing well, was talented, or studying hard, I might have grown up feeling loved.

Mama gave some good. She gave her gift of fashion sense and her stature. When I walk in the woods, I search out plants and birds and look up at clouds, sunsets, and the evening star with the same innocence as a child. I have a small aqua butterfly pin from her, a present in high school, and a housewarming gift at the bayou—a wooden rolling pin.

From her, I have my beloved cousins, aunts, uncles, and grandparents. Half of her creativity and curiosity joined Daddy's common sense making me a unique individual. Her well-proportioned frame and good health merged with Daddy's intellect granting me tenacity on my chosen career.

Did Charles love me? Not at all. His thievery robbed my virginity. For decades the name Charles left a bitter taste in my mouth. Did Mama pave the way for him? I wasn't hard to control. I never challenged her and him—only once. Inner strength empowered me enough to leave.

And Danny? I was already performing, setting riggings, and driving when I met Danny. I fooled myself thinking I needed him. Did he love me? Only on special occasion cards signed, "Love, Danny." Danny didn't love himself, no alcoholic does.

These people did not love me. The healing process taught me to stop trying to love them. To stop seeking what they couldn't give. I wanted to know why I recognized positive male qualities, yet didn't attract stable men. Was there truly someone to appreciate me without putting a price tag on my head? If I met a nice man, did that mean I had to marry him? Could I live knowing if Jesus confronted me, like the woman at the well, could I say I wasn't married?

My secrets were another thing. I didn't know how to live guilt-free. I consumed abuse as it happened. Therapy helped me let go of Danny and keep a safe distance from Mama. It didn't resolve what she did to us. It didn't justify Merritt's unthinkable whipping. My kids knew a little bit about their grandmother hitting me. I never told them about Charles. Only I knew about him. I wished when people asked me about my life I could say "Its fine," without scrunching up inside. It wasn't time to deal with those secrets.

Maybe balance wasn't the best thing for me. Maybe it enabled me to block out life. Maybe I needed the out-of-balance years to get me in tune. Psychotherapy helped with self-expression, promoted emotional healing, and taught me appropriate problem solving skills. That didn't mean my path would be smooth. I hoped each new experience had a positive lesson.

As my vision of reality cleared, it wasn't necessary to modify it with my inner voice. The illusion of unworthiness spirited out of my mind, replaced with the idea of finding balance through trial and error, without battering myself. Gone for good was coulda, woulda, shoulda thinking. Hafta, gotta, and must zapped out too. Saying "It would be nice..." put me where I intended, without pressuring myself.

If it was a bummer day, I refreshed with Psalm 27:1 *The Lord is my light and my salvation; whom shall I fear?* If that didn't soothe me, I had my angel vision, renewing my strength and courage. Strength to go on. Courage to celebrate. I had tools for whatever lay down the road.

For too many years I believed my destiny was with the circus because the circus gave me solace. Yet the circus isn't a place to find oneself. It's a place to be, an illusion of reality. I wasn't bound to the circus, so leaving was probable and accepted. A few brave souls transition back to town-life carrying their circus memories. I was one of them. For those who remain, the show goes on.

Made in the USA
Middletown, DE
21 February 2015